THE BATTLE OF NEGRO FORT

THE
BATTLE
OF
Negro Fort

THE RISE AND FALL OF A
FUGITIVE
SLAVE COMMUNITY

MATTHEW J. CLAVIN

NEW YORK UNIVERSITY PRESS

New York

NEW YORK UNIVERSITY PRESS
New York
www.nyupress.org

References to Internet websites (URLs) were accurate at the time of writing. Neither the author nor New York University Press is responsible for URLs that may have expired or changed since the manuscript was prepared.

Library of Congress Cataloging-in-Publication Data
Names: Clavin, Matthew J., author.
Title: The Battle of Negro Fort : the rise and fall of a fugitive slave community /
Matthew J. Clavin.
Description: New York : New York University Press, [2019] |
Includes bibliographical references and index.
Identifiers: LCCN 2018052782 | ISBN 9781479837335 (cl : alk. paper)
Subjects: LCSH: Negro Fort, Battle of, Fla., 1816. | Florida—History—To 1821. |
West Florida—History. | Fugitive slaves—Florida—History—19th century.
Classification: LCC E83.817 .C58 2019 | DDC 973.5/1—dc23
LC record available at https://lccn.loc.gov/2018052782

New York University Press books are printed on acid-free paper, and their binding materials are chosen for strength and durability. We strive to use environmentally responsible suppliers and materials to the greatest extent possible in publishing our books.

Manufactured in the United States of America

10 9 8 7 6 5 4 3 2 1

Also available as an ebook

For the loves of my life:

Gladys, Madeline, Joseph, and Joshua

CONTENTS

FIGURES

INTRODUCTION

> Had this thing happened during the war, it would
> have resounded from one end of the continent to
> the other, to the honor of those concerned in it;
> for it yields in gallant daring and complete success
> to no incident that happened in the late contest.
>
> —*Niles' Weekly Register*, 1816

IN the spring of 1816, Major General Andrew Jackson wrote the governor of the Spanish colony of West Florida. His letter addressed events that had taken place below the southern border of the United States since the War of 1812 had ended a year earlier. It began, "I am charged by my government to make known to you that a negro fort erected during our late war with Britain has been strengthened since that period and is now occupied by upwards of two hundred and fifty negroes many of whom have been enticed away from the service of their masters—citizens of the United States." Because the fugitives at the fort were armed, disciplined, and daily increasing their numbers by encouraging slaves from the southern states and territories to join them, the general insisted that the Spanish government return "those negroes now in the said fort and which have been stolen and enticed from" their American owners. A refuge for fugitive slaves near the republic's southern boundary was entirely unacceptable, Jackson explained, and if the Spanish government refused to eliminate it, then the United States would do so.[1]

Despite its apparent diplomacy, Jackson's gesture was purely symbolic. The military marvel, who fifteen months earlier had led

American troops to a decisive victory over the British at the historic
Battle of New Orleans, had already decided to assault the heavily
armed fortress that sheltered as many as one thousand fugitive slaves
from both the United States and Spanish Florida. "I have very little
doubt of the fact that this fort has been established by some villains
for the purpose of murder rapine and plunder and that it ought to be
blown up regardless of the ground it stands on," Jackson had written Brigadier General Edmund Gaines two weeks before reaching
out to the Spanish governor. The hero of New Orleans then added
forcefully, "If your mind should have formed the same conclusion,
destroy it and restore the stolen negroes and property to their right-
ful owners."[2]

The result of Jackson's directive was the Battle of Negro Fort, a
deadly clash involving hundreds of American troops, Indian warriors, and black rebels that took place in the Florida wilderness from
July 15 to July 27, 1816. Occurring a year and a half after the Treaty
of Ghent brought the War of 1812 to an end, the historic encounter was a remnant of the lengthy imperial struggle between Britain
and its former American colonies. But it was also part of the larger
fight over freedom and slavery that raged throughout the Americas
at the turn of the nineteenth century. Though it is rarely remembered
alongside the legendary battles of early American history like Bunker
Hill, Yorktown, and New Orleans or the unforgettable slave revolts
and conspiracies led by Gabriel, Denmark Vesey, and Nat Turner, the
Battle of Negro Fort marked an important milestone in the history
of the early American republic.

Understanding the battle's importance requires acknowledg-
ing that the American government had always sanctioned slavery. During and immediately after the American Revolution, the
Articles of Confederation placed no restrictions on the practice and
allowed the thirteen individual states to deal with the issue as they
saw fit. The United States Constitution, which replaced the Articles

in 1789, legitimized slavery by counting three-fifths of enslaved people when determining congressional representation and direct taxes. It also authorized the federal government to suppress slave insurrections and recognized fugitive slaves as the legal property of their owners even if they escaped to free states and territories. The Fugitive Slave Act of 1793 further committed the republic to slavery. As historian David Waldstreicher puts it, "In growing their government, the framers and their constituents created fundamental laws that sustained human bondage."[3]

Still, the new government's stance on slavery was contradictory.[4] In July 1787, while still operating under the authority of the Articles of Confederation, Congress adopted the Northwest Ordinance, banning slavery in the territories north and west of the Ohio River. That same summer, delegates meeting at the Constitutional Convention in Philadelphia empowered the federal government to abolish the Atlantic slave trade in twenty years, which it eventually did. The delegates also agreed to exclude the word "slavery" from the Constitution. As James Madison explained in his notes from the convention, it was wrong "to admit in the Constitution the idea that there could be property in men."[5] Though a lifelong slaveowner, Madison at times displayed the same ambivalence over slavery as the nation he helped establish.

And he was not alone. Before becoming the first president of the United States, George Washington confided to a friend about slavery, "There is not a man living who wishes more sincerely than I do, to see a plan adopted for the abolition of it."[6] The Mount Vernon planter was a harsh taskmaster who routinely used violence to secure a tractable labor force. At the same time, he contemplated ways to liberate his slaves while providing them with the skills required to succeed as free people. Long incapable of finding an ideal solution to the problem of slavery, Washington, in his last will and testament, stipulated that his slaves be emancipated upon the death of his wife, Martha.[7]

Thomas Jefferson was also ambivalent about slavery. In addition to enslaving hundreds of black people at his Monticello estate, he suspected that African Americans were inferior to European Americans "in the endowments both of body and mind."[8] Yet he fathered several children with Sally Hemings, one of his slaves, and communicated strong antislavery sentiments throughout most of his political life. Jefferson was particularly outspoken against the Atlantic slave trade, which he referred to in the first draft of the Declaration of Independence as a "cruel War against human Nature itself."[9] More than two decades later, while in the White House, President Jefferson proudly signed the bill outlawing the transatlantic trade to the United States.[10]

In many ways, Jefferson embodied the paradoxes and complexities not only of American slavery but of American antislavery as well. While admitting the institution's immorality, he recommended gradual abolition along with colonization, meaning the removal of freed slaves from the United States to Africa, the West Indies, or some other place beyond the republic's borders. As historians of the colonization movement have amply demonstrated, early white antislavery activists generally despised black people and dreaded their presence in the new republic, whether slavery existed or not.[11] Indeed, Jefferson revealed a racism that was common in both the North and the South when he famously used a disturbing metaphor to describe his own fear of slaves: "We have the wolf by the ear, and we can neither hold him, nor safely let him go."[12]

Madison, Washington, and Jefferson were incapable of imagining a society in which African Americans and European Americans lived together peacefully and as equals—but they still considered slavery an evil. Consequently, they rarely spoke out or wrote strongly in defense of the practice lest they impede what they hoped and assumed was its inevitable demise. But many of their contemporaries were far less patient. Fearful of leaving such an important matter to chance, they decided to act. Slaveowners across the republic, who were taken with the enlightened rhetoric of the American Revolution, manumitted thousands of their slaves in the last quarter of the eighteenth century. At the same time, every northern state passed legislation against slavery, and thus began the slow and deliberate process of abolishing the institution throughout the region. Despite these developments, slavery did not disappear from the new republic.[13]

To the contrary, the demand for slave labor increased in the decades following American independence. After Eli Whitney invented his cotton engine, wide-eyed entrepreneurs from the eastern seaboard headed south and west, hoping to turn the rough country that stretched from the Georgia backwoods to the Mississippi River and beyond into a slave society ruled by King Cotton. To make this happen, settlers needed unfettered access to the waters that flowed south from these territories to the Gulf of Mexico, so they could more speedily bring their product to market. The Louisiana Purchase of 1803 helped in this regard by doubling the size of the republic and transferring control of New Orleans—and the massive river that flowed past it—from France to the United States. Yet a significant obstacle remained below the United States' southern border: Spain refused to part with the immense colonies under its control, what the explorer Ponce de León had referred to centuries earlier as the Land of Flowers, or La Florida.[14]

At the turn of the nineteenth century, Florida consisted of two separate colonies on the northern edge of Spain's American empire. West Florida stretched more than one thousand miles from the lower Mississippi River along the northern Gulf Coast to the Apalachicola River, which forms at the confluence of the Chattahoochee and Flint Rivers in Georgia and cuts through the Florida panhandle before emptying into the Gulf of Mexico. East Florida extended from the Apalachicola River to the Atlantic Coast and included the entire Florida peninsula. Over time, the outer portions of both colonies

FIGURE I.1. The southern frontier of the United States in 1816.

resembled the American South. At Baton Rouge on the Mississippi River and St. Augustine near the St. John's River, a small group of wealthy white planters, including many who had migrated from the United States, established large plantations that employed hundreds and eventually thousands of slaves.[15]

The rest of Spanish Florida, on the other hand, remained a frontier inhabited by groups of people opposed to American expansion. Among them was the colony's free, Spanish-speaking, Catholic population, which included a diverse group of European- and African-descended people known as Creoles. Multiethnic polyglots who resided primarily in coastal seaports like Mobile, Alabama, and Pensacola, Florida, they were artisans, shop owners, and shipbuilders. Joined by a significant immigrant population that derived from the breadth of Spain's Atlantic empire, they struggled for survival in a harsh and unforgiving colonial world. Because of their isolated position, however, they enjoyed a modicum of social, political, and economic freedom. They also experienced a fluid racial system, which they knew would disappear should the United States extend its boundary southward.[16]

Native Americans also resisted the spread of southern people, institutions, and ideas into Florida. During the four decades of Spanish rule following the American Revolution, indigenous people claimed much of the land along the United States' southern border. Most numerous were the Creeks, an ethnically diverse, Muscogee-speaking people considered "more powerful than any nation" at the time.[17] By the turn of the nineteenth century, a confederation of several dozen Creek towns had divided into two separate societies. The Upper Creeks inhabited land along the Coosa and Tallapoosa rivers in the eastern Mississippi Territory (present-day Alabama). The Lower Creeks resided primarily in southwestern Georgia between the Chattahoochee and Flint rivers. Because of their proximity to foreign people and cultures, some Creeks experienced "a new order of things" and altered their customs and traditions accordingly. Others did not—and they would sacrifice their lives rather than suffer the loss of their land or culture to the United States.[18]

In Florida, Creeks who migrated southward into the Spanish territories joined other militant Indians to create a new people known as the Seminoles.[19] In many cases, they had originated in the volatile and hotly contested borderlands between the southern United States and northern New Spain, and then established themselves in the dense woods and nearly impenetrable swamps that European colonists and American settlers normally avoided. Violently predisposed to resist any threat to their way of life, they were "the most savage indians of the South," according to one frontiersman, "and also the most hostile."[20]

The Seminoles derived not only from indigenous people but also from fugitive slaves who had escaped from their Spanish and American owners over the course of many years. Though slavery existed in colonial Florida, Spanish law granted enslaved people rights that were often unthinkable in the United States, including the ability to marry, to own property, and to purchase one's own freedom. Through the last decade of the eighteenth century, Spanish officials offered freedom to escaped slaves and their families in exchange for military service. As a result, Florida became, in historian Jane Landers's memorable words, "a haven for runaways" who fled from Britain's North American colonies and, later, the South.[21] By the opening of the nineteenth century, African Americans living independently in Spanish Florida earned the moniker "maroons," a corruption of "*cimarrónes*," the Spanish term used to describe fugitive slaves. Allied and in many cases integrated with the Seminoles, the maroons similarly posed a significant challenge to anyone threatening their freedom.[22]

British Loyalists were the final group that challenged Americans' ambitions in Florida. During the War of Independence, several

FIGURE I.2. This engraving reflects the conspicuousness of fugitive slaves among Florida's Seminoles. *The Seminoles in Florida*. From Caroline Mays Brevard and Henry Eastman Bennett, *A History of Florida* (1904). Courtesy of the Library of Congress.

thousand inhabitants of England's thirteen rebellious colonies fled
to East Florida and West Florida, as both then belonged to Great
Britain.[23] After the war, some of these partisans—who reviled the
United States and stayed loyal to the British Empire—remained in
the Floridas despite Spain's reacquisition of both colonies as part
of the Treaty of Paris of 1783. Though initially unsure of how to
treat these Loyalists, the colonial governments of East and West
Florida eventually welcomed their arrival and offered them in-
centives to stay. In 1783, for example, Spanish officials granted a
monopoly on Indian trade throughout its colonies to the Loyalist-
owned trading firm Panton, Leslie & Company, thwarting the
efforts of most American merchants to secure a foothold in the
Florida colonies.[24]

   With Spanish Creoles, Native Americans, African Americans,
and British Loyalists opposed to American expansion into Spanish
territory, US officials struggled to find a way to acquire East and
West Florida peacefully. Among those offering a solution was
Thomas Jefferson. In 1791, the then secretary of state informed
President George Washington of his desire to see "a hundred thousand of our inhabitants" settle in the sparsely populated Spanish
colonies, as their presence would "be the means of delivering to
us peaceably what may otherwise cost us a war."[25] The migration
scheme never materialized, so with every passing year, the likelihood of a confrontation between the United States and Spain increased. However, because the ideology of Manifest Destiny—the
idea that the United States had the God-given right to conquer the
continent—had not yet taken hold, national support for southern
expansion into Spanish Florida was neither automatic nor assured.
As a result, southern slaveowners came to believe that in order for
the United States to acquire Florida, they had to convince the federal government to use military force on their behalf. In the end,
they were successful because of two separate but related events.[26]

First was Andrew Jackson's emergence as a national and sectional leader. When war broke out between the United States and Great Britain in 1812, the middle-aged Tennessee militiaman saw an opportunity for the young republic to secure and expand its southern border. In order to accomplish this, Jackson spearheaded American intervention in the Creek Civil War (1813–1814), which resulted in the United States' acquisition of millions of acres of the Indians' land.[27] The Creeks' demise proved of great benefit to many Americans but especially slaveowners, whose dreams of expanding their peculiar institution into Florida were on the verge of becoming a reality.[28]

Jackson's attainment of slaveowners' ambitions is a reminder that despite his much-deserved reputation as a frontier nationalist, he was also "truly a southerner."[29] From his earliest days in the North Carolina and South Carolina backwoods to the eight years he spent in the White House, Jackson strongly identified with southern interests and ideas. Because he shared none of the ambivalence over slavery that troubled the first generation of national leaders from the South, contemporaries considered him "SOUTHRON—a slaveholding man, from a slave holding State," whose interests aligned with theirs.[30] Inspired by a love of both country and section, the "Hero of the South" would prove indispensable in persuading the federal government to use military force on slaveowners' behalf.[31]

The second event was the rise of Negro Fort. When Great Britain withdrew the balance of its forces from the northern Gulf Coast in 1815, it left its recently built defensive fortification atop a steep bluff overlooking the Apalachicola River to several hundred armed and determined fugitive slaves. In the coming months, the fort's founding black population welcomed hundreds of additional American and Spanish maroons into their community, while allying themselves with the Creeks, Choctaws, Seminoles, and other indigenous people throughout the region. Having in many cases won their freedom by serving in the British Colonial Marines during the late war, these black veterans and the community they defended vowed to resist any effort to refasten the shackles of slavery around their limbs.

That being said, Negro Fort's denizens were not slave revolutionaries out to destroy the nefarious institution that sought to keep them in bondage. Nor were they determined to restore or recreate a traditional way of life recalled from their youth or inherited from their African ancestors.[32] Instead, like other maroons who struggled to survive in the southern United States or adjacent territories, "Their actions show that self-determination, self-reliance, and self-rule were their key objectives."[33]

While American slaveowners abhorred Negro Fort because it drew fugitive slaves from their own homes, farms, and plantations, they exploited its existence by using it as a pretext for war. Playing on white racial fears, they portrayed the fort as the base of operations for rebellious slaves, Indian savages, and foreign emissaries, who threatened the peace and security of the United States' southern border. With federal officials and military personnel prominent among those disseminating this imperialist pro-slavery propaganda, the federal government embraced the idea that Negro Fort needed to be eliminated. Therefore, it did nothing to stop Jackson when, in his capacity as the commander of the United States' southern forces, he ordered an illegal joint army-navy expedition into Spanish Florida to destroy the fort and reenslave or kill its defenders.[34]

Given these objectives and the unprecedented use of the military to achieve them, the assault on Negro Fort provided early evidence of what came to be known as the Slave Power—that is, a political alliance of southern slaveowners and their northern allies who used the federal government to promote and protect slavery. From the late eighteenth century, northerners feared losing political power to southerners as a result of the Three-Fifths Compromise and other constitutional provisions. Thomas Jefferson's victory over John Adams in the presidential election of 1800 confirmed these fears, as the slaveowning southerner would not have defeated the antislavery northerner without the benefit of the "Negro votes" in the Electoral College.[35] Decades later, abolitionists' resistance to what they termed the "Slave Power" helped raise tensions between the North and the South to a boiling point. This led some historians, who derided the abolitionists for their radicalism, to dismiss the idea of a federal government dominated by slavery's supporters as just another absurd antebellum conspiracy theory. Yet the destruction of Negro Fort proves that the Slave Power existed long before the sectional conflict erupted into civil war.[36]

Though largely forgotten, the Battle of Negro Fort formed a crucial chapter in the history of the early American republic. By eliminating this refuge for fugitive slaves—the largest that ever existed within the borders of the present-day United States—the federal government closed an escape valve that African Americans had utilized for generations. While slaves would continue to run away, they would never again find a sanctuary so close to the nation's borders and so secure. At the same time, the government intensified the subjugation of southern Native Americans. Forced to choose sides in a conflict between an emerging nation and a small but determined group of fugitive slaves, Creeks, Choctaws, and Seminoles responded in a variety of ways, from leading the joint army-navy assault on Negro Fort to sacrificing their lives to resist it. However, no strategy proved effective in stopping American expansion into their lands.

The battle was important for another reason as well. During its year-long existence, Negro Fort was a powerful symbol of black freedom that subverted the racist foundations of the slave society being expanded across the southern frontier. That the US government felt compelled to destroy this symbol proved the nation's growing

commitment to slavery while illuminating the extent to which ambivalence over the institution had disappeared since the nation's
founding. Indeed, four decades after declaring that all men were created equal, the United States destroyed a fugitive slave community in
a foreign territory for the first and only time in its history. In so doing,
it accelerated its transformation into a white republic, which served
both the interests and the ideology of an emerging Slave Power.

WAR AND RESISTANCE

I
N January 1815, Andrew Jackson's motley collection of army regulars, militiamen, Indians, pirates, and free people of color were engaged in defending New Orleans from an invading British force more than twice its size. At the same time, *Niles' Weekly Register*, a popular national periodical published in Baltimore, Maryland, warned of a simultaneous attack against the southern United States originating in Spanish Florida. Though nominally neutral during the War of 1812, the colonial governments of East and West Florida seemed to have chosen sides when they allowed a British naval fleet to gather at the mouth of the Apalachicola River with fourteen thousand troops, "a considerable part of them blacks." The vessels brought arms, ammunition, and other "presents," which the British intended for the Indians and slaves they expected to recruit nearby. With the American army focused on New Orleans, the redcoats planned to arouse "the *savages* and *negroes*" along Florida's Gulf Coast "for the purpose of murdering women and children on the inland frontiers of Georgia." Or so claimed *Niles' Weekly Register*.[1]

For American settlers, the fear of Indians and slaves was part and parcel of life on the southern frontier. But British actions during the

War of 1812 made the possibility of a combined Indian-slave assault across the United States' southern border a distinct reality. When the American government declared war on Great Britain in June 1812, the British responded indifferently. The Napoleonic Wars in Europe had diverted the empire's attention from its former American colonies for more than a decade, and now the government was reluctant to join another costly military campaign. Only an American invasion of Canada in June 1812 succeeded in arousing Great Britain, initiating a prolonged fight between the two rivals. With resources stretched thin, Great Britain early decided on a policy of arming and recruiting Native Americans, African Americans, and anyone else willing to volunteer for His Majesty's Service. By filling their ranks with America's subject people, the British hoped to produce a form of "psychological warfare to force the American government to terms."[2]

From the opening of the war, Indians across North America rallied to the British cause because of their common enemy. Westward expansion meant that by the opening of the nineteenth century, some four hundred thousand American citizens—roughly 10 percent of the US population—lived west of the Appalachian Mountains. In the Northwest Territory, white encroachment on Indian land increasingly brought native people into contact with British merchants and officials, who manned a series of forts along the Canadian border and who also abhorred the new arrivals. In an effort to slow the Americans' advance, the British provided food, weapons, and other essential goods to the territory's indigenous people, who then harassed and intimidated settlers. "We have had but one opinion as the cause of the depredations of the Indians," read an article circulated on the eve of the War of 1812. "They are instigated and supported by the British."[3]

Among the beneficiaries of Great Britain's generosity were the Shawnee, an Algonquian-speaking people who in the eighteenth century migrated from various points to the Ohio River Valley. At the opening of the nineteenth century, the Shawnee were inspired by their leader Tecumseh, a charismatic war chief, and his religiously inspired brother, Tenskwatawa, or the Prophet. Under their leadership, the group launched a historic movement to unite Indian people across tribal lines and to join the British in vanquishing the United States. Tecumseh thought violence was the best way to fight for the Shawnees' interests whereas his younger brother sought a religiously inspired cultural revolution, but both dreamed of an expansive pan-Indian alliance extending from Canada to the Gulf of Mexico.[4]

In 1811, Tecumseh traveled hundreds of miles to convince Indians below the Ohio River to join the anti-American confederation. In a fiery speech before hundreds of Creek chiefs and warriors in the old Indian town of Tuckabatchee, Alabama, the Shawnee leader challenged his listeners to reclaim the land and culture of their ancestors. The Muscogee were once a powerful people, Tecumseh began, but they had buried their bows and arrows in the graves of their fathers. Because the "white race" had seized their land, corrupted their women, and trampled on the bones of the dead, Tecumseh demanded, "War now! War always! War on the living! War on the dead!" Referring to Great Britain and Spain, Tecumseh informed his rapt audience, "Two mighty warriors across the seas will send us arms—at Detroit for us, at Pensacola for you." When this happened, he declared, "I will stamp my foot and the very earth shall shake." The impact of the emotional address was palpable. According to one eyewitness, "Not a word was uttered when he closed; no one applauded; no one replied; but a thousand warriors, the 'stoics of the woods,' shook with emotion, and many a tomahawk was brandished in the air."[5]

Despite his plea, Tecumseh failed to unite diverse Indian groups against the United States. After the Shawnee helped the British lay siege to Fort Detroit in eastern Michigan in one of the first major engagements of the war, American victories along the Canadian border forced the British and Indians to retreat into Canada. There, important disagreements emerged between the two allies over strategy and tactics. While Tecumseh's dream of halting American expansion died with him at the Battle of the Thames in October 1813, the Anglo-Indian alliance he spent the last years of his life cultivating continued.

In the spring of 1814, Napoléon Bonaparte abdicated the French throne, temporarily bringing peace to Europe and enabling Great Britain to focus its attention on the American war. Momentum soon turned in favor of the British. In August, after capturing Washington, D.C., redcoats burned and destroyed the city's most prominent public buildings, including the recently completed US Capitol. Among the incendiaries in the nation's capital were fugitive slaves from the Chesapeake Bay area, referred to as the "internal enemy" by Alan Taylor in his study of the War of 1812 in Virginia. Numbering in the hundreds, they served the British in a variety of capacities, including as scouts, spies, soldiers, and sailors.[6]

The courage and determination of these fugitives along the eastern shores of Maryland and Virginia initially surprised the British, who immediately arranged for the conveyance of these refugees aboard one of His Majesty's ships. "The slaves continue to come off by every opportunity," wrote Royal Navy captain Robert Barrie before revealing his plan to send the women and children to the British colony of Bermuda for safety. The men he intended to use militarily, noting, "Amongst the Slaves are several very intelligent fellows who are willing to act as local guides should their Services be required in that way, and if their assertions be true, there is no doubt but the Blacks of Virginia & Maryland would cheerfully take up Arms & join us against the Americans." Barrie allowed slaveowners to approach their slaves under flags of truce and try to convince them to abandon the British, but, he noted with a bit of pride, "Not a single black would return to his former owner."[7]

Though sparse, some evidence of the fate of the fugitive slaves who climbed aboard the British ships survives. In 1837, Charles Ball penned one of the important fugitive slave narratives of the antebellum era, *Slavery in the United States: A Narrative of the Life and Adventures of Charles Ball, a Black Man*, but decades earlier he was serving as a free man in the US Navy when he witnessed "several thousand black people" disappear beyond British lines. Ball recalled in his memoir, "None of these people were ever regained by their owners, as the British naval officers treated them as free people." After a local slaveowner lost almost all of her one hundred slaves, Ball joined a "deputation of gentlemen" that approached the British fleet "for the purpose of inducing her slaves to return to her service." Once on board one of the vessels, Ball encountered hundreds of escaped slaves on the main deck and encouraged them to return to their owners. Because "their heads were full of notions of liberty," however, they refused and instead tried to convince him to accompany them to one of Britain's Caribbean colonies. For reasons never explained, Ball declined these entreaties, choosing instead to continue his service in the American rather than the British armed forces.[8]

Ball incorrectly asserted that all of the slaves who embarked on British vessels headed for the West Indies. To the contrary, many men of fighting age volunteered in the Corps of Colonial Marines, a unit of black enlisted men and white officers organized by Vice Admiral Alexander Cochrane. To attract recruits, the commander-in-chief of the Royal Navy's North American Station issued a proclamation in April 1814, which British agents distributed to black people along the southern Atlantic and Gulf coasts. "WHEREAS it has been represented to me, that many Persons now resident in the United States, have expressed a desire to withdraw therefrom," the official decree began, "all those who may be disposed to emigrate from the UNITED STATES will, with their Families, be received on board of His Majesty's Ships or Vessels of War, or at the Military Posts that may be established, upon or near the Coast of the UNITED STATES." Once under the protection of the British, the former slaves "would have their choice of either entering into His Majesty's Sea or Land Forces, or of being sent as FREE Settlers to the British Possessions in North America or the West Indies, where they will meet with all due encouragement."[9]

The reasons behind Cochrane's abolitionist plan were several, though two in particular stand out. First was military necessity. While the Americans hesitated to employ large numbers of black troops for fear they would inspire further slave resistance, the British quickly seized the opportunity just as they had done four decades before. At the outset of the American Revolution, the royal governor of Virginia, Lord John Murray Dunmore, issued a proclamation similar to Cochrane's that promised freedom to all "Servants, Negroes, or others" who aided in the suppression of the colonial rebellion.[10] Several years later, the commander-in-chief of the British Army, General Sir Henry Clinton, offered freedom to all slaves who escaped to the British, regardless of whether they volunteered for military service. As a result of these and other actions, thousands of enslaved colonists undermined the American independence movement by joining the British and depriving their owners of a valuable source of labor and military manpower.[11] History seemed to repeat itself during the War of 1812, when Cochrane's proclamation prompted as many as five thousand fugitive slaves to emigrate from the United States and become free British subjects.[12]

The second motive behind the decision to liberate and enlist American slaves was British exceptionalism. Britons prided themselves on Great Britain's status as a world power and its advancements in the area of political freedom. Yet the revolt of the thirteen North American colonies challenged the idea that Great Britain was in the vanguard of liberty. After American independence, therefore, the British relished opportunities to assist those who were denied freedom in the United States—the new and self-proclaimed land of the free. Writing about Great Britain's early efforts to secure black volunteers, historian Gerald Horne concludes that London gained important advantages over its former colonies "by staking out a more progressive position on abolition."[13]

Whatever the reason, the results of the British policy were profound. During the War of 1812, a knowledgeable American sailor summarized the frustration many American troops felt when confronting an enemy that better epitomized the ideals they claimed as their own. The British, he confessed, were the true republicans. "It is all liberty and equality with them; they fight the battles of the world all for freedom." Unlike the Americans, who resisted fighting alongside darker-skinned people they believed to be inferior, the British took "all sorts in their camp—the Indians, the mulattoes, negroes, and whomsoever they can get."[14]

The practice of arming slaves led to some unexpected results, such as convincing British combatants to reconsider their negative views of black people. While stationed along the Chesapeake shore, Rear Admiral George Cockburn begged Cochrane to reconsider his plan to free slaves regardless of whether they chose to enlist in His Majesty's Service. Cockburn believed that slaves lacked courage and would never risk "joining us in Arms."[15] Within a matter of days, however, his attitude changed. Upon the first sight of British vessels, slaves in Maryland and Virginia abandoned their owners and overseers by the thousands, despite the risk of being captured or killed. Those enslaved men who reached the British and enlisted as soldiers were "getting on astonishingly, and are really very fine Fellows," Cockburn noted. "They have induced me to alter the bad opinion I had of the whole of their Race."[16] The admiral's change of mind was so extreme that after several engagements with the American army, he claimed to prefer the newly minted black Colonial Marines to the more seasoned white Royal Marines, admitting, "They are stronger Men and more trust worthy for we are sure they will not desert whereas I am sorry to say we have Many Instances of our Marines walking over to the Enemy."[17]

While the British took great pride in His Majesty's black volunteers, the sight of fugitive slaves in redcoats horrified American citizens and officials, prompting charges that Great Britain had crossed the bounds of civilized warfare. In an essay on the causes of the War of 1812, US secretary of the treasury James Alexander Dallas accused the British of inciting a slave insurrection. To make his point he invoked the Haitian Revolution—a revolt of nearly half a million slaves at the turn of the nineteenth century, which birthed the independent nation of Haiti. Dallas argued that basic humanitarian impulses should have discouraged the British from trying to subject the South to a similar cataclysm, one that would result in the extermination of the white race, as it had done in Haiti. Referring to Cochrane's decree, he remonstrated, "Yet, in a formal proclamation issued by the commander in chief of his Britannic majesty's squadrons, upon the American station, the slaves of the American planters were invited to join the British standard, in a covert phraseology, that afforded but a slight veil for the real design."[18]

Despite Dallas's claim, the British had no intention of inciting a slave revolt and actually discouraged such an event from taking place.[19] They wanted black volunteers, however, and during the war's second year intensified their recruiting efforts by opening an additional front against the United States along Florida's Gulf Coast. From there they intended to recruit, arm, and train fugitive slaves from Georgia and South Carolina and then send them back across the American border alongside regular British troops and allied Indian warriors to destroy the South. To put this plan into motion, British officials ordered the establishment of a headquarters on the eastern bank of the Apalachicola River. Located fifteen miles from the Gulf of Mexico atop a ten- to fifteen-foot-high cliff, the site was called Achackwheithle by local

Indians, but the Spanish referred to it as "the hill of beautiful view or Prospect Bluff."[20]

Construction of the British Post began after British forces arrived at Prospect Bluff in May 1814, seized a trading post belonging to John Forbes & Company, and welcomed several of its enslaved employees into their ranks. Over the next several months, British soldiers, Indian warriors, and fugitive slaves carved an opening out of a vast swampland lying beneath a canopy of hundred-foot-tall pine trees. By the end of the summer, the compound consisted of a square-shaped moat enclosing a large field several acres in size. A four-foot-tall wooden stockade ran along the entire length of the moat and included two bastions on its northeastern and southeastern corners. Scattered near the shore were several stone structures, including soldiers' barracks and a "large store building" measuring forty-eight by twenty-four feet.[21] Several hundred feet inland stood a substantial circular armory—known as a magazine—designed to protect the 73 kegs of gunpowder and 180 stands of arms recently delivered to the site.[22]

To attract recruits to this stronghold, British operatives visited the Creek, Seminole, and "negro settlements" scattered along the Apalachicola River and its tributaries, distributing guns, uniforms, and other goods.[23] Surprised by the success of these early missions, Captain Hugh Pigot reported that from the British Post to Pensacola, more than one hundred miles to the west, there were nearly three thousand "Warriors of the Creek Nation" who were anxious to don British red coats and take up arms against the United States. Besides that, "There is every reason to suppose the Negroes of Georgia knowing the Creeks are armed will come over to them in great numbers, many have already taken refuge with these tribes."[24]

Encouraged by Pigot's report, Cochrane reached out to Indian leaders across Spanish Florida, informing them of His Majesty's intentions. Vowing that "Father King George will not suffer his Indian children to be made slaves of by his rebellious subjects," Cochrane promised to support the Indians "by every means" in his power. All he asked in return was the fulfillment of two requests. First, he beseeched the warriors to talk to their "deluded brothers" who sided with the Americans, and tell them that by joining the enemy they were "forging chains for themselves and their children." Second, Cochrane implored the Indians to encourage by every means the flight of fugitive slaves from Georgia and the Carolinas. The British would arm as many black men who arrived at the post as possible, and with their assistance the war against the United States could not possibly "fail of Success."[25]

The response of Indian leaders to Cochrane's entreaty was unequivocal. In an extraordinary document forwarded to the admiral, several of the most feared chiefs in all of Indian country, including Kinache (Capichi Micco), "the Prophet" Josiah Francis (Hillis Hadjo), and Peter McQueen, vowed to assist the British in defeating the United States. The chiefs recalled their loyalty to Great Britain since the days of the American Revolution, adding that because of the redcoats' recent return, the Creeks and Seminoles were again walking "like Men in their Streets." Regarding Cochrane's plea, the chiefs promised to "get all the black men we can to join your Warriors." They would also strive to unite their "red brethren and form a strong arm that will be ready to crush the wicked and rebellious Americans."[26]

As a result of these communications, the British Post was a beehive of activity in the spring and summer of 1814. The site's superintendent, Captain George Woodbine, an eccentric backwoods trader and interpreter originally from Jamaica, welcomed hundreds of Creek and Seminole warriors and their families. Though eager to launch an offensive against the United States, many of the Indians were in no condition to fight. "They have not a morsel of any description of their own to eat," Woodbine wrote in one of a series of letters begging his superiors for additional provisions. He further added that "Negroes are flocking in from the states & I make no doubt that I shall have occasion for a considerable supply more of musquets." Because Cochrane's proclamation had been distributed across Florida, Georgia, and Louisiana, Woodbine reported that two hundred slaves were already en route to the post, and he anticipated many more "joining our standard the moment it is raised."[27]

With Woodbine in charge of recruitment, responsibility for organizing the new recruits into an effective fighting force fell to Edward Nicolls. This thirty-five-year-old marine officer, in the words of historian Nathaniel Millett, "devoted most of his life to fighting slavery."[28] In July 1814, Cochrane ordered the Irish-born lieutenant colonel to raise a force of five hundred warriors from among the Creek and "other Indian nations," teach them to use firearms "in an organized mode of Warfare," and convince them to cease the practice of scalping prisoners and committing "other species of cruelties." Cochrane moreover directed Nicolls to enlist in the Colonial Marines "such Negroes and others as may be induced to desert from the territory of the United States to whom you are to hold out every Encouragement." To assist in this process, Cochrane forwarded additional copies of his proclamation for distribution among the "Black population." He also ordered Nicolls to inform the fugitive slaves he encountered that in return for their service, they would receive land in a British colony and, regardless of the war's outcome, would never "be returned to their former Masters."[29]

After only a month of training at the British Post, Nicolls rushed several hundred white, black, and Indian troops to Pensacola to stop a rumored American invasion. When the force disembarked in late August, the Spanish governor, Mateo González Manrique, allowed them to occupy the city and take possession of the adjacent Fort San Miguel, a large hilltop fort located about a mile from the city's shoreline. The British then hoisted a Union Jack atop the Spanish flag, which had flown over the city for more than three decades, and waited for a confrontation. American troops, who watched the arrival of the British from just miles away, were surprised and perhaps intimidated by the British occupation and promptly relocated to Mobile, Alabama, the closest American port.[30]

Whereas Spanish officials welcomed the diverse British force, Americans were outraged. A writer in the Mississippi Territory complained of having received numerous reports from Florida of "an attack upon some part of the southern country." With the British arming Indians and slaves, he feared nothing could be done to "save the intermediate country in which we reside from falling into their hands, and becoming the prey of their savage coadjutor."[31] Captain Parker McCobb was equally terrified at the prospect of a multiracial army originating from Florida's Gulf Coast. The St. Mary's, Georgia, resident informed US secretary of war John Armstrong and Georgia governor Peter Early that under the leadership of the fanatical "Irishman" Nicolls, the British planned "to arm the Indians and all others that would Join them, which was understood to Mean the Negros of this Country."[32]

To secure the United States' southern border with Florida, the American government initially turned to Benjamin Hawkins, one of the most influential public servants in the history of the early republic. Born into a wealthy North Carolina family, Hawkins enjoyed a privileged youth. After working as an interpreter on George Washington's staff during the American Revolution, he served as a North Carolina assemblyman, Continental Congress delegate, and United States senator. A brief stint as a federal commissioner to the Cherokees, Choctaws, and Chickasaws earned Hawkins an appointment by President Washington as the United States' principal agent for Indians residing below the Ohio River. The appointment occurred in 1796, and "from this time," writes a biographer, "the remainder of the life of Benjamin Hawkins was devoted entirely to the Indians."[33]

At the Creek Agency on the eastern banks of Georgia's Flint River, Hawkins spent two decades instructing the Creek people in the agricultural and industrial arts, which led them to adopt many of the characteristics of their American neighbors. They organized a central government that served to unite more than a dozen Lower Towns, and they cultivated farms, nurseries, and orchards of various sizes that produced all sorts of goods, including wheat, cotton, strawberries, apples, and peaches. In addition to raising cattle, sheep, goats, and hogs, they tanned leather, spun and wove cotton, and processed cooking oil from acorns and nuts. While teaching the Creeks "the benefits of civilization," Hawkins found the time to compile one of the most important ethnographies of the Creek people ever written. *A Sketch of the Creek Country in the Years 1798 and 1799* described the origin and language of the Creeks while offering a detailed description of the culture and geography of the more than three dozen towns that comprised Creek country. Though written in a patronizing tone, the essay still stands out for its thoughtful and even sympathetic perspective.[34]

This makes Hawkins's antipathy toward African Americans striking. At the same time that the agent tried to save Indians from extinction, he owned a large plantation cultivated by black slaves and encouraged the practice of slavery among the Creeks. Though biographers and historians have often ignored the fact, Hawkins was a ruthless slave trader. He transformed the Creek Agency and Fort Hawkins, the closest army installation, into holding stations for fugitive slaves by offering Indian trackers cash payments of as much as $12.50 (approximately $250 in today's currency) for every black captive delivered to either location. Though slaveowners who recovered their property were expected to reimburse Hawkins the full amount of the reward, the arrangement nevertheless revealed a great deal about the early American government and slavery. Decades later, in the middle of the nineteenth century, southern slaveowners would threaten disunion if the government did not further assist them in the recovery of fugitive slaves. But such threats were unnecessary at the turn of the nineteenth century with federal agents, including Hawkins, serving as slave catchers.[35]

Because of his proximity to so many Indians and slaves, Hawkins particularly dreaded the arrival of British troops on the Gulf Coast. Shortly after learning that the enemy was training "Indians and some negroes for purposes hostile to us," he ordered the Lower Creek chief Little Prince (Tustennuggee Hopie) and the Upper Creek chief Big Warrior (Tustennuggee Thlucco) to invade Spanish Florida and stop the British intrusion.[36] Hawkins preferred that the warriors avoid any conflict with their fellow tribesmen for fear of exacerbating an already existing internecine tribal conflict, but he demanded that they "attack and take or destroy all the white and black people you find in arms." To avoid any misunderstanding, Hawkins added a note of clarification: "Take such white people as you see encouraging the black to mischief, and bring them prisoners to me, if they refuse to surrender to you, fire on them and compell them." In return for their assistance, Hawkins promised the Creeks a bounty of black men, women, and children. He declared, "The negros you take who have no white masters will be your property, and those who have white masters shall pay you 50 dollars a head."[37]

In addition to quadrupling the bounty for fugitive slaves, Hawkins put Chief William McIntosh (Tustennuggee Hutke) in charge of the mission to improve its chance of success. Known as the "White Warrior," this son of a Scottish father and Coweta Creek mother was a strong advocate of Hawkins's acculturationist schemes and long served as one of the agent's most trusted allies. With an ability to thrive in both the Indian and the white worlds, McIntosh experienced much personal success. Though the Creek's matrilineal social structure made him a bona fide chief, he adopted "the lifestyle of an antebellum southern gentleman," owning more than one hundred slaves on two Georgia plantations.[38] McIntosh's acquisition

FIGURE 1.1. While working at the Creek Agency to help Native Americans assimilate into European American culture, Benjamin Hawkins enslaved dozens of African Americans and used his authority as a federal Indian agent to hunt fugitive slaves and return them to their owners. "Benjamin Hawkins" (undated). Courtesy of Wikimedia Commons.

of property and power supports the ethnohistorical argument that Indian leaders of mixed parentage, whom the Spanish referred to as "mestizos," compelled the transformation of Native American culture along the European American model. Nevertheless, in contrast with McIntosh and others like him, there were powerful mestizos like Josiah Francis, Peter McQueen, and William Weatherford (Red Eagle) who resisted such change.[39]

During the War of 1812, McIntosh fought alongside Andrew Jackson at the Battle of Horseshoe Bend. He then further demonstrated his loyalty to the United States by affixing his name to the Treaty of Fort Jackson. Subsequently, McIntosh maintained immense power among the Lower Creeks by controlling the distribution of federal annuities among them. Given his privileged position, it is not surprising that when Hawkins offered McIntosh another chance to prove his fidelity to the United States by invading Spanish Florida, the chief promptly accepted. But before any sort of confrontation could commence, the British embarked from Prospect Bluff for Pensacola with their black and Indian allies beside them.[40]

Despite their best intentions, Hawkins and McIntosh lacked the resources and power to permanently secure the southern border against a British invasion. Therefore, the task fell to an extraordinary lawyer, planter, and politician, about whom little was known outside of his home state of Tennessee prior to the War of 1812. Born along the North Carolina–South Carolina border in 1767, Andrew Jackson grew up fatherless in the southern backcountry. There he acquired a deep hatred both for Indians, who refused to forfeit their land to the United States, and the British traders who encouraged the Indians and enabled them to resist American expansion. Jackson's animosity towards Indians and Britons intensified during the Revolutionary War, which took the lives of his mother and two brothers and shaped the adolescent patriot into a serious and solemn young man. Orphaned and alone at age fourteen, Jackson inherited

FIGURE 1.2. Among the most powerful Native American leaders on the southern frontier, William McIntosh was an ardent supporter of US expansion and a close confidant of Andrew Jackson and Benjamin Hawkins. He would lead the United States' assault on Negro Fort in July 1816. "William McIntosh" (undated). Courtesy of State Archives of Florida, Florida Memory, www.floridamemory.com.

two hundred acres following the war. However, ambition drove him to Charleston, South Carolina, where he began the process of trading his backwoods culture and heritage for the exalted status of a proper southern gentleman.[41]

Though Jackson possessed the drive necessary to join the ranks of the South's planter elite, he did not always look the part. From the age of eighteen, the aspiring pioneer stood tall among his peers at more than six feet in height. But weighing less than 150 pounds, with an unusually large head and perfect posture, he resembled a flag pole. This, combined with a long face, wild hair, and uncommonly deep and piercing blue eyes, resulted in an appearance "far from handsome." Yet what Jackson lacked in looks, he more than made up for with talent and tenacity.[42]

If, as historians suggest, honor was the edifice upon which southern white men carved out their names and reputations, then slavery was its cornerstone, providing the economic and racial foundations of the South's peculiar social order.[43] In his ascent to the gentry class, Jackson fully embraced the region's peculiar institution. The future president's personal involvement with slavery began in 1788, when, after settling in North Carolina and earning a law license, he purchased a young "Negro Woman named Nancy."[44] Fifteen years later, Jackson owned almost twenty slaves and was well on his way to owning more than 150 black men, women, and children on plantations in Tennessee, Mississippi, and Alabama. Like most slaveowners, Jackson was an active participant in the domestic slave trade, which, in the decades before the Civil War, brought hundreds of thousands of enslaved people from the tobacco farms and wheat fields of the Upper South to work on the sweltering sugar and cotton plantations of the Lower South. Throughout his political career, Jackson disparaged rivals for trafficking in human flesh. Yet he made no apologies for the role he played in the trade throughout his entire adult life.[45]

FIGURE 1.3. "GENL ANDREW JACKSON. THE HERO OF NEW ORLEANS." The undated lithograph by Nathaniel Currier epitomizes the heroism and bravery most Americans ascribed to the southern general following the Battle of New Orleans. Courtesy of the Library of Congress.

As a slaveowner, Jackson could be considerate. He formed close personal relationships with some of his servants and at times rejected potentially profitable slave sales to keep enslaved families intact. But there was a sadistic side to his personality, as an infamous case involving one fugitive slave makes clear. The absconder was a light-skinned man named Tom Gid, who left Nashville with forged papers intended to prove his status as a free man. To retrieve him, Jackson placed an advertisement in the classified section of a local newspaper, offering fifty dollars "to any person that will take him, and deliver him to me, or secure him in jail, so that I can get him." The advertisement was typical of the time and place, with one exception. In addition to the stated sum, Jackson promised anyone who captured the recalcitrant slave "ten dollars extra, for every hundred lashes any person will give him, to the amount of three hundred."[46]

Despite Jackson's unequivocal pro-slavery stance, his racial beliefs were inconsistent. Though convinced that Native Americans and African Americans were intellectually, physically, and socially inferior to European Americans, he respected their martial ability. Throughout his military career, Jackson employed Indians or slaves in nearly every significant military engagement in which he participated, including the Battle of New Orleans. In an earlier instance, Jackson even armed his own slaves. This occurred after an overzealous Indian agent named Silas Dinsmoor began detaining slaves whom settlers and traders were moving through the Mississippi Territory without the required papers. Jackson considered such actions a threat to his rights and liberties as a slaveowner, and while passing through Indian country tried to provoke a confrontation. According to one account, Jackson "armed two of his most resolute negro men, and put them in front of his negroes, and gave them orders to FIGHT THEIR WAY, if necessary."[47] Due to Dinsmoor's absence, no blood spilled on the southern frontier that day, but it would soon flow across the region with the arrival of thousands of British redcoats and their black and Indian allies.

FIGURE 1.4. While many citizens revered Andrew Jackson, some reviled him for his pro-slavery politics as well as his reputation as a ruthless slaveowner and trader. In *A Brief Account of General Jackson's Dealings in Negroes* (1829). Courtesy of the William L. Clements Library, University of Michigan.

Jackson, for his part, welcomed a second war with Great Britain. In addition to providing the young republic an opportunity to vanquish its nemesis, the conflict significantly increased the United States' chances of acquiring Spanish Florida and securing the lives and property of settlers across the southern frontier. "I hope the government will permit us to traverse the Southern coast and aid in planting the American eagles on the ramparts of Mobile, Pensacola and St. Augustine," Jackson wrote confidently in the first year of the War of 1812. "This alone will give us security in that quarter and peace on our frontiers." Unless the British influence over Spanish Florida was eliminated, Jackson averred, "We will have the whole Southern tribe of Indians to fight and insurrections to quell in all the Southern states."[48] This "triple alliance of British soldiers, Indian warriors, and slave rebels" was "the southern citizenry's ultimate nightmare," concludes southern frontier historian Adam Rothman.[49]

Jackson was not alone in his desire to extend the southern boundary of the United States to Florida's Atlantic and Gulf coasts. Several weeks after the United States declared war on Great Britain, settlers in southern Georgia petitioned President James Madison to take "immediate possession of the Floridas." The group apologized for addressing the commander-in-chief directly but felt that failing to do so constituted "a dereliction of duty, as good Citizens." The petitioners informed the president that the lives of American citizens were in grave danger if Great Britain acquired Florida from Spain, for the British would incite "the merciless and unrelenting Savages, immediately bordering upon us." They would, moreover, seduce "our black population, exciting them to abandon their owners, and perhaps to rise up in rebellion against them."[50]

As these petitioners perfectly understood, American expansion into Spanish Florida required subjugating a violent faction of the Creek Indians known as the Red Sticks. So called because of their red war clubs, the militant group launched a vicious civil war in July

1813 against fellow tribesmen who thought resistance to American expansion was futile. The Creek Civil War escalated dramatically a month later as hundreds of Red Sticks under the leadership of Peter McQueen and William Weatherford attacked Fort Mims. Fort Mims had recently been built at a site on the Alabama River, where hundreds of Indians and white settlers were protected by US troops. The Red Sticks' surprise attack resulted in a devastating defeat for the Americans. "The slaughter was dreadful," read one account sent from the Mississippi Territory to Washington. Beside the approximately one hundred slaves who absconded with the Red Sticks, only a handful of the three hundred men, women, and children who hid in the fort survived. "The rest lie scalped and mangled in the most horrid manner . . . the sheep, cattle, hogs & other animals which were within reach lie round about, together with the human bodies in a state of decay."[51]

Revenge for the massacre at Fort Mims was swift and exact. In Tennessee, Jackson alerted citizens that the Red Sticks were heading towards their "frontier with their scalping knives unsheathed, to butcher your wives, your children, and your helpless babes." Soon, more than one thousand militiamen followed him into northern Alabama, where they laid waste to every Creek town and village in their path.[52] The following spring, Jackson's force, which now numbered more than two thousand federal troops, militiamen, and allied Indians, met more than one thousand Red Sticks who had retreated with their families to a small U-shaped peninsula along the Tallapoosa River in central Alabama known as Horseshoe Bend. A bloodbath followed. In about five hours, Jackson's army overwhelmed the one thousand Red Sticks who defended the peninsula before commencing a terrible slaughter of the retreating survivors that "continued until it was suspended by the darkness of the night."[53]

For defeating the Red Sticks, Jackson earned a promotion to major general of the United States Army. To demonstrate his gratitude, he continued the undoing of the Creek nation. In August 1814, Jackson secured the signatures of more than two dozen Upper and Lower Town chiefs, including William McIntosh, Little Prince, and Big Warrior, on the Treaty of Fort Jackson. This treaty stripped the Creeks of twenty-three million acres of land in exchange for a temporary supply of necessities.[54] It was a devastating blow from which the Creeks, including those allied with the United States, would never recover. Jackson then planned to visit Pensacola, where hundreds of Red Sticks had taken refuge. But after learning of the British occupation of the West Florida capital, he instead proceeded to Mobile and began plotting his next move.[55]

In the meantime, public pressure mounted on the American government to unleash Jackson and his army on the gathering multiracial forces that threatened the safety and security of the southern frontier. This pressure is apparent in a letter written by John Smith, former US senator and resident of the Louisiana Territory. Smith feared that with the British occupation of Pensacola, "The Spaniards will coalesce with Creeks, Choctaws, Negro's & English in Offensive War." Since frontier militiamen were no match for the overwhelming force gathering in Florida, Smith believed that only "Gen. Jackson with 10,000 regular troops would be able to repel [the] invasion & save the Country." If the government failed to send Jackson and his army, the entire region would be lost to the enemy, as many settlers refused to "serve a tour of duty & leave their families to be plundered & Butchered by Negro's &c."[56]

Willie Blount also thought that Jackson was the only man capable of eliminating the threats emanating from Spanish Florida. In a panicked letter to Secretary of State James Monroe, the Tennessee governor insisted that recent British actions on the Gulf Coast justified "the U.S. in taking possession of Pensacola, and continuing in the occupation thereof." If the British remained in the West Florida capital, the southwestern section of the United States would remain

FIGURE 1.5. In this rendering of events following the Battle of Horseshoe Bend, the Red Stick Creek chief William Weatherford, or Red Eagle, surrenders to Andrew Jackson and agrees to the Treaty of Fort Jackson. "Treaty of the Hickory Ground." From John Frost, *Frost's Pictorial History of Indian Wars and Captives* (1873). Courtesy of the Library of Congress.

vulnerable to depredations by "straggling parties of hostile Indians, by disaffected white men, and by run away and plundered negroes, who have an asylum there, and who will flock to the British standard." Blount believed that the violent plots forming among these deranged people could only be averted "by the gallant patriot and friend to his Country Major Genl. Jackson, who is, at all times, on the alert, and promptly acts against such workers of mischief."[57]

With the likelihood of a Jackson-led American assault on Pensacola increasing every moment, the city became a cockpit of Great Britain's radical interracial agenda.[58] Nicolls and Woodbine enacted martial law and recruited several hundred volunteers from the town and surrounding areas. Within several weeks, Woodbine claimed to have organized a force of several hundred "White Men, Mulattoes & Blacks," as well as eight hundred Indian warriors. No ordinary imperial army, these men yearned "to free all these Southern Countries from the Yoke of the Americans."[59] William H. Robertson, an American citizen imprisoned in Pensacola during the British oc-cupation, confirmed Woodbine's claim, adding that in addition to Indians and slaves, the redcoats also recruited a number of "American deserters." Robertson also considered especially notable an address Nicolls delivered in the city plaza to a large crowd of "Indians, ne-groes, royal marines, and inhabitants of Pensacola."[60]

Nicolls began his speech by reminding his regular troops that fight-ing against the United States would carry on the tradition established in Europe of assisting "all those who lingered in oppressions bonds." As Britons, they would honor the flag of the British Empire by fight-ing for Indians, "who had robberies and murders committed on them by the Americans," and slaves, who had long "been oppressed by cruel taskmasters." Nicolls then commended the fugitive slaves in his corps for having escaped from captivity and then taken a vow to "unrivet the Chains" of those still held in bondage. He reminded them that because of their bravery, they would soon enjoy all "the rights of a

British man" in one of Great Britain's colonies, where "the ground you will then cultivate will be yours and your Childrens for ever."[61] It was a revolutionary speech that "used timely and poignant language to attack American slavery, encourage American slaves to flee, and assert these same slaves' humanity."[62]

Niles' Weekly Register published a copy of Nicolls's speech to document the subversive activities of the British below the southern border. The paper mocked the growing multiracial army that comprised "his majesty's forces in the FLORIDAS," insisting that "their *impudence* is equaled only by their folly." Then, in a curious case of editorial sleight of hand, it deleted the portion of Nicolls's speech dealing with the recruitment of fugitive slaves and their rights as British subjects. In the United States, it seemed, the best way to address the news of a foreign power spreading freedom throughout the republic—which was founded on that very ideal—was to suppress it.[63]

By the end of the summer of 1814, a clash of American and British forces along the Gulf Coast was inevitable given the deployment of so many men and resources. Yet Jackson's and Nicolls's divergent views on Indians and slaves meant that much more was at stake than the outcome of any single military contest. Though sharing a love of military service and a deep devotion to their respective countries, the two men were polar opposites: "Old Hickory" was a backwoods brawler committed to killing Indians, defending slavery, and spreading the institution to the south and west; "Fighting Nicolls" was a citizen of the world, a racial egalitarian dedicated to protecting Indians from colonizers and delivering slaves from bondage.[64] With Jackson and Nicolls preparing to square off, the fate of the southern frontier hung in the balance. It would become an integral part of America's racially ordered southern slave society, or it would remain a refuge for enslaved people escaping therefrom.

The first of several battles between the United States and Great Britain along the northern Gulf Coast occurred in September 1814, when Nicolls's troops launched a surprise attack on Fort Bowyer, a small stockade at the mouth of Mobile Bay, Alabama. According to an American eyewitness, the Royal Marines left Pensacola with 750 Indian warriors as well as "about 40 recruits of negroes, mulattoes, American deserters and refuse Spaniards."[65] Believing the size of the British force to be greatly exaggerated and fully confident that the troops he had stationed on the coast would "give a good account of the enemy," Jackson remained at his headquarters several miles away in downtown Mobile.[66] His assumptions proved correct. After a brief seventy-two-hour engagement, the larger American force easily repulsed the British invaders, who beat a hasty retreat to Pensacola.

The British were devastated. Besides failing to take the fort, they lost more than sixty men killed or wounded, as well as their largest ship, the HMS *Hermes*.[67] Colonel Nicolls survived the battle but suffered near-fatal injuries to his head and leg, while grapeshot from an American cannon left him permanently blinded in his right eye.[68] Still, he persisted. In anticipation of a rematch with Jackson, he spent several weeks in Pensacola recovering from his wounds, while his troops continued searching for recruits.

By the fall of 1814, the continued enlistment of slaves had drawn the ire of local residents, who initially welcomed the British presence. John Innerarity, a Scottish immigrant and prominent Pensacola businessman, recalled that as soon as Nicolls's troops returned from Mobile, "They began to exert all their faculties of deceit, to set all their traps, to put all their tools to work, to catch negro Slaves." With the "American fugitive slaves" who had already joined them, the British "visited the negro cabins in the town, attended their meetings and by every means that the genius of seduction could invent endeavoured to entice the slaves of the Spanish citizens to join them."[69] The recruitment effort succeeded, and Pensacola's citizens watched helplessly as former slaves wearing distinctive uniforms of scarlet red caps and coats, white shirts, and blue leggings drilled on the city's streets along-side their white and Indian allies.[70]

In a protest forwarded to the British government, Innerarity's business partner, John Forbes, detailed how Pensacola's slaveowners suffered at Nicolls's hands. Across the city, the "Demon" colonel welcomed into his corps "whatever Black man he could inveigle whether free or Slave the property of friend or foe, of Spaniard, English or American." When the owners of these recruits tried to regain possession of their valuable chattels, they were "treated with the grossest abuse for dareing to claim them." During the three-month British occupation, "No man could be secure of his Negro property for a day or an hour; to every discontented or capricious slave Col. Nicolls's troop offered a secure asylum, and their owners dared scarcely utter a murmur from dread of the Indians who he held at his beck."[71]

Nicolls, Woodbine, and the other British officers directed the recruitment effort throughout Pensacola, yet some of the most effective recruiters were not even British subjects. The most notorious was Sergeant Hugh McGill, a member of the Second Infantry Regiment of the United States Army who had deserted from Fort Stoddert in the Mississippi Territory to Spanish Florida. During the British occupation of Pensacola, McGill helped "take away all negros that could be got at" and made his home an important "rendezvous" for the redcoats and their allies.[72] Another successful recruiter was Delisle, an "Indian chief" from the Seminole town of Miccosukee hired by Nicolls and Woodbine as an interpreter at the British Post. After disembarking in Pensacola, Delisle thought he would only assist the British in communicating with the local indigenous population but soon found himself enlisting "Negros as would be suitable for the service."[73]

African Americans also counted among Great Britain's local agents. It is unknown whether the "mulatto, called London" and "a negro called Boston" were free or enslaved, but both men helped the marines procure beef, water, "and some other things" from the woods surrounding Pensacola.[74] A free black man named John Bennett received a sergeant's stripes and one hundred dollars when he accepted Woodbine's offer to serve in the "Volunteer Regiment." He quickly became one of the captain's closest confidants.[75] A particularly successful operative was an enslaved carpenter named Prince, who belonged to Don Eugenio Antonio Sierra, a prominent Spanish doctor. After escorting several slaves from a local lumberyard to the British, Prince became a lieutenant in the Colonial Marines with orders to "persuade all sorts of Negroes whether Freemen or Slaves" to join the corps.[76]

Though estimates vary slightly, Nicolls's troops freed at least 135 slaves from Pensacola and the vicinity during their three-month occupation of the city. The figure is remarkable given that Pensacola's total population rarely surpassed one thousand at any point during the Spanish colonial era.[77] Still, the number of fugitive slaves may have been even higher. A petition signed by Pensacola's leading citizens accused the British of evacuating the city with "at least Two-Thirds of our Slaves," including men, women, "and their infant children." Regardless of the actual number, the petitioners acknowledged that their losses would have been even greater if not for the arrival in November of "the Army of the United States of America Commanded by Major General Andrew Jackson."[78]

In October 1814, Jackson informed Washington that Spanish governor Mateo González Manrique and "the citizens of Pensacola have become tired" of their British guests. The final straw occurred when Colonel Nicolls, "to convince the Governor of his power and prowess, paraded his savage force, marched it through the town, saluting his excellency with the war whoop, and threatening to scalp all the inhabitants." With British authority in Pensacola unchecked, Jackson wanted to invade the city and claim all of Spanish Florida for the United States in the process.[79] President Madison disagreed. Preferring a diplomatic solution to the problem, he informed Jackson unequivocally, "You should at present take no measures, which would involve this Government in a contest with Spain."[80]

Believing himself more than capable of handling the crisis as he saw fit, Jackson completely ignored the commander-in-chief's order. On November 6, 1814, he arrived on Pensacola's outskirts with an army of four thousand militiamen, army regulars, and allied Choctaws, greatly outnumbering the force of one thousand British marines, Spanish regulars, and Indian warriors that defended the capital. When the Americans stormed the town the following day, the Spanish government quickly surrendered its army. The British flew to the shore, where they blew up several coastal fortifications, including the stronghold that guarded the entrance to Pensacola, Fort San Carlos de Barrancas. Then, along with several hundred Indians, fugitive slaves, and some seventy black Spanish troops, they embarked for the British Post.[81]

The British had failed again, but by returning to their Apalachicola River base, they announced their intention of maintaining a strong presence on the southern frontier. After learning of the outcome of the Battle of Pensacola, the *Georgia Journal* informed readers that their lives and property were still in grave danger. "Yesterday, a dispatch was received by the Governor," the piece began, "of the arrival at the mouth of the Appalachicola in Florida of a large British fleet, having on board according to the enemy's statement, *fourteen thousand troops*, and a considerable portion of them *****." The flotilla consisted of seven large vessels and several others of smaller size, all of which contained arms, ammunition, and other articles for their Indian allies. The British having established a defensive post with a garrison of three hundred men, "All the Indians have been invited to receive presents—the Redsticks and many runaway ******* have gone."[82]

As indicated by the writer's insistence on using asterisks instead of the words "black" and "negroes" to refer to the African American population at Prospect Bluff, white settlers were never going to allow an asylum for fugitive slaves to exist so close to their homes, farms, and plantations. But for the British troops stationed in Spanish Florida, the establishment of just such a sanctuary had become an integral part of their southern strategy. In the coming months, the interracial alliance of British troops, fugitive slaves, and Indian warriors at the British Post not only prospered but reached a level of success that in the era of the early American republic was rarely if ever surpassed.

• 2 •

THE BRITISH POST ON PROSPECT BLUFF

UMBLED by their losses at Mobile and Pensacola, the British returned to Prospect Bluff to regroup. In the coming months, nearly fifteen hundred Royal Marines, Colonial Marines, and allied Indians lived at the post, where they worked and trained under the leadership of Edward Nicolls and George Woodbine. The disparate group undertook several fortification projects, including enlarging the moat surrounding the complex and constructing an octagonal-shaped internal fort on a massive dirt mound at the center of the compound. This new edifice, which was encircled by a stockade and a moat of its own, enclosed the "Powder Magazine" built months earlier.[1] Its walls were imposing. Consisting of large timbers stacked horizontally with dirt and debris as mortar, they stood nearly thirty feet tall and were a dozen feet thick, with mounted cannon. Upon its completion, this immense inner fort—what Nicolls called a "citadel"—had an interior diameter of sixty feet and an exterior diameter twice that distance, making it the largest man-made structure in Florida between St. Augustine and Pensacola, the capitals of East Florida and West Florida, respectively.[2]

Besides fortifying their Prospect Bluff post, the British continued to win the hearts and minds of Indians and slaves. In a proclamation published in December 1814 and addressed "To the Great and Illustrious Chiefs of the Creek and Other Indian Nations," Admiral Cochrane beseeched Indians across the southern frontier to "join the British standard,—the signal of union between the powerful and the oppressed." The proclamation explained that the British had come to America to wage war against "the People of the Bad Spirit," and the result was a series of major military successes, including the capture of the "Capital City of Washington." Still, defeating the Americans required the assistance of "ye brave Chiefs and Warriors," and what did Great Britain ask of its Indian volunteers? "Nothing more than that you should assist us manfully in regaining your lost lands,— the lands of your forefathers,—from the common enemy, the wicked People of the United States."[3]

The appeal worked. Within two weeks of its publication, officers at the British Post reported a "vast number of Indians, pouring in upon us daily."[4] By the start of the new year, Nicolls noted the presence of some of the most powerful Indian leaders in the entire southeast. The list included the Creek chiefs Josiah Francis of the Tuskegees, Peter McQueen of the Tallassees, and Old Factor of the Euchees. Representing the Seminoles were Thomas Perryman and Hopoy Micco. Of all the great men assembled at Prospect Bluff, Nicolls was particularly fond of Kinache, the widely regarded king of the Miccosukees. The "brave and faithful old" Seminole chief "has adhered to England throughout all difficulties," the colonel informed Admiral Cochrane proudly, and "is here with me and 70 of his men helping me to build the Fort."[5]

To increase the number of black volunteers, the British commanders at Prospect Bluff concocted one of the more extraordinary abolitionist schemes in American history: they offered to purchase slaves belonging to the Creeks and Seminoles. Before leaving Pensacola, Woodbine had asked Nicolls for permission "to purchase such slaves as the Indians may be at present possessed of, and also those they may capture in war, with the intention of giving them their liberty, and enlisting them in the Corps, you have done me the honor of ordering me to raise." Woodbine insisted that the slaves claimed by the Indians would "each have their chains struck off for a very low sum," and he pledged "one hundred guineas" of his own money to set the process in motion.[6] When Nicolls and Woodbine returned to the British Post, they began negotiating with the Indians, who agreed to sell their slaves for as little as twenty-five dollars each.[7] While it is not certain how many slaves British officers purchased from their Indian allies at Prospect Bluff, Captain Robert Henry later asserted that the Indians never relinquished ownership of any of "their Negroes" without being paid.[8]

The scheme is a reminder that slavery flourished in America long before the arrival of Europeans and Africans. Though various forms of bondage had existed in Native American culture, it was not until the turn of the nineteenth century that Indians embraced a racialized version of slavery based on the American model. This resulted in their holding thousands of African Americans captive. While any form of bondage is cruel, inhumane, and degrading, black people owned by southern Native Americans generally experienced a less severe form of slavery than black people enslaved by whites in the South.[9] Of all the forms of black slavery that developed among the South's indigenous people, the one adopted by Seminoles appears to have been the most benign. As US Indian agent Wiley Thompson described the Seminoles' black vassals, "They live in villages, separate, and, in many cases, remote from their owners, enjoying equal liberty with their owners, with the single exception that the slave supplies his owner annually, from the product of his little field, with corn in proportion to the amount of the crop."[10]

The unique relationship between the southern Indians and their slaves often revealed itself on the battlefield, where the two groups fought alongside each other when one or both of them felt threatened.[11] The story of one of Nicolls's black volunteers at the British Post illustrates this phenomenon. According to Chief Josiah Francis, the individual had distinguished himself during the Red Stick assault on Fort Mims the previous year. "The blacks were the first in," Francis told Nicolls, and among them was this unnamed fighter, who "killed seven Americans in that affair."[12] When considering why Creeks' slaves would fight alongside their owners, a Red Stick writer recalled that these enslaved warriors expected to become free. "Their freedom would come about when the Negroes and the Indians would conquer and destroy the white people, according to the say of the prophets."[13]

For some recruits at Prospect Bluff, the motivation for joining the British was not freedom but revenge. When asked if he could help locate the American army, an elderly Creek man who had traveled "about 300 miles" to the post responded affirmatively, adding that while the journey would take seven days, "he could not miss the way, for it was marked by the graves of his four children." When Nicolls offered the aged warrior a musket and bayonet, the man rejoiced. He revealed that in previous engagements he had always wasted time loading and reloading his firearm, but now that he had a bayonet, he "would rush on the Americans when he was sure of victory."[14]

Owing to their common American enemy and the concerted effort of the British to cultivate strong relationships among their allies, Native Americans and African Africans at Prospect Bluff got along famously. "The Indians and the blacks are on very good terms and cooperate bravely together," Colonel Nicolls observed during his command. This led him to believe that both groups would play a key role in the British assault on New Orleans. By December 1814, as the final preparations for the invasion began, Nicolls informed Admiral Cochrane that while the British could not rely on the assistance of New Orleans's French and Spanish residents, the Indians at the bluff had already offered their assistance. Moreover, in addition to the hundreds of slaves currently enrolled in the Colonial Marines, he expected New Orleans's black inhabitants to "join us the moment we appear."[15]

British invaders saw their effort to recruit among New Orleans's free and enslaved black population as a humanitarian component of a much larger imperial war effort. American citizens, on the other hand, interpreted it as the opening salvo of an unthinkable race war. Such fears were not unrealistic. Only a few years earlier, several hundred slaves had revolted on the eastern bank of Louisiana's German Coast just north of New Orleans, taking the lives of two white men and leaving a path of destruction in their wake. Considered today by some historians as "the largest slave rebellion" in US history, it affected the way many in New Orleans perceived the war with Great Britain.[16] But it was not just locals who feared a British-inspired slave revolt.

The views of American soldiers and sailors stationed in New Orleans reflected those of the local white population. Midshipman Daniel Patterson, commander of the United States Navy Station at New Orleans, argued that once the British had provoked a war between the Indians and Americans along the Florida border, they would rush to New Orleans and spark an insurrection among the city's slaves, "for after inducing the Savage to raise the Tomahawk and draw the Scalping knife, they will descend to tamper with negroes."[17] French-born Arsène Lacarrière Latour, who as a young man survived the unprecedented slave revolt in Haiti before immigrating to New Orleans, likewise feared a British-inspired slave revolt along Louisiana's Gulf Coast. The US Army major claimed that an "insurrection of the negroes," to whom the British had promised freedom, "was one of the chief means they intended to employ, being confident of its success."[18]

General Andrew Jackson also feared that the British assault on New Orleans would produce a slave revolt. After being presented with a British musket that was "given to a friendly Indian by those at Apalachicola Bay," he alerted Louisiana governor William Claiborne to the likelihood of a traditional military assault by the British, who would also employ the tactic of "exciting the black population to insurrection & massacre."[19] Claiborne responded that Louisiana's citizens were greatly distressed by the possibility of a domestic disturbance; he insisted that there was "every reason to believe that the Enemy has been intriguing with *our* slaves, and from a variety of circumstances, we have much cause to suspect that *they* on their part, meditate mischief."[20] Historians have generally dismissed Americans' fears of a British-inspired slave uprising on the eve of the Battle of New Orleans. However, the shared concerns of the general and governor are noteworthy, for they reveal just how much these fears weighed on the minds of American citizens and their leaders when British forces finally began landing on Louisiana's shores during the last several weeks of 1814.

Contrary to popular belief, the Battle of New Orleans lasted more than a single day. In reality, it was a month-long engagement that began in mid-December when the navies of Great Britain and the United States clashed on Lake Borgne just east of the Crescent City. Over the course of the next several weeks, British and American ground troops skirmished along Louisiana's swampy southern shore, which allowed the bulk of Jackson's army the time to take up strong defensive positions on both sides of the Mississippi River. Consisting of army regulars, marines, sailors, and militiamen from Louisiana, Mississippi, Tennessee, and Kentucky, as well as Choctaw warriors, Baratarian pirates, local slaves, and free men of color, the hastily organized American force totaled more than four thousand men. The

British force was more than twice the size of Jackson's and equally diverse. Commanded by Major General Edward Pakenham, it included some of Europe's most experienced professional soldiers, along with hundreds of black men from Jamaica, Barbados, and the Bahamas, who served in distinct units known as the West India Regiments.[21] Nicolls volunteered his marines to lead the ground assault on New Orleans, but Admiral Cochrane feared the loss of one of his most important officers. He denied Nicolls's request, forcing the colonel to watch the battle from a safe distance offshore.[22]

The last major battle of the War of 1812 culminated on January 8 when Pakenham's troops, despite being closed in by the Mississippi on the left and an unnavigable cypress swamp on the right, advanced towards New Orleans. The deeply entrenched Americans unloaded their rifles and cannon on the exposed invaders, and in less than an hour sent Pakenham to his grave and forced the entire redcoat army to retreat. In repulsing the invaders, Jackson's American force suffered about a dozen casualties, while the British lost more than two thousand dead, wounded, or captured. It was, as battle historian Robert Remini asserts, a shocking outcome by any measure: "Who could believe this band of frontiersmen, privateers, men of color, local citizens, state militiamen, and army regulars had annihilated the most modern and most powerful army in the world?"[23]

Some have cited the contributions of six hundred of New Orleans's free men of color to the city's defense as a symbol of the new republic's democratic promise. However, it was more accurately a sign of its growing commitment to slavery. By all accounts, the free black men Jackson asked to help defend New Orleans were citizens of property and standing who shared little in common with slaves other than African ancestry.[24] In fact, some were slaveowners in Haiti before the revolution on that island nation forced them to take refuge in the United States. "They were almost all men who had long and bravely defended their native country, St. Domingo, against the British, and

against the rebels, who at length subdued it," wrote Major Latour, a
first-hand witness to the heroism of these volunteers in Louisiana.[25]
Shortly after arriving in New Orleans, some of these free men of
color continued to fight against slaves seeking their freedom when
they assisted their white neighbors in suppressing the German Coast
revolt of 1811.[26] By assisting the American army in its opposition to
the British invasion of New Orleans, they would continue to fight in
slavery's defense.

Despite the potential for subversion, Jackson's decision to arm
slaves reinforced the racial status quo. Unlike his British counterparts,
the American general did not recognize military service as a path to
citizenship for enslaved people. In fact, according to the only published account of a slave who served under Jackson's command, the
general offered freedom to slaves who assisted in the defense of New
Orleans and then reneged on the agreement afterwards. The author
of the narrative, James Roberts, was a plantation laborer in Natchez,
Mississippi, when Jackson "came into our section of the country" and
promised five hundred slaves that if they helped defeat the British,
"we should be free after the battle." Roberts seized the opportunity
and fought heroically at New Orleans, killing six British soldiers in
close hand-to-hand combat while suffering the loss of a finger and
receiving a "deep wound on my head from a British sword." In return for their sacrifices, Roberts and the other enslaved volunteers
were stripped of their weapons, jailed, and ordered by Jackson to "go
home to your masters." Roberts regretted his decision to assist the
American army, convinced that the contributions of slave soldiers like
him determined the battle's outcome: "Had there been less bravery
with us, the British would have gained the victory, and in that event
they would have set the slaves free; so that I now see how we, in that
war, contributed to fasten our chains tighter."[27]

Service in the American army at New Orleans only tightened
slaves' bonds. But for those who cast their lot with the British, the

result was permanent release from the shackles of slavery. When the redcoats began arriving on the coasts of Louisiana and Mississippi, they encouraged slaves to enlist in His Majesty's armed forces in exchange for the freedom of all enlisted men and their families following the war's conclusion. As a result, approximately 250 slaves embarked from Louisiana and Mississippi with the British after the defeat at New Orleans, leaving their owners at a loss as to how to resume their livelihoods.[28] "The result was that they carried almost all the negroes off with them," Latour complained in his memoir. "And those negroes were private property, and without them their masters could not cultivate their plantations."[29]

The British fleet sailed about one hundred miles eastward to Dauphin Island, a small island at the mouth of Mobile Bay, where it remained for several months. In February, Jackson promised American slaveowners that he would do everything in his power "to procure a restoration of their property," including authorizing several planters to go to the island and meet with Pakenham's successor, General John Lambert, to discuss the matter.[30] Whereas Jackson anticipated that the British would assist the Americans, given the outcome at New Orleans, Lambert resisted. Regarding the black people on the island as being under the protection of the British flag, he told the Americans that they could speak with the slaves and embark with any who chose to return—but that the use of force would not be tolerated. One of Lambert's aides then met with the slaves, informing them directly, "Your masters come for you, you are at liberty to follow them, but recollect that you are as free as themselves."[31]

With the might of the British Empire behind them, the slaves at Dauphin Island spurned the offer to return home. While some declined the offer respectfully, others openly defied those who would dare to reenslave them. Among the most "insolent" was Jean-Baptiste, a thirty-five-year-old carter, or wagon driver, believed to be worth an incredible twelve hundred dollars. In a face-to-face encounter with Colonel Pierre Lacoste, a member of the Louisiana General Assembly, the proud bondsman refused the offer of the slaveowning legislator, telling him, "You may carry my head along with you but as to my body it shall remain here."[32] Days later, Jean-Baptiste and the other former slaves at Dauphin Island left the shores of the "slave country" and began their new lives either as British subjects in the Colonial Marines or as free settlers in the colonies of the Bahamas or Trinidad.[33]

Not every slave at Dauphin Island sailed for the West Indies. Just prior to the British departure, Lambert tried to mollify Jackson's concerns over the loss of so many slaves by informing the American general that the British had tried to convince the slaves to return to their owners "and many have done so."[34] The statement was an exaggeration. In a deposition taken several years later in New Orleans, a local resident refuted Lambert's claim, complaining that only "a few of the negroes" ever returned from the island.[35] Regardless of the actual number, it is clear that a percentage of the slaves at Dauphin Island allowed their own reenslavement.

As to the reason why any enslaved person would voluntarily return to bondage, the answer is complex. Throughout the War of 1812, as historian Gene Allen Smith details in his examination of the conflict, fugitive slaves took an incredible "gamble" by running away.[36] For them, nothing—not even the good fortune of reaching enemy lines—guaranteed them any assurances of their future. In an era of global racial slavery, the lives of African-descended people were precarious, regardless of whether the law of any particular nation considered them free. Consequently, when some slaves who escaped to the British Post chose not to sail to the West Indies and instead agreed to return to their previous homes, it was a testament to both the universal plight of enslaved people and the powerful bonds of family and community that sustained them. It was not evidence of the allegedly benign nature of American slavery.[37]

In the end, Jackson failed to help slaveowners from Louisiana and Mississippi reclaim more than a fraction of their fugitives. However, he successfully protected America's slave society and further paved the way for its expansion. Indeed, Jackson's victories at Mobile, Pensacola, and New Orleans augured a new era in American history when slave-produced cotton dominated the southern economy, providing the region both "its power and sense of nationhood."[38] Still, much work remained to ensure the rise of the Slave Power. The Treaty of Ghent, which brought the war to an end, was ambiguous about millions of acres of land claimed by the Americans yet still inhabited by the Creeks. The treaty also left Spain in control of the Floridas, where British troops, Indian warriors, and fugitive slaves remained.

Like their American counterparts, slaveowners in Spanish Florida also failed in their bid to recover escaped slaves living under the protection of the British flag. The struggle began during the Battle of New Orleans, when a delegation sent by West Florida governor Mateo González Manrique traveled to the British Post to meet with Nicolls and negotiate the return of their property. The two delegates, José Urcullo, a Spanish Army lieutenant, and William McPherson, a representative of John Forbes & Company, expected to resolve the matter quickly, since Admiral Cochrane's wartime offer of freedom to fugitive slaves only applied to absconders from the United States. The delegates were also optimistic because they carried a letter from Cochrane to Colonel Nicolls in which the British commander-in-chief agreed to return "to their respective owners at Pensacola" any and all escaped slaves claimed by Spanish subjects.[39]

Despite Urcullo's and McPherson's optimism, they were soon disappointed as both the British officers and their black charges refused to cooperate. Because Nicolls was still with the British squadron at New Orleans, the post's temporary commander, Captain Robert

Henry, ignored Cochrane's instructions, choosing instead to defer "the measure" until Nicolls returned. When Urcullo and McPherson produced a roster including the names of slaves believed to have come from Pensacola and vicinity, the slaves not only failed to answer to the names on the list but openly brandished their British-manufactured weapons, making it clear that they preferred to remain at the bluff.[40] The moment these suspected fugitives learned of the Spanish delegation's arrival, Henry recalled, "they expressed their sentiments of disapprobation in strong terms, such as to convince me of the danger which might attend those who would attempt to take them in a vessel unarmed."[41]

Henry did allow Urcullo and McPherson to speak to the black men and women believed to have escaped from Pensacola, with the understanding that the delegates could board only those people who chose to return voluntarily. In the face-to-face conversations that followed, the officials persuaded twenty-five people to agree to leave the post, but only ten women boarded the Spanish vessel the following morning.[42] Why these women agreed to return with the delegates is a mystery. As for the fifteen others who changed their minds overnight, they decided to remain at the bluff because "if they returned to Pensacola they would be slaves & there they were free."[43]

Following the departure of the Spanish delegation, things returned to normal at Prospect Bluff. Upon his return from New Orleans, Nicolls compiled an informal census, which revealed the number of people the British had recruited to their cause. In "Return of Muscogee or Creek Indians under the Command of Lieut. Col. Nicolls," Nicolls identified more than thirty-five hundred pro-British fighters. Already at the bluff were 130 Red Stick warriors and 150 "Black Troops," while more than two thousand Creeks, Chehaws, Seminoles, and "their negroes" were either en route to the site or preparing to come to its defense. The remaining Indians and slaves, whom Nicolls considered loyal to the British cause, remained in one of fifteen towns "on or close to" the upper Apalachicola River, the three largest being Euchee, Ockehochne, and Fowltown.[44]

In correspondence attached to the report, Nicolls predicted that even the Indians who had previously sided with the United States would soon change their allegiance. "I was long enough in the Country after the Peace to hear the Indians of the American side declare they would wear Red Jackets next war," he assured Admiral Alexander Cochrane. He added that "the Muscogee Indians bear a fixed hatred against the Americans and Spaniards and properly managed the British Government may at all times depend on them against these powers."[45] Encouraged by Nicolls's report, the British intended to avenge the loss at New Orleans by launching an invasion across the southern frontier from Spanish Florida.[46]

But they never got the chance. When word of the United States' ratification of the Treaty of Ghent reached the Gulf Coast in February 1815, Nicolls began preparing his troops for a complete withdrawal. The Creek and Seminole chiefs, as well as the thousands of warriors who had pledged themselves to the British cause, were devastated by the cessation of hostilities. Having lost faith in their long-time allies, they began drifting away from the British Post in search of safety and security deep in the Florida forests.

Before the British and Indian withdrawal was complete, the new West Florida governor, José de Soto, ordered another delegation to the bluff in a second attempt to recover slaves belonging to Spanish subjects. This time, the group consisted of Spanish Army captain Vicente Sebastián Pintado, the survey general of West Florida; Eugenio Joseph Sierra, Pensacola's respected royal surgeon; and William McPherson, who again stood in for the partners of John Forbes & Company. In addition to recovering fugitive slaves, the three delegates were directed to gather intelligence on the army of "Whites, Indians, Mulattoes and free Negroes and Slaves" still under Colonel Nicolls's command. They were additionally ordered to observe "the state and class of the establishments that they had formed on that river, the other fortifications that had been made, the artillery, equipment, munitions &c. that they have there" and to "give an exact count of each."[47] What the Spanish government expected to do with this information is unclear, though taking possession of the post following the British withdrawal was a distinct possibility.

When Pintado, Sierra, and McPherson disembarked at the British Post in early April, their spirits were buoyed by the appearance of Robert Spencer. A British marine captain, he had recently assisted many of Pensacola's property owners in receiving compensation from the British government for losses suffered during the British occupation of their city the previous fall. In the case of John Forbes & Company, for example, Spencer eventually secured a cash payment of eighteen hundred dollars for boats, hogsheads, and other property appropriated by Nicolls's troops. The only lost or stolen possessions Spencer failed to reimburse the company for were its slaves, but he promised "to do everything that lay in his power to bring back the negroes."[48]

At the post, Spencer proved a man of his word. He allowed the three delegates to meet with the suspected fugitives from Pensacola. Furthermore, he ordered some of these individuals to be moved to St. Vincent Island at the mouth of the Apalachicola River so the delegates could interview them "without the presence of the other negroes." Just as Captain Henry had instructed the first Spanish delegation at the post four months earlier, Spencer informed the delegates that they could do everything in their power to persuade the black people they interviewed to return to Pensacola voluntarily. The use of force, however, was strictly forbidden.[49] Due to this policy, Spencer cautioned the delegates about expecting much from their effort, for "the blacks are very violent & say they will die to a man rather than return."[50]

Despite Spencer's apparent good faith, the prohibition on forced removal meant that the British had no intention of assisting in the reenslavement of African Americans who had volunteered for His Majesty's Service. Indeed, following the debacle at New Orleans, Admiral Cochrane again reversed his position on the fugitive slaves at the post; he informed the Spanish governor that he was now powerless to do anything about the absconders for fear they would turn violent. He stated matter-of-factly, "Situated as I am with so few white troops at Apalachicola, it would be attended with much hazard the making use of forcible measures, which accordingly I must entirely decline." As for the escaped slaves who had abandoned the post with the Indians, Cochrane was equally uncooperative, adding, "Your Excellency must make application to their Chiefs."[51]

Though Cochrane's about-face decreased their chances of success, Pintado, Sierra, and McPherson went forward with the interviews, confident in their powers of persuasion. For nearly a week at Prospect Bluff and St. Vincent Island, the three men interviewed scores of slaves believed to have absconded from West Florida, encouraging them to trade the discomfort and insecurity of the Florida wilderness for the comfort and security of their former homes. As an enticement, the delegates promised the slaves a full pardon for having run away. They also warned that if any individuals declined the offer and were later returned to Pensacola by force, their owners would punish them severely.[52]

Some of the slaves who met with the Spanish delegation were considering returning to Pensacola, but Nicolls tried to convince them to stay. When the interviews began, he at first seemed to be interested in assisting the Spanish by "faintly" encouraging the slaves to return to their owners. But when the slaves rejected the offer, it appeared that they had already reached a secret agreement with Nicolls to remain at the bluff regardless of the conditions of their possible return. The delegates complained of Nicolls that "this apostle of liberty" had already promised the fugitives land in a British colony, as well as "a well constructed fort to defend them in the interim."[53]

Running out of options, the delegates argued that the British had no right to harbor slaves who came from Florida or were owned by Floridians, since Cochrane's original proclamation only offered freedom to fugitive slaves from the United States. Nicolls stipulated the point before making the extraordinary claim that the absconders from West Florida did not escape from a Spanish territory at all. Instead, Nicolls proclaimed that they were fugitives from the United States because they had fled Pensacola "when the Americans occupied it with their army under the command of General Jackson."[54] He applied the same claim to a group of about ten escaped slaves who belonged to the Pensacola-based John Forbes & Company. Nicolls would not even allow these individuals to meet with the delegates, for they had joined the British on the Alabama shore in the Mississippi Territory and therefore had also run away from the "American country." Thus, by the terms of Cochrane's proclamation, Nicolls claimed, they were free people.[55]

Nicolls's argument was a spurious one, yet it helped scores of slaves from Spanish Florida and the Mississippi Territory remain free. After hearing Nicolls's conversation with the delegates, many of the absconders claimed that despite their having come from Pensacola with Hispanic names and accents, they were fugitives from the United States. To prove their case, "They said they were Americans and took names of such."[56] Nicolls continued the lie years later. Recalling the slaves who fled Pensacola with the British and eventually reached Prospect Bluff, he asserted, "They arrived at our head Quarters one or two at a time reporting themselves as having come from the United States, all speaking good English." Nicolls claimed that because of their uncanny skills at deception, "it was a long time before" he realized they actually derived from West Florida.[57]

According to surviving notes of the interviews at Prospect Bluff and St. Vincent Island, although dozens of slaves simply refused to meet the delegates, more than seventy-five men, women, and children did. Of this group, more than half rejected the Spanish delegates' offer to embark for Pensacola by simply declaring that "he/she did not want to return" or "they did not want to return."[58] Others provided a reason. Samson, a fifty-year-old carpenter belonging to a member of one of Pensacola's most prominent families, explained that he had no choice but to stay at the bluff as his owners "would kill him if he came back."[59]

Several slaves participated in the interviews even though their owners were among the delegates. For example, the laborer Moises, the carpenter Simon, and the sawyer Lucas all informed their former owner, Dr. Sierra, that they were staying at the post. There is no record of the emotions they felt when they told him that they were now free men. In a similar fashion, Sally, a mulatto woman owned by John Forbes & Company, informed the firm's agent, McPherson, that she and her three children would not be embarking with the delegates and were thus permanently severing their relationship with the company.[60]

For some slaves, the decision whether to return to Pensacola or remain at the bluff was complicated. A nineteen-year-old mother named Flora Miller agreed to return to Pensacola with her two-year-old daughter and even boarded one of the Spanish vessels for that purpose. But when her husband discovered that his wife and child were on board, he convinced them to disembark. Francois, a thirty-six-year-old mulatto cook owned by Don Manuel Gonzalez, strongly considered returning to Pensacola, given that he joined the British only after "the Indians took him by force and tied him." But having become accustomed to freedom at the bluff, he informed the delegation that he had decided to stay.[61]

In a handful of cases, the suspected fugitives denied being slaves at all. Ruben Nelson, a thirty-five-year-old carpenter, swore that he was a free man and "presented some papers intended to prove it even if indirectly." The twenty-six-year-old shoemaker Ambrosio made a similar argument; he professed that he was free "by virtue of a certificate signed by a Justice of the Peace, and issued by the Pensacola Secretary in the English language." The delegates thought the document was a forgery, writing in their notes that it lacked authenticity and in other ways "seemed funny." Though Tomás Thompson lacked free papers, he also denied being a slave. The twenty-six-year-old servant "said he was free" and that before coming to the post "only used to work for a wage."[62]

In one instance, Nicolls demonstrated the lengths he was willing to go to defend the freedom of the black people under his command. "Carlos Mulatto" claimed that prior to leaving Pensacola with the British, he had arranged with his owner to purchase his own freedom, asserting that an additional payment of two hundred pesos would make him a free man. Hearing this, Nicolls offered to pay the sum to Carlos's owner so that the bondsman would be "granted complete freedom." The delegates rejected the buyout as they did not have the owner's permission to make such a deal. It was a decision the owner would regret. When the delegation embarked for Pensacola several days later, the highly valued twenty-five-year-old carpenter stayed behind, leaving his former owner without her former slave or the two hundred pesos Nicolls had offered to pay her.[63]

Nicolls provided a record of their service to the fugitive slaves who had enlisted in the Colonial Marines. His purpose was to establish "full British rights and liberties for the former slaves."[64] In a brief public ceremony, the colonel paid these black volunteers "their earnings as soldiers" and officially discharged them from the corps. He then handed them signed discharge papers, which documented their length of service as well as their receipt of all the pay and clothing to which they were entitled. The Spanish delegates suffered through the ceremony in silence but later protested the issuance of these "licenses," declaring that each of them was "a certificate of freedom" that would allow these men to pass for free "in whatever place that they presented themselves with this document."[65]

Given the long and varied paths the Colonial Marine veterans would eventually travel, it comes as no surprise that very few of the certificates Nicolls issued at the British Post survive; nevertheless, one found in the Andrew Jackson Papers at the Library of Congress—which suggests that the general was aware of events unfolding at the British Post—offers an example. The first page bears Nicolls's signature, the date March 31, 1815, and the name of the unit, "His Brittanic Majesty's first Battalion of Colonial Marines." It reads, "Parish Lane—Private in the Battalion aforesaid and in the Rifle—or Captain Spurin's—Company has served Honestly and faithfully for the space of Six—Months and Twenty Six—days, is hereby discharged in Consequence of the Preliminaries of Peace with the United States of America." On the second page, the illiterate soldier marked an "X" alongside the signatures of two witnesses, officers William Allen and James Chapman, below the following text: "I Parish Lane—Do Acknowledge that I have received all my clothing, Pay, Arrears of Pay, and all demands of Pay whatsoever— from the time of my enlisting in the Battalion and Company mentioned on the other side to this present day of my Discharge."[66]

Ultimately, the results of the Spanish delegation's mission to the British Post were mixed. Of the more than three hundred fugitive slaves still believed to be on the bluff, the delegates returned to Pensacola with only twelve.[67] As was the case both at the post and at Dauphin Island several months earlier, there is no extant evidence explaining why these seven men and five women chose to return to their owners. All Governor de Soto offered was that some came by choice and others were "won by persuasion."[68] Either way, what is important to remember is that in the five months after the Battle of New Orleans, hundreds of fugitive slaves from the United States and

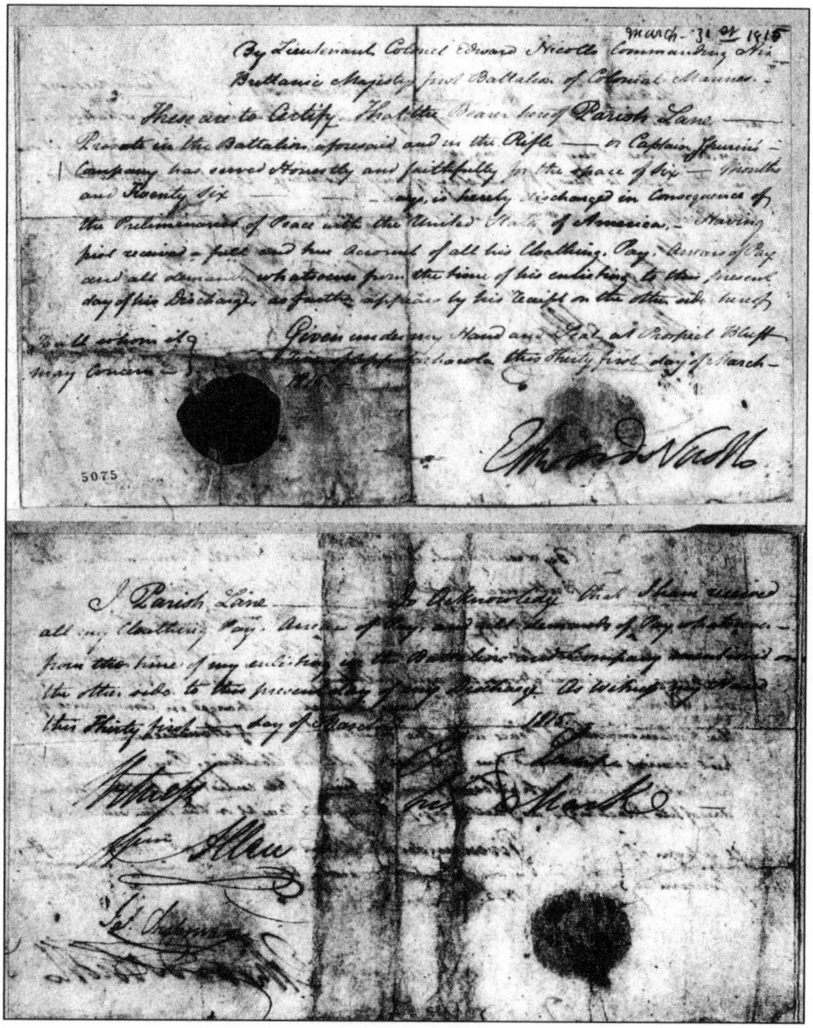

FIGURE 2.1. Beyond recording the discharge of enlisted men from Great Britain's Corps of Colonial Marines, the two-sided document was a "certificate of freedom" for black veterans of the corps. Andrew Jackson Papers, Courtesy of the Library of Congress.

Spanish Florida who escaped with the British had every opportunity to return to their owners—and only a handful did.

The delegates had much more success recovering the seventy free black Spanish soldiers originally from Havana, Cuba, who comprised the Spanish garrison at Fort Barrancas in Pensacola but had evacuated the city with the British. Whether these troops abandoned their posts voluntarily is unclear. Spanish leaders claimed that these men were taken against their will, but Nicolls denied the charge. He swore that he only "embarked such of the Spanish troops as chose to save themselves the mortification of falling in to the hands" of their acknowledged enemy—the United States.[69]

Where the delegates proved most adept was in gathering intelligence on the British Post and its black population. Pintado recorded that the compound was encircled by a "shallow ditch" and wooden stockade. At the center, an estimated sixty "toesas" (nearly four hundred feet) inland, stood an imposing octagonal structure with several cannons mounted on its walls. Closer to the water were "a considerable number of huts" and four six-caliber cannons resting on mobile gun carriages. Along the shore was a "Redan"—a V-shaped defensive structure with openings for artillery. Comprised of earth and wood, it pointed westward across the river. A number of boats and canoes rested at an adjacent dock alongside the frigate *HMS Cydnus*, which had recently brought to the post four cannons, four hundred cannonballs, "and boxes of grapeshot and powder," weighing as much as several thousand pounds. As for the post's armed inhabitants, Pintado estimated 250 fugitive slaves from East and West Florida, along with those "from the American or Indian settlements." While the British expected as many as three hundred black families to remain at the site permanently, Pintado learned that in anticipation of the British withdrawal, some of the escaped slaves were planning to abandon the bluff and "establish themselves in Tampa Bay."[70]

When Pintado, Sierra, and McPherson returned to Pensacola, slaveowners took the news of the mission badly. Among the most distressed were the partners of John Forbes & Company, who collectively lost as many as one hundred slaves to the British from their four trading posts at Pensacola, St. Augustine, Prospect Bluff, and Mobile. Unwilling to give up, they ordered Edmund Doyle, the former manager of their Prospect Bluff store, to the British Post to try yet again to convince "as many of the negroes as he can persuade to return." While they waited for the results of Doyle's trip, the partners wondered if they would be able to reopen their Prospect Bluff store after the evacuation of the British—but they were beginning to realize that it would be "impossible to do until this hornets' nest of negroes is broke up."[71]

As Florida's slaveowners were well aware, the colonial governments of East and West Florida were in no position to eliminate the black settlement on Prospect Bluff. The Florida colonies had never been a priority for the Spanish Empire, which had been unraveling for decades, and now, revolutionary convulsions in Europe and the Americas made both Florida colonies an afterthought. Consequently, Spanish troops were incapable of seizing the post when Nicolls and the rest of the British forces finally abandoned it in April 1815.

The same could not be said of the United States, which seemed well suited for such a mission given its recent victories over the Creeks and British along the Gulf Coast. Anticipating the withdrawal of British forces, American officials stayed abreast of the situation through two widely circulated reports. The first came from William Hardridge. The frontier trader and interpreter spent three days "in the British Fort" in late February and witnessed five hundred black and Indian fighters drawing rations "the same as soldiers." The British were "determined to keep the negros," Hardridge informed agent Benjamin Hawkins. "They have joined them as soldiers and they have given them their freedom."[72]

In the second report, a British deserter named Samuel Jervais also described the post as having been placed in a state of permanent readiness for war. The former sergeant recalled seeing several cannon, including four twelve-pounders and a howitzer, along with "about three thousand stands of small arms, and near three thousand barrels of powder and ball." In addition to an unknown number of Indians, he estimated that there were "between three and four hundred negroes, taken from the United States, principally from Louisiana." Jervais was mistaken in claiming that a large portion of the bluff's black population derived from Louisiana, but more important than their origins was what they and their Indian allies intended to do with the stockpile of weapons at their disposal. According to Jervais, "The arms and ammunition were for the use of the Indians and negroes, for the purposes, as it was understood, of war with the United States."[73]

Among those who believed Jervais's account was the commander of Fort Stoddert in the Mississippi Territory, Brigadier General Edmund Pendleton Gaines. Immediately after reading the text and personally meeting with its author to confirm its contents, the general forwarded copies of the report to Andrew Jackson in Nashville and Alexander James, the acting secretary of war, in Washington. In attached correspondence, Gaines warned that despite the departure of the British, the "deluded savages" who remained at the bluff contemplated "a renewal of the war upon our frontier inhabitants." To preempt such an event, the general proposed organizing as many as one thousand troops and an equal number of allied Indian warriors across the southern frontier. Then, should any additional forces be provided, he would "make a decisive stroke upon the depots at Appalachicola." Gaines pointed to Spanish inaction as justification for the invasion of a sovereign territory. With Spain failing to stop "our enemy," he asked rhetorically, "can she blame us then, for restraining them, ourselves?"[74]

More than war, what Benjamin Hawkins most feared was that some or all of the fugitive slaves at Prospect Bluff would join the British evacuation. To prevent that from happening, he forwarded a letter to Nicolls, reminding the colonel of Article 1 of the Treaty of Ghent, which required the return of all private property captured during the war. The agent protested the removal of "any negroes belonging to the Indians within the United States or citizens thereof," and he demanded that the British embark without these people so "that their proper owners may get possession of them." Nicolls fired back that neither he nor any other Briton would be returning anyone to slavery. "On the subject of the negroes lately owned by the citizens of the United States or Indians in hostility to the British forces," he offered proudly, "I have to acquaint you, that, according to orders, I have sent them to the British colonies, where they are received as free settlers and lands given to them."[75]

Article 1 was not the only part of the treaty between the United States and Great Britain that set Nicolls and Hawkins at odds with each other. Another controversial part of the accord, Article 9, required the American government to return all the land acquired from the Indians during the war to those Indians—and only those Indians—who were still officially at war with the United States at the time of the treaty's ratification. Since the Creeks who had joined the British at the bluff never agreed to peace with the United States, Nicolls considered them to still be at war with the United States at the time of the Treaty of Ghent. He therefore believed that Article 9 entitled them to the millions of acres of land taken from them in the Treaty of Fort Jackson. Hawkins took the opposite view, insisting that the Treaty of Fort Jackson made all Creek people ineligible to reclaim any land lost to the United States during the war.[76]

In a heated exchange, Nicolls blasted Hawkins for allowing settlers to move onto Indian lands and commit a variety of crimes against the

Indians, including murder. The colonel explained that while his Indian allies had temporarily agreed to stand down, he had sent them "a large supply of arms and ammunition, and told them *to put to death without mercy any one molesting them*." In addition to their weapons, Nicolls continued, the Indians also had a "strong hold" at the bluff, where they were guaranteed protection. Therefore, he encouraged Hawkins to bring the perpetrators of crimes against the Indians to justice or consider "the miseries that may be suffered" by those living along the southern frontier.[77] Hawkins responded forcefully to these taunts. Revolted by the thought that "good and innocent citizens on the frontiers are to be the victims of such barbarity," he promised Nicolls that any acts of aggression against American citizens would be "speedily met and speedily crushed."[78]

Though Nicolls only wanted Indians to use violence in self-defense, his militant rhetoric was all some southerners needed to call for a renewal of hostilities with Great Britain. One Georgia editorialist decried the lasting influence of British troops in Florida, holding them responsible for the failure of American officials to run the new boundary lines established in the Treaty of Fort Jackson. The writer asserted, "Being guilty of a flagrant violation of the late treaty of peace, Colonel Nicolls and his *banditti* should be instantly driven off at the point of the bayonet."[79] Another Georgia writer concurred. "This is a circumstance our government cannot overlook, and will doubtless claim its immediate and serious attention," he declared. "If colonel Nicholls be authorized to do what he has done, so flagrant an infraction of our rights would warrant an immediate appeal to arms."[80]

By July 1815, Nicolls's widely publicized comments prompted an official complaint from Washington to London. Secretary of State James Monroe asserted that the security of the southern frontier had been compromised ever since the British had established their "military Station" on Prospect Bluff and organized a massive force of

Indians and fugitive slaves, "evidently for hostile purposes against the United States." The situation only worsened after the war when Nicolls refused to accept the terms of the treaties of Fort Jackson and Ghent. Because these actions were entirely unacceptable to the United States, Monroe demanded that Great Britain "put an end to proceedings of a nature so unwarrantable, and which have already produced such injurious effects."[81]

British officials eventually agreed with the United States on the subject of Indians. In a conversation with John Quincy Adams in London, the British secretary of state, Lord Bathurst, dismissed Nicolls as "a wild fellow." He informed his American counterpart that the British government rejected Nicolls's interpretation of Article 9 and was abandoning its alliance with the Creeks. He further offered that while government leaders still sympathized with the Indians' plight, the British government was powerless to do anything about it.[82] In a final symbolic act, Bathurst stated that he refused to meet with the Creek leaders, including Chief Josiah Francis, who had journeyed to London with Nicolls to ask for assistance. Though the visiting Indians were "in great distress," Bathurst ordered them to return home and "make their terms with the United States, as well as they can."[83]

The British position on fugitive slaves was far less conciliatory. While remaining silent on Nicolls's interpretation of Article 1, the government honored its promise of both land and freedom to the roughly five thousand fugitive slaves from the United States who escaped to British lines during the war. Because these individuals had fled from their American owners voluntarily, and in many cases had taken up arms in His Majesty's Service, the British government recognized them as free subjects entitled to the full protection of the law—despite the loud and angry protests from abroad.[84]

The British left no record of the fugitive slaves they removed from Spanish Florida, making it difficult to determine the number who joined the British withdrawal from Prospect Bluff. After Nicolls and the last of his troops embarked from the post, *Niles' Weekly Register* reported that "about 50 *slave troops*" arrived with the British fleet at Bermuda several days later. An anonymous observer on the island believed that the number was closer to two hundred when taking into account the soldiers' wives and children, who were promptly transported to Trinidad aboard the HMS *Carron*.[85] Regardless of the number, it is clear that a sizeable group of black soldiers and their families sailed out of Apalachicola Bay with the British and never returned.

It is also apparent that many others remained at the bluff. Explaining why is a matter of some speculation. Nicolls claimed that a lack of adequate transports made the evacuation of the black population of "350 men, women, and children" impossible. He further asserted that these people remained at the site because they were waiting for the redcoats to return and retrieve them.[86] But it is just as likely that the hundreds of fugitive slaves Nicolls left behind had no intention of leaving their new homes. With slavery still flourishing throughout much of the British Empire, the possibility of migrating to a Caribbean island renowned for its sugar plantations must have weighed heavily on the minds of these recently enslaved people. Indeed, it is easy to imagine that after receiving their freedom certificates from Nicolls, the marine veterans and their families and friends preferred to remain at the isolated frontier fortress rather than remove to a British colony that sanctioned slavery.[87]

By the summer of 1815, the British Post on Prospect Bluff was gone. But the large citadel, surrounding structures, and a massive store of arms and ammunition remained in the possession of hundreds of fugitive slaves and a small group of Indians who remained allied with them. The situation terrified white southerners, who sounded the alarm that both their lives and their property were in danger. Blinded by their racist ideology and insatiable quest for land, they could not imagine that the people on Prospect Bluff simply wanted to be left alone. A resident of the Mississippi Territory spoke for many white people in the South when, after learning of the British evacuation, he proclaimed that the southern frontier was still in danger—because on the eastern shore of the Apalachicola River, there was "a large body of Indians and Negroes, well supplied with every thing necessary for war."[88] Something had to be done.

• **3** •

A FREE BLACK COMMUNITY

O N the Fourth of July in 1815, while Americans celebrated the republic's thirty-ninth anniversary, William McGirt, a mestizo Creek friendly to the United States, made his way from the Georgia backcountry into Spanish Florida toward Prospect Bluff. As he approached the bluff, McGirt encountered a British lieutenant named William Hambly, whom Colonel Edward Nicolls had appointed to oversee the recently evacuated British Post.[1] Having been ordered "to confine every white man that comes from the U. States," Hambly arrested McGirt but then released him when McGirt insisted that he "was not a white man." After quickly surveying the area and returning home, McGirt related that while the Indians had vacated the bluff along with the British, they still refused to abide by the terms of the Treaty of Fort Jackson. Therefore, if the Americans attempted to establish new boundary lines it would produce "another War Between the US. & Great Britain."[2]

McGirt further revealed that the former British Post was now inhabited exclusively by fugitive slaves—many of them from the United States. "I was not permitted to go inside the fort," McGirt reported, but the structure appeared strong and secure. On the matter of British troops, none were there presently "but negros." Unable to get an accurate count of the fort's occupants, McGirt estimated that inside the stockaded perimeter there were at least one hundred black men "under arms," who kept guard over several buildings filled with food, weapons, and ammunition. Others were "about and off from the Fort" planting fields of corn. Regardless of their proximity to the fort, none of these former slaves showed any deference to McGirt. To the contrary, he reported, "The negros were saucy and insolent, and Say they are all free."[3]

Albeit unintentionally, what McGirt documented was the trans- formation of the British Post into something truly historic. With only one British operative remaining in the area, with Indians dis- persed into the surrounding wilderness, and with armed and uni- formed black soldiers in command, the heavily fortified base along the boundary of East and West Florida had become the largest fugitive slave settlement in the history of the present-day United States. After reading McGirt's account, Benjamin Hawkins called it "the negro fort on Apalachicola," coining the term that would forever define the compound after the departure of the British and Indians.[4] Almost immediately, "Negro Fort" became a part of the American lexicon, while the fort itself emerged as a symbol of slave resistance and revolt—a symbol that frontier officials felt compelled to eradicate.

As they began contemplating how to eliminate the sanctuary for escaped slaves, Andrew Jackson immediately came to mind. In a let- ter sent from the Mississippi Territory to Jackson in July 1815, Harry Toulmin, a prominent frontier planter, politician, and judge, ap- plauded Jackson for his recent military successes and bemoaned the fact that the "conqueror could not be at the same time in Orleans, in Mobile, and everywhere else that his talents & energy were wanted." Toulmin informed Jackson that although the British had with- drawn from Spanish Florida, "There is still a body of negroes forted there,—with a white man at their head, & several pieces of artillery at their command." Although he was unsure of the "meaning of this establishment," Toulmin proclaimed, "its operation must be highly prejudicial to the interests of the southern states and . . . its continuance will, on the occurrence of another war, if not before,—be found very repugnant to the welfare & policy of the union at large." The elimination of this fugitive slave community and the adjacent Indian settlements was necessary, Toulmin insisted, to get the land acquired from the Creeks in the Treaty of Fort Jackson "ready for sale as soon as possible."[5]

Benjamin Hawkins also contacted Jackson after learning of Negro Fort's emergence. Writing from the Creek Agency, the agent informed the general that while some Indians were willing to reach "an amicable agreement" with the United States concerning the new boundary lines established by the Treaty of Fort Jackson, others continued to threaten the treaty's execution. They were reportedly encouraged to do so by Lieutenant Hambly, who had one hundred black troops under his command at the former British Post, as well as by orders from Colonel Nicolls "to attack the Commissioners if they attempt to run the line."[6]

Despite the warning sent to Jackson, the lone British officer remaining at Prospect Bluff in the summer of 1815 had no evil intentions toward the United States. Prior to the War of 1812, William Hambly lived on the eastern shore of the Apalachicola River and worked as a clerk for John Forbes & Company's Prospect Bluff store. Life was good for this second-generation go-between until the summer of 1814, when Nicolls's troops sacked the store and enlisted several of its enslaved employees in the Colonial Marines. Happy to be alive, Hambly impressed the British by demonstrating a facility with Indian languages and accepted a lieutenancy in the corps, along with the title of Head Interpreter of the Creek Nation.[7] Following the British evacuation of Prospect Bluff in May

1815, Nicolls promised his allies that he would return in six months to resume his command.[8] In the meantime, with the Creeks and Seminoles leaving the site and returning to their homes, he appointed Hambly to look after the free black community that remained. Instead, the double-crossing backwoodsman began plotting its demise.

Hambly's treachery was revealed by Kendal Lewis and William Hardridge, two of Benjamin Hawkins's American "spies." Shortly after the two men departed for "the British Fort kept up by the negros at Apalachicola," they stopped at the home of "a well informed half breed" named Alexander Durant. The mestizo explained that it was too dangerous for the two men to continue any further because Hambly had abandoned the former British Post, leaving it in the sole possession of the "Negros." Taking Durant at his word, Lewis and Hardridge proceeded to Hambly's farm, where their old acquaintance treated them "with all manner of friendship & Civility." In the conversation that followed, Hambly confessed that despite being left in command of the former British Post, he "wished the place destroyed" but dared not tell anyone because doing so "would cost his life." Hambly added that Nicolls and the British were unlikely to ever return to the site, so if the Americans endeavored to eliminate it, he would "give them every assistance."[9]

If the United States refused to destroy Negro Fort, Hambly vowed to initiate a military operation himself with the help of his Creek and Seminole allies. The plan consisted of two parts. First, he would invite the headmen to send their warriors to the fort and take what was rightfully theirs, meaning both the former British Post and "the negroes" inside of it. Second, he would provide the Indians with the keys to the fort's storehouses of weapons and provisions. In response, "The Negroes will then oppose the Indians of opening the houses which will raise a dispute between the negroes & Indians, and will lead to destruction of the place."[10]

For a colonial go-between like Hambly, the decision to destroy Negro Fort with Indian assistance was an obvious one. European settlers and their American descendants had long employed the principle of divide-and-conquer to diminish the violent threats posed by Indians and slaves. Indeed, European Americans routinely instigated conflicts between Native Americans and African Americans. As one expert concluded in an important early study, "Whites willfully helped created the antagonisms between Indians and Negroes in order to preserve themselves and their privileges."[11]

One of the successful tactics used to preempt alliances among people of color was to employ Indians as slave catchers. With their own survival at stake, Native Americans developed a major interest in hunting fugitive slaves and consequently played an essential part in encouraging slavery's expansion across the southern frontier. Nevertheless, before Indian slave catchers would target Negro Fort, they had to be convinced that their interests lay not with the black fugitives who resided at the fort but rather with the white settlers who desperately wanted the fort destroyed and its inhabitants reenslaved.[12]

Responsibility for this important task would eventually fall to Benjamin Hawkins, but initially the agent simply needed to share the available intelligence with his superiors. After receiving Lewis and Hardridge's report, he forwarded a copy to Washington under the title "Confidential report of occurrences at Apalachicola." In a brief note attached to the file, the agent vouched for the two sub-agents who had risked their lives by traveling nearly the entire length of the Apalachicola River to obtain as much information as possible. Then, perhaps in an effort to save officials the trouble of reading the entire document, he summarized the situation at Prospect Bluff with the following comment: "The establishment is negroes altogether."[13]

As Hawkins's statement demonstrates, the transformation of the British Post into Negro Fort was complete by the end of summer 1815.

Still, more than two hundred years later, it is difficult to reconstruct life inside this extraordinary free black community. As is typical of any society of fugitive slaves, whose lives and freedom depended on secrecy and silence, African and African American sources are practically nonexistent. At the same time, the surviving accounts of Europeans and European Americans are often biased and in some cases completely unreliable. Nevertheless, carefully interrogating a variety of Spanish and American sources provides an image of Negro Fort and its people.

Before bringing the image into focus, it is worth noting that communities of fugitive slaves had existed and frequently thrived throughout the Americas since the earliest days of the Atlantic slave trade. They were called "*palenques*" by the Spanish and "*quilombos*" by the Portuguese, while the English referred to them as "maroon" colonies or settlements. More than just random encampments for escaped slaves, these societies shared several traits. Among them were geographic isolation; relative political and economic autonomy; and a diverse population of African and African-descended people. The establishment of good relations with neighboring indigenous groups was another common characteristic. In these ways, Negro Fort was a typical maroon community.[14]

But it was also exceptional. As Nathaniel Millett determines in his study of Prospect Bluff, the British Empire played an unprecedented role in its creation by establishing the British Post and then leaving it and all of its materiel in the possession of the former Colonial Marines and their families, friends, and allies. Perhaps even more helpful to these former slaves was Great Britain's recognition of their freedom. This recognition gave them both the right to resist their reenslavement and the expectation that the empire would further assist them in the process. Millett may exaggerate when he asserts that the Negro Fort maroons derived their "guiding principles and identity" from their British allies, but their real and imagined connection to an imperial European power did differentiate them from every other maroon society before or since.[15]

Two lists compiled by West Florida slaveowners provide biographical information on the portion of the fort's residents who, with British assistance, had come to Prospect Bluff from Pensacola, Mobile, and adjacent areas. The group consisted of eighty-three men, nineteen women, and twenty-three youths under age eighteen. Their ages ranged from two to fifty-five, and at least four couples were married. The names on this list indicate a disparate group of people with international backgrounds. Spanish names like Eduardo, Maria, Francisco, Pedro, and Santiago reveal the Hispanic origins of most of the fugitives, yet Francophonic names like Dominique, Jaque, Moises, and Paris suggest a French heritage. The names Billy, Betsey, Frank, Sam, and Tom indicate that some had spent at least a portion of their lives in the United States, while Congo Tom, Carlos Congo, and Carlos Mayumba were almost certainly African born.[16]

The people cited on these lists possessed a wide variety of skills based on their former occupations. In addition to common laborers and field hands, the men were blacksmiths, carpenters, coopers, masons, sawyers, shoemakers, shipwrights, and sailors. Women worked as cooks, house servants, seamstresses, and washers.[17] As Jane Landers concludes in her seminal study of Spanish East Florida, the range of skilled workers is important to consider because "if this group is representative, and there is no reason that it should not be, the blacks who lived at this settlement were certainly equipped to be self-sufficient."[18] Though essential for survival, the skills possessed by the Negro Fort maroons would have mattered little in a wilderness setting without any resources. But the British left behind a plethora of implements and equipment, including dozens of axes, carts, harnesses, hoes, shovels, and saws.[19]

Probably more important for the survival of the Negro Fort maroons than talents or tools was the large cache of arms and ammunition provided by the British. Among the long list of military stores were a brass howitzer, eight cannons with their carriages, ranging in size from six to thirty-two pounds, and hundreds of muskets, bayonets, and cartridge boxes. Several hundred pairs of shoes, uniforms, belts, and other "accoutrements" undoubtedly made the residents of Negro Fort among the best-dressed fugitives in the history of American slavery.[20]

Whether they were the best fed is a different story.[21] Since the days of the British Post, the supply of beef at Prospect Bluff had been abundant. This was due to the herds of wild cattle that roamed the woods as well as the two hundred head of cattle stolen from John Forbes & Company.[22] Spanish subjects also unwittingly supplied several thousand pounds of sugar, flour, coffee, corn, rice, and salted pork, which the British had appropriated when they evacuated Pensacola.[23] As the number of British marines, fugitive slaves, and Indians grew into the thousands, however, the situation grew difficult and eventually desperate as food supplies ran low. Even the once reliable source of beef proved unreliable as "driving the cattle out of the swamp" became increasingly difficult.[24] The lack of sustenance at least partly explains why, during the winter of 1814–1815, many Indians began deserting the post and "dispersed in the woods."[25]

That being said, once the British and Indians left Prospect Bluff, the Negro Fort maroons produced a consistent food supply for themselves and a constant influx of fugitive slaves. As navy commodore Daniel Patterson later wrote, "The force of the negroes was daily increasing, and they felt themselves so strong and secure that they had commenced several plantations on the fertile banks of the Appalachicola, which would have yielded them every article of sustenance."[26] Another soldier described these plantations as consisting of "green corn, melons, &c," while the Creek informant William McGirt saw several houses inside the fort filled with "every thing plenty corn and Rice a side; no scarcity."[27] Perhaps in an effort to utilize two corn mills left by the British, the fort's farmers focused their energy on the cultivation of corn, so much so that their cornfields eventually "extended fifty miles up the river."[28] The situation was similar below the fort, where a Spanish official spotted the "planting of all kinds of provisions" as far south as Apalachicola Bay.[29]

Basic food crops provided only a part of the maroons' daily diet. In addition to corn, melons, and rice, all varieties of marine life and wild game provided essential sustenance. Fish, alligators, deer, and wild turkeys, which teemed in the water and woods surrounding Negro Fort, regularly drew hunters and fishers deep into the woods.[30] (This may have played a role in the settlement's demise, for according to Nicolls, the fort's defenders were out "fishing and hunting" when the American military launched its fateful assault on the compound.)[31]

Besides securing their own food, the Negro Fort maroons received sustenance from Indians living along the Apalachicola River. From the northern part of the waterway, near the confluence of the Chattahoochee and Flint rivers, Lower Creeks and Seminoles provided cattle taken from American settlers on both sides of the US-Florida border.[32] From the southern part of the river a group of anti-American Choctaws provided additional fare. "They are supplied by the Choctaw Indians," one informant explained of the maroons, "and give British goods in return."[33] As for the specific goods the Indians received in exchange for food, a Spanish official learned that it was "powder and ball, left for them by the English."[34]

George Robert Gleig's diary describes the type of food the Choctaws traded with the Negro Fort maroons. In the spring of 1815, the British Army lieutenant visited a small village near Apalachicola Bay that "consisted of upwards of thirty huts, composed of reeds and branches of trees, erected in the heart of a wood, without any regard to form or regularity." Women appeared to do all the work at this remote settlement, while more than one hundred warriors waited imperiously for their next meal. On the menu this day were minced meats and "Buffalo flesh, barely warmed through, and swimming in blood; with cakes of Indian corn and manioc." Also available for consumption was "an abundant supply of rum, which these people had received from our fleet."[35]

The identities of these Choctaws remain one of the great mysteries surrounding Negro Fort, for they not only contributed to the fort's survival but later died in its defense. Since before the War of 1812, when Tecumseh traveled to the Mississippi Territory to unite disparate Indians against American expansion, the Shawnees and Red Sticks had tried to recruit the Mississippi-based Choctaws to the cause, but to no avail. The Choctaws sided with the United States during the war, and under the leadership of chiefs Pushmataha and Mushulatubbee, they aided in several important American victories, including the one at New Orleans.[36]

Even so, not all Choctaws thought alike. As early as the summer of 1813, frontier officials learned that dozens of warriors from the Choctaw towns along the Tombigbee River and Yahnubbee Creek were preparing to "aid the creeks against us."[37] This was probably the same group of Choctaws who traveled with the Red Sticks to Prospect Bluff the following spring to meet with redcoat officials, leading the site's superintendent, Captain George Woodbine, to boast, "Some of the Choctaws, the most numerous tribe the Americans have, are now with me, they tell me that the moment it is known in that Nation that the British intend to aid them with arms & ammunition, they will all come over to us."[38] In 1815, prior to the British evacuation of their post, the Choctaws were conspicuously absent from Colonel Edward Nicolls's roster of the site's residents. This indicates that they had already moved several miles southward to the headwaters of Apalachicola Bay, where they must have remained.[39] Presumably this was the group of Choctaws Gleig described in his diary.

In any case, extensive trade networks reveal that despite their iso-lated location, Negro Fort's maroons maintained strong trade ties with their Indian neighbors, especially the dozen or so Seminole towns that extended many miles from the Apalachicola River east-ward. Two maps drawn by the surveyor general of West Florida, Vicente Sebastián Pintado, reveal the proximity between the Negro Fort maroons and their Indian allies. The maps show two roads, or footpaths, running parallel in a north-south direction for nearly one hundred miles from the edge of Negro Fort to the US border. The western road, labeled "Path from the Hill of Good Vista to the Flint River," ends at Nicolls's Fort, a small, British-built redoubt near the junction of the Flint and Chattahoochee rivers. The eastern road, marked "Path of the Micasukies to the Hill of Good Vista or Prospect Bluff," takes a sharp turn to the east and branches into what Pintado labels the "Path that goes to the Micasukies." Having con-venient access to both a deep-water river and one of the largest and most powerful Seminole towns, the Negro Fort maroons were well situated to acquire all of the goods necessary to survive and maintain their independence indefinitely.[40]

Negro Fort was commanded by several elite slaves from Pensacola, who had gained invaluable experience in military tactics and the maintenance of law and order while serving in the Colonial Marines. The first to emerge as a leader was the mulatto Cyrus, a twenty-six-year-old carpenter and cooper distinguished by his ability to "read & write." After Hambly's departure in midsummer 1815, Hawkins's spies reported that Cyrus was the lone "Commander of the Fort." However, several weeks later, Francisco Caso y Luengo, a Spanish officer sta-tioned some fifty miles away at Fort St. Marks (Fort San Marcos), claimed that there were two other "captains" who ruled alongside Cyrus.[41] Prince was a twenty-six-year-old master carpenter who, during the British occupation of Pensacola, had earned a lieutenancy in the Colonial Marines for helping to recruit large numbers of black

volunteers for the corps.[42] Garçon, a thirty-year-old carpenter who
quickly rose to the level of sergeant major in the Colonial Marines,
became the most renowned of the fort's three commanders. With a
Francophonic name and other personal traits that earned him the
appellation "French Negro," this militant commander must have inspired many white Americans' fears that the horrors of the Haitian
Revolution would be repeated in their country.[43]

Comparing Negro Fort with other maroon colonies throughout
the Americas, Nathaniel Millet argues persuasively that this community was exceptional because it conceived of itself as a "sovereign
enclave of British subjects." He is on much shakier ground, however,
when insisting that the fort's government constituted "a sophisticated and modern political system, even if it was not a formal democracy." While plausible, the claim relies on evidence from events
that occurred after the fort's demise. Moreover, Millett misquotes
William Hayne Simmons as referring to the fort as a "democracy"
of slaves.[44] In fact, the American army doctor used the expression
"dulocracy"—an archaic term describing a society ruled by slaves.[45]
As for other contemporaries who were familiar with Negro Fort,
few ever commented on its government. An exception was Captain
Pintado, who referred to the fort and its inhabitants as "a new republic of bandits."[46] But even this observation, Millett admits, was
sarcastic and contemptuous.[47]

In reality, the government of Negro Fort can best be described as
martial law. For more than a year, uniformed veterans of the Colonial
Marines controlled the fort's resources, oversaw maintenance and
construction projects, monitored traffic to and from the site, and
daily prepared for a possible invasion. According to a free black man
known only as Ned, who lived briefly at the fort before making his
way to the Mississippi Territory, there were as many as 250 black
soldiers under Garçon's command during the winter of 1815–1816.
Wearing the bright red jackets provided by their former allies, they

> Statement of Ned, a free man of colour.
>
> Fort appalachicola is situated on the east side of the river appalachicola about sixty miles below the junction of the chattahoochee and Flint rivers.
>
> The walls of the Fort are made of Timber filled in with dirt and are about thirteen foot through — The space within the walls is about Twenty yards square — There is nine large pieces of Cannon mounted on the walls
>
> There is Three hundred and eighty casks of Powder and about Five hundred Casks of Cartridges in the Fort
>
> There is Two hundred and fifty negroes armed with muskets Commanded by a French negro called Garscon — They are drilled and perform regular Guard Duty
>
> They are supplied by the choctaw Indians and give British goods in return

FIGURE 3.1. Early in 1816, General Edmund Gaines received a copy of this eyewitness account of Negro Fort from "a free man of colour" known as Ned. In addition to describing the fort's citadel, the number of armed combatants, and the size of the arsenal at their disposal, the informant noted the command of "a French negro called Garscon" and the trade of supplies and "British goods" between the fort's maroons and their Choctaw allies. Courtesy of the National Archives and Records Administration.

were a disciplined and spirited unit that drilled and performed guard duty daily.[48]

Though united in the same cause, many of the Negro Fort maroons differed from their leaders in a number of ways. First, not all of them were fugitive slaves. According to eyewitnesses, when Colonel Nicolls and Captain Woodbine were in Florida, the duo had tried "to persuade all sorts of Negroes whether Freemen or Slaves to enter" their corps.[49] Among those persuaded to enlist was a black corporal who spoke "nothing but Spanish." The free man had served in the Spanish garrison at St. Augustine before journeying to Prospect Bluff with "betwixt thirty and forty negroes principally men." Upon arriving at their destination, this Spanish army deserter and the other new British recruits "made no secret of having come from East Florida" and immediately donned redcoats and began drilling.[50]

Second, as the assertions of these volunteers reveal, a significant number of the Negro Fort maroons came from East Florida. According to Pensacola merchant John Innerarity, in one recruiting trip to St. Augustine, Woodbine convinced at least eighty slaves to desert their owners and then "picked up a few more belonging to" the Indians. While some of these absconders did not make it to Prospect Bluff because of "fatigue & hunger," as many as seventy did.[51] The exodus of fugitive slaves from St. Augustine and vicinity seems to have continued long after the British evacuation. During the summer of 1815, the maroons expected "about 100 more from E Florida composing of men, women, & children" to join them.[52]

Third, an indeterminable number of maroons came to Negro Fort from the United States. In November 1815, Innerarity learned that "a considerable number of Negroes" had successfully made their way from Georgia to the fort, or what he referred to as "that accursed hornet's nest at P Bluff." Since neither the American nor the Spanish government had taken any measures to recover these or any of the other hundreds of fugitives at the fort, the Pensacola

FIGURE 3.2. This mid-nineteenth-century engraving of a member of Great Britain's West India Regiments and his family indicates how the Negro Fort maroons may have appeared. From *Illustrated London News* (1858). Courtesy of the Library of Congress.

businessman considered sending a schooner "and perhaps a few soldiers" to the Apalachicola River. Once there, they would use "every practical measure to secure the Negroes."[53]

While the identities of the slaves who fled from the United States towards Negro Fort are in most cases unknown, fugitive slave advertisements offer some clues. Among the enslaved people believed to be escaping into Spanish Florida during the days of Negro Fort were Dick, a thirty-year-old African missing several of his teeth and one of his fingers; Simon, a bald, light-skinned, forty-five-year-old African with a cropped ear and badly dislocated ankle; and an unnamed sixteen-year-old boy known for his physical strength as well as his laughter.[54] Also thought to be headed for the "Spanish dominion" was Tom. A dark-skinned man no older than forty, Tom left southeastern Georgia with an extraordinary amount of clothing and bedding, which indicated that he would not be returning home any time soon. The stockpile included a "blue broad cloath coat, plain white metal buttons, twelve yards of white homespun blue grounded, overalls crossed with copperas and white, two pair died black, also, one white dimity waistcoat, several shirts, one with buttons down the bosom, one bed quilt pieced with calico and white, and one blanket."[55]

Because the southern frontier was heavily militarized, fugitive slaves heading toward Florida often belonged to state and federal troops. Three who attempted to escape from Georgia toward the end of 1815 were described in the *Georgia Journal*. One of these was Grigg, "the waiting man of General Clark—he is a small tolerable well made fellow, rather of a dark complexion, about five feet five inches high, thirty years of age, one of his upper teeth out, near one corner of his mouth." Another was Green, "the waiting man of Col. Dooly, a bright Mulatto fellow, well made, about five ten inches high, twenty-eight years of age." The third was Barrott, "the waiting man of Col. Carter, well made, dark complexion, about five feet, six or seven inches high, twenty-seven years of age." Having spent time with their owners at Fort Hawkins, the three bondsmen were "well acquainted with the country" nearby and likely to "pass down the river" toward Florida.[56]

Another absconder familiar with Fort Hawkins was Jim. Belonging to Major Philip Cook of the Eighth Regiment US Infantry, this twenty-year-old servant of medium height and a dark complexion stood out for the "old military coat" he wore and the way he combed his hair on the top of his head. Jim absconded from his owner just days after Grigg, Green, and Barrott had taken flight nearby, suggesting that the four men traveled southward together. Based on the advertisement Cook placed in the *Georgia Journal*, the army recruiter had no idea where Jim planned to escape to—though Negro Fort's proximity made it a likely destination.[57]

Federal agents also lost slaves to Negro Fort. In the winter of 1815–1816, agent Hawkins reported to Secretary of War William Crawford that in anticipation of a British return to Florida, "an invitation has come up from the Seminoles to invite the negros in the Creek nation and frontiers of Georgia to come down and be free." Among the first to accept the offer were eight slaves belonging to the Indian subagent and interpreter Timothy Barnard, and six others from the Georgia backcountry.[58] In the coming days, an estimated two dozen slaves from Georgia reached Negro Fort. The situation was dire, leading Hawkins to warn the secretary, "If that fort is not broke up soon by the red people or white the citizens of Georgia will loose a number of their negroes before the coming summer is over."[59]

For Hawkins, the crisis over Negro Fort was personal, as some of his own slaves counted among the community's residents. Near the end of the War of 1812, after accusing the Seminoles of launching a series of raids into the Georgia backcountry, the agent complained to Georgia governor Peter Early, "5 of my negros run off or were stolen."[60] Hawkins regained possession of three of the fugitives several months later, but the other two remained at large and in all likelihood enlisted in the British service.[61] Prior to leaving for England, Colonel Edward Nicolls informed Admiral Cochrane that while reviewing his black battalion, he noticed "several of Colonel Hawkins's negroes" among them.[62]

While both of these escaped slaves joined the Negro Fort garrison following the British evacuation, at least one of them may have embarked with the redcoats. At the Creek Agency, "Negro Phil" was a literate field hand and serial absconder with a remarkably defiant attitude for an enslaved man. Nonetheless, his religious zeal impressed two German Moravians, who after establishing a mission on the agency's grounds, welcomed this black preacher into their community. Phil proved an apt pupil in matters of religion, but his relationship with the Moravians soured when they helped a local blacksmith hide from authorities after killing a man. Finding the concealment of a confessed murderer patently un-Christian, Phil rebelled against the Germans by leading the agency's slaves in a boycott of the mission's religious gatherings. When Hawkins's wife learned of Phil's misbehavior, she ordered him "tied to a tree and given 50 lashes with a cowhide."[63] The flogging appears to have had an unintended effect on Phil, for he escaped into Florida during the War of 1812 and never returned. In July 1815, almost three months after the British evacuation, Hawkins learned from one of his subagents that "old Phil has gone off with Col. Nicolls."[64]

Regardless of their origins, the Negro Fort maroons lived according to their status as soldiers or civilians. The garrison of black troops resided with their families in the large citadel at the center of the complex or in one of the stone barracks or wood cabins that fronted the river. Noncombatants occupied the farms and villages that extended several miles beyond the fort's outer stockade. As for the number of people living inside the compound, multiple eyewitnesses confirmed Nicolls's estimate of 350. With a similar number of people thought to be living outside of the fort, the total number of Negro

Fort maroons probably never exceeded seven hundred, though *Niles'*
Weekly Register reported that "nearly 1000 negroes had taken refuge
from their masters" at the fort and in surrounding areas.[65]

With arms at the ready, the Negro Fort maroons guarded maritime traffic on the lower Apalachicola River with an extraordinary
collection of watercraft. They built some of their vessels with the assistance of the Royal Marines under the supervision of Nicolls, who
once boasted to his superiors that "with the assistance of the Black
men, I can build as fine gun boats at the bluff, as can be seen."[66]
Others they took from their former owners and employers when they
fled Pensacola with the British in the fall of 1814. Among these crafts
were more than a dozen schooners, barks, and canoes of various sizes.
From the proprietors of John Forbes & Company, the maroons acquired a small white-cedar boat and a forty-five-foot-long canoe,
along with a collection of rigs, sails, anchors, and other equipment
worth more than the considerable sum of 650 pesos.[67] While most
of the watercraft collected at Negro Fort was used for transportation,
a Spanish army officer remarked that "the negroes have armed with
their Cannon" two of these vessels, "one very regular in size, and the
other not much larger than a Bark."[68]

Having a number of boats at their disposal allowed the Negro
Fort maroons to raid foreign vessels on the lower Apalachicola River
and adjacent waterways with impunity. Francisco Caso y Luengo
complained that as far south as the mouth of the river, these black
buccaneers seized "all the boats that were not English." The maroons also took possession of a small Gulf Coast island known as
"la Isla de Perros" (Dog Island). From this location they guarded
the entrance to Apalachicola Bay and established an informal alliance with coastal pirates, whose communication and trade networks
reached across the Caribbean.[69] Pensacola's John Innerarity complained of the Negro Fort mariners, "They are now organized as
Pirates, have several small Vessels well armed, & some Piracies that

lately occurred in the Lakes are supposed to have been committed
by them."[70]

Waterborne soldiers, including a number of experienced sailors
and shipwrights who were skilled in the art of ship navigation, construction, and repair, bore much of the responsibility for defending
Negro Fort. However, two of the fort's distinguishing features made
it especially formidable. First, the large, wooden, V-shaped redan that
jutted out over the edge of the bluff about a dozen feet above the
river included embrasures on each side. These splayed openings for
firing artillery enabled the fort's protectors "to strike up and down
the river," Pintado observed.[71] Second, beyond the "deep ditch" surrounding the fort's outer perimeter lay a nearly "impenetrable swamp"
that extended from the rear of the fort "to the river above."[72] Given
these protections, it was clear that anyone who approached Negro
Fort did so at great risk.

Among the first to learn this was the Spanish supply officer, Felipe
Prieto. He sailed up the Apalachicola River at the head of a group of
traders early in the summer of 1815, searching for food for the small
Spanish garrison at Fort St. Marks. After approaching Prospect Bluff,
where the group expected to find British lieutenant Hambly, they instead met twenty-five armed and uniformed black soldiers under the
command of Garçon, who ordered the Spaniards to remain in their
vessels and present their passports. When asked who was in charge
of the former British Post, Garçon replied that while Hambly had
officially left an unnamed Indian chief in charge, the black troops
surrounding the Spanish vessel were "willing to execute anyone" who
challenged his (Garçon's) authority. Things remained tense until the
following day when Hambly returned to the bluff and encouraged
the visitors to abandon their mission, as neither the maroons nor
the Creeks and Seminoles still at the fort were willing to share their
food with the Spanish. Fearing for their lives, Prieto and his party
immediately departed.[73]

FIGURE 3.3. This hand-drawn illustration of Negro Fort shows the V-shaped redan and the large octagonal-shaped citadel used for both quartering troops and storing supplies, including gunpowder. Also visible are the "Comfortable barracks and large stone houses" described by General Edmund Gaines. The dotted line represents the trail to the Seminoles. Vicente Sebastián Pintado, *Plano del Rio Apalachicola, Territorio é Yslas Adyacentes* (1815). Courtesy of the Library of Congress.

Given the treatment Prieto and his contingent received, it is no surprise that Spanish officials, like their American neighbors, abhorred Negro Fort and sought its destruction. However, their enmity does not appear to have been primarily grounded in any racially inspired pro-slavery agenda.[74] Instead, it was the fort's negative impact on trade that most concerned Florida's political leaders. Ever since British troops had first arrived on Florida's Gulf Coast in 1814, they had challenged the longstanding economic alliance between the Spanish colonists and their indigenous neighbors by offering arms, food, and supplies to any Indians who visited Prospect Bluff. The situation only worsened when the British and Indians abandoned the site, for they left it "perfectly armed" in the hands of their black allies. In July 1815, West Florida governor José de Soto bemoaned Negro Fort's having become a home for "villains of all classes and Nations," as it undoubtedly made Great Britain "the master of trade" throughout the region.[75]

The partners of John Forbes & Company shared the economic fears of colonial officials, especially because Negro Fort was located at the site of one of the company's once successful trading posts.[76] In a letter to Forbes, John Innerarity explained how the Treaty of Fort Jackson offered extraordinary economic opportunities for their firm, given its vast land holdings along the Apalachicola River. But because the British had broken up the Prospect Bluff store, removed all of its property, and established a military post, the company's influence over the Indians was "dead, or expiring." Worse still, the British had trained fugitive slaves for war and left them "in possession of a well constructed fort, with plenty of provisions, & with Cannon Arms & Ammunition of every description, not only in abundance but in Profusion for their defense." Because of Negro Fort, Innerarity doubted that the company's business would ever return to normal. He wondered if he should begin selling the firm's immense Florida territory to land-hungry Americans, "who will settle them in spite of Indians, Negroes, or English."[77]

Because of their hunger for more land, Americans feared that Negro Fort's disruption of Spanish-Indian trade would enable Great Britain to seize East and West Florida. Indeed, just weeks after the British evacuated Florida, frontier propagandists began reporting that the British would soon try to add the Spanish territory to their global empire. A Georgia writer claimed that prior to departing for Europe, Royal Marine officers stationed at Prospect Bluff had confessed their government's desire to acquire Florida by the end of the summer, "peaceably if they can—*forcibly* if they must." If Spain was willing to sell its two colonies, the writer hoped the United States would pay the required amount regardless of cost, for "it should not be suffered to pass into the hands of the British."[78]

Following this initial report, the *Georgia Journal* claimed in a series of specious articles that Great Britain not only conspired to seize Florida from Spain but had actually succeeded in doing so. In June 1815, when a story circulated that Colonel Nicolls, Captain Woodbine, and the British marines were planning to return from England and "take possession" of the Floridas, the paper suspected the colonies had already been "secretly transferred by Spain to the British government."[79] Six months later, the journal further stoked readers' fears, declaring, "It is now asserted with confidence in London papers, that East and West Florida have been ceded by Spain to Great Britain as indemnity for services rendered by the latter to the former in the war with France."[80]

There were any number of reasons for Americans to be concerned about Florida's becoming British. For southern slaveowners, none was more important than the protection of their two most valuable commodities—land and slaves. As an anonymous commentator in the Mississippi Territory explained, "From the practice recently pursued by the British, with regard to negro slaves, it may be feared that their becoming neighbours to us, will not only reduce the value of that species of property in this southern country, but will render even landed property itself hardly worth possessing." Fearful that the reports of the Floridas' cession were true, the writer felt that the best way to protect these assets was to increase the number of white settlements across the southern frontier, "extending all the way from Georgia to the Mississippi, as the nature of the country will admit of."[81]

The possibility that Great Britain would purchase East and West Florida did not concern all Americans, as some believed that the two colonies would inevitably belong to the United States. This was the perspective of the *National Intelligencer*, which declared, "It may not happen this year, or next, or for a score of years to come: but it will in the course of time, if this government exists, which no man will dare to doubt." As for the rumor that Spain had already sold the Floridas to the United States' rival, the paper was skeptical but admitted that it was possible given recent British history. "We do not, we confess, like this rumor," concluded one editorialist. "It has an ugly appearance, especially when we connect it with the intrigues of the Nicholls's and Woodbines in that quarter during the last spring."[82]

If rumors of Great Britain's acquisition of Florida caused Americans some consternation regarding Negro Fort, the fact that hundreds of armed fugitive slaves inhabited a heavily fortified defensive structure near settlers' homes, farms, and plantations inspired great fear. As soon as this free black community emerged, white southerners decided to challenge its existence, primarily because it offered a safe haven for the people they enslaved. But there was another reason as well. As long as it survived, Negro Fort challenged the idea of white supremacy upon which the South's rapidly expanding slave society rested.

This is not to suggest that white supremacy was an exclusively southern phenomenon. To the contrary, the opposite was true. Racism pervaded the early American republic as European Americans

everywhere held Native Americans and African Americans in contempt. Nevertheless, the extent and intensity of this contempt varied
widely according to region. In the North, where Indians and slaves
were few, white supremacy often took a muted form. But in the
South, where Indians still posed a threat to settlers' lives and the
slave population grew at a historic rate, racism was explicit and often
accompanied by violence. On the southern frontier, where Red Sticks,
Seminoles, and fugitive slaves all lurked, white Americans' hatred of
nonwhite people was palpable. The hatred of African Americans was
especially intense. The Creeks' defeat during the War of 1812 suggested declining Indian opposition, but it did nothing to indicate the
end of slave resistance.[83]

Media coverage of Negro Fort's emergence revealed the depths
of white southerners' fears of the people they enslaved. Throughout
the summer of 1815, popular newspapers adopted the tradition
begun by the *Georgia Journal* of refusing to describe the fort's
residents as "slaves," "blacks," or "negroes," instead using asterisks
and other punctuation marks in place of these plural nouns. In
June, while providing an update on the situation at Prospect Bluff
following the departure of Colonel Nicolls's troops, *Niles' Weekly
Register* disclosed that according to Benjamin Hawkins, "The
British white force at Appalachicola, which was only 40 or 50, has
been somewhat diminished, and their number of ***** troops increased from 60 or 70 to about 300."[84] A month later, the *National
Intelligencer* published an anonymous letter from Georgia that similarly asserted that with the departure of the British and Indians,
the fort's population consisted of "three hundred —— well organized, with eight pieces of cannon." In a final comment, the paper
warned that if "energetic steps" were not taken to eliminate this
fort, "Our Southern —— property will not be worth holding."[85]
That two widely regarded national newspapers refused to mention
the kind of people who had taken sole possession of Negro Fort

reveals more than just racism; it reflects American citizens' inability to fathom an armed and independent community of black people so close to the southern border.

Still, any effort to eliminate this free black community by killing or capturing its members would have to wait. The American government's top priority remained running the boundary lines established by the Treaty of Fort Jackson across huge tracts of land in Alabama and Georgia.[86] Responsibility for this dangerous task fell to several federal commissioners, including army general Edmund Gaines, General John Coffee, and Captain William Barnet. The trio hoped to complete the running of the entire line by the end of summer or early fall. However, they were delayed by threats of violence from a contingent of Creek leaders, including some who had renounced their alliance with the United States. Among them was Big Warrior, who now disavowed the Treaty of Fort Jackson, which bore his own signature, claiming that it robbed his people of both their land and their means of survival. "If they suffered the line to be run," the great Upper Creek chief declared, "they had as well die by the sword as with famine."[87]

From his Nashville plantation, Andrew Jackson vowed to destroy those who resisted the running of the line, including his former Creek allies. Convinced that the British—and Colonel Nicolls in particular—were to blame for the Creeks' continued opposition, he reminded several prominent chiefs of the redcoats' failed promises, as illustrated by their withdrawal from the region. "Listen," Jackson admonished, "did not the British after exciting them to war, after promising them protection flee like cowards and leave the Indians to perish, and is there any of your nation after all this so crasy as to Listen to their wicked talks again." The line would be run, Jackson assured his Indian "Friends and Brothers," warning them that "if you attend to the lying talk of Colo Nicholls you will bring down upon you inevitable ruin."[88]

Throughout the fall of 1815, the treaty commissioners and a sizable contingent of army regulars ran the new boundary lines. As they did so, Jackson became even more convinced that if it were not for the British and their black allies, the Creeks would accept the terms of the Treaty of Fort Jackson. Believing that the Indians on their own lacked "the temerity to do any acts of Hostility," he authorized Gaines to deal harshly with any British or black interlopers found encouraging them to violence. "On the event of hostility or opposition to the running of the line, you must be ready to quell it, the line must be run," Jackson demanded, "and on the event of war with the Indians, every whiteman or negroe found in arms with the enemy must be put to the sword."[89]

Despite its bombast, Jackson's mandate was no idle threat. By the second decade of the nineteenth century, the American government was committed to protecting its southern border, while slaveowners were intent on expanding their peculiar institution across it. Once the boundary lines of the Treaty of Fort Jackson were established, Negro Fort would provide the perfect pretext for the United States to accomplish both of these objectives. Approximately one year after Negro Fort became the largest independent community of fugitive slaves in the history of the present-day United States, Jackson endeavored to bring about its ruin. Ordering a combined army-navy invasion of Spanish Florida, he launched an illegal, unconstitutional, and undeclared war against fugitive slaves.

4

FIGHTING TO THE DEATH

IN February 1816, Colonel Powell, Captain Daniel Johnston, and John McGaskey were prospecting land in the Mississippi Territory, which the United States had acquired in the Treaty of Fort Jackson but which the Creeks refused to abandon. Suddenly, shots rang out, and in an instant, Johnston and McGaskey were dead. Powell escaped unharmed, though several bullets passed through his clothes as he fled the small band of Indians who wanted him dead. After scurrying several miles through the woods, Powell eventually made it to safety. The bodies of his companions were never recovered, and the horses and slaves belonging to the three prospectors vanished with the Indians.[1]

Though occurring hundreds of miles away from Negro Fort, the murders of Johnston and McGaskey permanently altered the American government's perception of the fort and its inhabitants. When news of the ambush reached Major General Edmund Gaines at Fort Mitchell in eastern Alabama, he suspended the running of the new boundary lines established by the recent treaty, moved an army battalion from Georgia to the Mississippi Territory, and ordered his troops to build a small fleet of boats to assist in conveying men and provisions. He also forwarded a report to the War Department, which described in great detail the layout of Negro Fort, the size of its population, and the strength of its armaments. The implication was clear: Negro Fort provided not only sanctuary for fugitive slaves from the United States but a base for their Indian allies to commit violent depredations across the southern frontier. As long as it survived, neither the American people nor their property was safe.[2]

On the basis of this line of reasoning, in the coming months Gaines continually warned of the dangers of Negro Fort and called for its destruction. While a love of country and an oath to protect its citizens help explain Gaines's early and enthusiastic support of the use of military force against this foreign free black community, a deep commitment to slavery and its racist ideology was also a contributing factor. Like so many army officers in the early American republic, the general was a native southerner and lifelong slaveowner; as such, he vehemently opposed the idea of a multiracial society without slavery. Hence, it was a love of both nation and race that compelled Gaines to spend the first half of 1816 trying to convince the federal government to unleash its forces on Negro Fort.[3]

Benjamin Hawkins also blamed Negro Fort for fueling the growing Indian insurgency. Several days after the murders of Johnston and McGaskey, the Indian agent sent a message to the secretary of war, informing him that slaves were still escaping to the fort and had joined the Red Sticks and Seminoles in resisting the running of the line. According to Hawkins's sources, the Indians had declared that "if the country is checkered off they will fight." Moreover, the Indians vowed to protect the slaves who joined them, saying that "none are to be given up or to be taken from them." More alarming than the disruption of the running of new boundary lines was that the Indians and slaves were together performing the Red Stick dance in anticipation of a violent confrontation with the United States.[4]

To both stop the flight of fugitive slaves and secure the southern frontier, Hawkins beseeched the American government to eliminate Negro Fort. But its reluctance compelled him to act. In March, the agent sent an Indian detachment into Florida under the command of the "half breed" subagent Captain Timothy Barnard— their mission was to hunt "runaway negroes" believed to be living in the Florida Seminole town of Miccosukee.[5] He also prepared a delegation of eight Creek chiefs, led by the ever-faithful Coweta headman William McIntosh, to visit the White House and ask the president directly about the fate of their people. Unfortunately for Hawkins, both efforts proved complete failures. Barnard and his slave hunters returned to the agency several weeks later empty-handed, while McIntosh and the chiefs headed for Washington never left the agency at all. Hawkins claimed that the trip to the nation's capital was postponed due to the "want of an interpreter." A more likely reason, however, was that some of the chiefs were insisting on regaining "part" of the land taken from them in the Treaty of Fort Jackson.[6]

In response, Hawkins threatened to send American troops against the Creeks. When their chiefs asked why, he claimed that the Indians were responsible for allowing the British to establish a fort in their territory, "making it an asylum for runaway negros belonging to people of the United States." Because of the recent hostility of the Seminoles and their slave allies, he asserted, the United States had no choice but to use force. If the Creeks suffered as a result, they had no one to blame but themselves. Hawkins asked the chiefs indignantly, "As you have no leave for establishing a negro fort on your land, why was not a stop put to it" and "the negros belonging to people of the U. States restored back to them?" Given the state of peace that now existed between the United States and Great Britain, he demanded, "Why was not this banditti driven off?"[7]

Authorization for an attack on Negro Fort could only come from Washington, and before the War of 1812, President James Madison had provided similar authorization in response to two separate armed uprisings in Spanish Florida. In the fall of 1810, when residents of the far western portion of West Florida revolted against the Spanish government and declared the independence of the Republic of West Florida, Madison issued an official proclamation in support of the rebels, annexing all of the disputed land along the Gulf Coast between the Mississippi and Perdido rivers. Two years later, when American revolutionaries sought to wrestle East Florida from Spanish control, Madison provided financial and military assistance for the so-called Patriot War, a violent and "bedeviling two-year conflict" that, according to historian James Cusick, "slowly merged with the war of 1812."[8]

Clearly, given Madison's support of these rebellions, he was not opposed to military intervention in Spanish Florida. Throughout the spring of 1816, however, he decided to exercise patience, preferring that the Spanish government assume the many risks involved in contending with Negro Fort. In March, the president ordered General Andrew Jackson to inform Mauricio de Zúñiga, the newly appointed West Florida governor, that the laws of nations required colonial officials "to put an end to an evil of so serious a nature." If the Spanish declined to move against the fort's inhabitants, the president would determine what if any action he could "adopt in relation to this banditti." If Madison decided that the fort's destruction did not require legislative approval, he—and only he—would let Jackson know what "measures will be promptly taken for its reduction."[9]

Instead of waiting for instructions from the commander-in-chief, Jackson decided to launch the military operation that would culminate in the Battle of Negro Fort.[10] Writing from New Orleans, where he was inspecting the area's defenses, Jackson informed General Gaines of the insecurity of the southern frontier, arguing, "Half peace half war is a state of things which must not exist." Citing the deaths of Johnston and McGaskey, he said he wanted every "town or village" that offered asylum to their murderers destroyed. As Negro Fort was just such a refuge, Jackson authorized Gaines to annihilate it. "You possess the power of acting on your own Discretion," he explained, "which I hope you will exorcise on this."[11]

To justify the illegal invasion of a sovereign territory, Jackson depicted Negro Fort as the base of operations for fugitive slaves, Indian warriors, and murderous outlaws who threatened the lives and property of the American people. Since the fort was established for the perpetration of a series of outrages across the southern frontier, the general demanded its destruction. Notwithstanding Jackson's commitment to protecting the southern border, the actual objective of the offensive against Negro Fort was neither national security nor justice for the two murdered settlers. Rather, it was the capture and return of the fugitive "Negroes of our citizens or friendly Indians living within our Territory" to their owners.[12]

Subsequent correspondence reveals that although Jackson had left it to Gaines's discretion whether or not to attack Negro Fort, he fully expected Gaines to do so. In a letter written two weeks after he had empowered Gaines to act independently, Jackson informed Secretary of War William Crawford that he hoped Gaines had already "attended to the subject of this negroe fort and put an end to the lawless Depradations of this Banditti of *Land Pirates*." Jackson further explained that while he officially gave Gaines "Discretion to act on this subject," the fort needed to be destroyed. Then, in a moment of candor, he admitted freely, "I trust he has taken the Hint."[13]

Jackson's delegation of such an important decision to a subordinate officer was inconsistent with his usual imperiousness. However, the seemingly uncharacteristic action is easily explained. Since rising to national prominence in the War of 1812, the military icon was already being considered for the presidency, though some critics believed that his authoritarian style disqualified him from holding high public office. The decision to assault Negro Fort presented the southern commander with an opportunity to hone his skill in the art of republican politics, demonstrating an awareness of what is today referred to as plausible deniability. By formally delegating responsibility to Gaines, Jackson hoped to avoid culpability if the assault proved unsuccessful or particularly controversial. If it was successful, he could and would take credit.

Eager to get started, Gaines moved a battalion of the army's Fourth Infantry Regiment to the eastern shore of the Chattahoochee River in southwestern Georgia. There, under the direction of Lieutenant Colonel Duncan Clinch, the troops erected Fort Gaines, a "small work" about fifty miles north of the Florida border. When local Indians complained, Gaines responded that he had "brought the pipe of peace for our friends,—and for our enemies the *cannon* & *bayonet*."[14] Gaines then met with agent Hawkins, who insisted that an army expedition into Florida was unnecessary because a small contingent of Creek warriors, led by the Cusseta chief Little Prince, had already agreed to the undertaking. For a mere three hundred bushels of corn, Hawkins explained, the Indians were "making an effort of themselves to aid the Seminolie Chiefs in destroying the negro establishments in that country, and capturing and delivering all Negros belonging to Citizens of the United States, to me, or some of our military establishments."[15]

Hawkins was overly optimistic. Just days after agreeing "to go down to the fort of the blacks, and take them out of it, and give them to their masters," Little Prince hesitated because the construction of Fort Gaines proved the Americans' intention to establish an even greater presence on the Indians' land.[16] The agent responded by reminding the chief and his warriors of the benefits of slave catching. He recalled that when he was first sent by "Gen'l Washington" to live among the Creeks, the reward for each of the "runaway ne-groes" brought to the agency or Fort Hawkins was only $12.50; now the bounty was fifty dollars per black captive. Besides cash rewards, another benefit of slave hunting was the appeasement of American slaveowners, who would otherwise be forced to swarm across Indian country in pursuit of their property and in the process claim even more land. Hawkins assured the Creeks that if they continued to capture fugitive slaves, "Their masters will stay at home and be peaceable and friendly and your paths of peace and trade will be free and open."[17]

With Little Prince and his Cusseta warriors unconvinced, Hawkins enlisted the former Prospect Bluff store clerk and site su-pervisor William Hambly to help the chief find indigenous volun-teers for the proposed expedition against Negro Fort. While traveling through the Lower Towns, however, the two men nearly lost their lives. The Indians at Fowltown (Tuttalosa) "were crazy," Little Prince reported, for in addition to refusing to "go against the Negro Fort," they chased the two visitors out of their town, making it known that if they captured Hambly, they would burn him alive.[18]

Despite the failed mission, Hawkins felt that he and William McIntosh would eventually find "a respectable force" to take Negro Fort. On May 3, 1816, the agent asked General Gaines to inform General Jackson that he was counting on the southern army for their support as well. With or without Little Prince, Hawkins de-clared, "I will take my stand below, and take by force the negroes with the Creek warriors." As to the question of whether he pos-sessed the power to lead such an expedition, the agent responded, "I feel myself clothed with the authority of the nation for the purpose."[19]

While waiting for Gaines's response, Hawkins also asked West Florida governor Mauricio de Zúñiga for assistance. In the process, he offered an absurd explanation of his motivation for taking aim at

Negro Fort. Calling the "runaway negro establishment" an annoyance
to both Spanish Florida and the United States, he asserted that it
was the Muscogee people—rather than the Americans—who wanted
to attack the fort in order to "restore the negros to their masters."
To help the Indians, Hawkins was offering a fifty-dollar bounty on
every captured fugitive slave, and he encouraged the Florida governor to offer "a like premium for the negros belonging to the subjects
of Spain on delivery at St. Marks or Pensacola." Hawkins reminded
Zúñiga that more than a decade earlier, American troops had helped
the Spanish squash an Indian and slave uprising led by the frontier
revolutionary, William Augustus Bowles. Consequently, he hoped the
Spanish would return the favor by coming to the aid of its "friendly
neighbour."[20]

While it is not entirely clear why, General Gaines indulged
Hawkins's intrigues with the Creeks and Spanish for several weeks.
But he soon lost patience, informing Jackson that he would avail
himself "of the discretionary power which you have been pleased
to confide to me" and take the necessary measures to break up "the
Negro establishment." Gaines fully understood that the task would
be difficult. In addition to its secure location between the river on
one side and an impassable swamp on the other, the fort was rapidly "acquiring strength and additional numbers." No ordinary refuge
for fugitive slaves, it was an organized society defended by an army
of more than three hundred black soldiers "with a large quantity of
British muskets, Powder and other supplies" at their disposal.[21]

With his mind set on taking decisive action, Gaines revealed his
plan for a three-pronged assault on Negro Fort. First, American
troops would erect a defensive fortification near the junction of the
Apalachicola River and the US-Florida border. Known as Camp
Crawford, and later Fort Scott, it would serve as the base of Colonel
Clinch's Fourth Infantry Regiment. Second, Commodore Daniel
Patterson, the commander of the United States Navy station at

New Orleans, would send a convoy of supply vessels and gunboats from the Louisiana coast to the mouth of the Apalachicola and then upstream to Camp Crawford. Besides thirty thousand rations for Clinch's men, the vessels would also convey two eighteen-pound cannons, one howitzer, "with fixed ammunition, and implements complete," as well as fifty thousand musket cartridges, some rifles, and swords. Third and last, as the naval convoy ascended the river, one of Clinch's army boats from Camp Crawford would descend the river to meet the convoy and help escort it safely to its destination. "Should the boats meet with opposition at what is called the Negro fort," Gaines declared, "arrangements will immediately be made for its destruction."[22]

Gaines's instructions demonstrate that he also understood the controversial nature of the plan to deploy American troops against fugitive slaves in a foreign territory without proper authority. By sending armed vessels past Negro Fort, he fully expected to provoke a confrontation. He ordered Patterson to place one of the gunboat commanders in charge of the supply convoy from New Orleans and defend the vessels against any and all "opposition" from the shore. Upon commencement of the expected firefight, the army and navy would assault the fort from both land and water. It was an ingenious plan. Having successfully drawn fire from Negro Fort, the United States could assert a claim of self-defense despite having instigated the conflict.[23]

While Gaines set his plan in motion, Jackson dispatched a representative to Pensacola as he had been instructed to do by the president two months earlier. During the last week in May, US Army captain Ferdinand Amelung arrived in the West Florida capital with an important communication from Jackson. The letter informed the Spanish governor that Negro Fort had become a base for hundreds of fugitive slaves, who were training for war and encouraging "negroes from the citizens of Georgia, as well as from the

Cherokee and Creek nations of Indians," to join them. Because so many settlers had lost valuable slave property, the Spanish government needed "to destroy or remove from our frontier this Banditti, put an end to an evil of so serious a nature, and return to our citizens and the friendly Indians inhabiting our territory those negroes now in the said fort and which have been stolen and enticed from them." With a patronizing tone reflecting his contempt for the Spanish government, Jackson's communication encouraged Zúñiga to act promptly, "particularly when I reflect that the conduct of this Banditti is such as will not be tolerated by our government, and if not put down by Spanish Authority will compel us in self Defense to destroy them."[24]

Zúñiga's response must have surprised Jackson, as it revealed the Spanish government's shared commitment to Negro Fort's demise. Insisting that colonists in East and West Florida suffered more from the fort's existence than American citizens did, the governor professed that he also wanted to see both the destruction of the fort and the return "to their Lawful owners all negroes that may be retaken." However, he explained, he was unable to employ his own troops in the project until he received permission from his superiors in Cuba. Zúñiga added that as most of the Negro Fort maroons belonged to Spanish subjects, and their fort was built without the knowledge of the Spanish government, he considered them "Insurgents or Rebels against the authority not only of H.C.M. [His Catholic Majesty] but also of that of the proprietors from whose Service they have withdrawn." In closing, Zúñiga reiterated his intentions to defend the rights of all slaveowners, whether American or Spanish, and promised that he would do whatever was necessary to preserve the harmonious relationship that existed between Spain and the United States.[25]

Having tried to allay Jackson's concerns, Zúñiga expected the United States would not move against Negro Fort until Spanish officials in Cuba had an opportunity to directly address the matter. He was wrong. As soon as the American general received Zúñiga response, he forwarded it to Secretary of War William Crawford. Buoyed by the fact that the Spanish governor considered the Negro Fort maroons "rebels," Jackson proclaimed that there were no more obstacles to "destroying the negro fort, and restoring to the owners the negroes that may be captured."[26]

If there were any doubts that the attack on Negro Fort was a slave-hunting expedition, they were dispelled by an editorial published in the *Georgia Journal* just prior the assault—which newspapers across the South quickly copied onto their pages. Ever since the withdrawal of British forces from Spanish Florida, the piece began, a substantial fort left standing at the site of the former "British station" on Prospect Bluff had been occupied by "runaway negroes and hostile Indians." While it was surprising "that an establishment so pernicious to the Southern States, holding out to a part of their population temptations to insubordination, would have been suffered to exist," it did. As slaves from Georgia, Tennessee, and the Mississippi Territory continued to escape to the fort more than a year after the British had abandoned it, the question arose, "How long shall this evil, requiring immediate remedy, be permitted to exist?" Clearly, it was the duty of the Spanish government to "disperse this horde of ruffians, and deliver up the slaves to their owners." But as they refused to take action, there was no reason why American troops "should not be ordered on that service with the least possible delay."[27]

After months of preparation, the United States' operation against Negro Fort began in the last week of June 1816, when US Gunboat 149, under the command of Sailing Master Jarius Loomis, sailed eastward out of New Orleans. Several days later, the vessel rendezvoused with US *Gunboat 154*, commanded by Sailing Master James Bassett, as well as the schooners *General Pike* and *Semilante* at Bay St.

Louis on Mississippi's Gulf Coast. The entire convoy then proceeded
to Apalachicola Bay, arriving on July 10. While the schooners served
exclusively as supply vessels, carrying all of the provisions, stores,
and ordnance destined for Camp Crawford, the gunboats were ready
for a fight. Weighing an estimated twenty-five tons and extending
some sixty feet in length, they together carried about fifty sailors and
several large cannons. Like all gunboats built at the opening of the
nineteenth century, they were, despite their modest size and defensive nature, important components of the new republic's emergent
foreign policy.[28]

After arriving at the mouth of the Apalachicola River, the navy convoy met the mestizo Creek chief known as John Blount (Lafarka), who
carried orders from Colonel Clinch to hold their positions. As the sailors awaited further instructions, Clinch began his descent down the
river from Camp Crawford on July 17 with 116 army troops. Traveling
in several heavily armed flatboats with reinforced wooden sides and
roofs, the soldiers were divided into two companies commanded
by Brevet Major Peter Muhlenberg Jr. and Captain William Taylor.
Within hours of their embarkation, Clinch's unit met 150 Coweta
warriors commanded by Chief William McIntosh. The following day
they joined another sizable contingent of Creeks led by chiefs Captain
Isaacs and Mad Tiger (Kotchahaigo), bringing the total number of
American and Creek ground forces to more than three hundred.[29]

Though Clinch would later deny the arrangement, he had planned
to meet McIntosh's warriors at the head of the Apalachicola River
and descend the watercourse together.[30] In return for their assistance,
the Creeks were to be generously rewarded. The official agreement
reached between Clinch and the three war chiefs, McIntosh, Captain
Isaacs, and Mad Tiger, generally repeated what Creek leaders had
already agreed to receive when apprehending fugitive slaves, that is, a
cash award of fifty dollars for "every grown negro" taken captive. But
there was more. To sweeten the deal, the agreement authorized the

Indians to take from Negro Fort anything they could carry, with the exception of cannons and related ordnance.[31]

For the United States, the enlistment of McIntosh's Creek fighters could not have come at a better time—because the Battle of Negro Fort had already begun. Early on the morning of July 15, at the northeastern edge of Apalachicola Bay, Sailing Master Loomis spotted several individuals pulling a small craft out of the river. In an effort to ascertain his convoy's ability to ascend the river "peaceably," he dispatched a boat with one officer to approach the vessel, but "nearing her, she fired a volley of musketry into my boat, and immediately pulled in for the river." In retaliation, Loomis's men returned fire at the small craft, which quickly disappeared. There were no casualties in this first brief exchange between US troops and the Negro Fort maroons. But that would soon change.[32]

Two days later, at dawn, Loomis sent a small boat manned by Midshipman Alexander Luffborough and four sailors, who were armed with a swivel gun and muskets, up the river in search of fresh water. Shortly after the men distanced themselves from the rest of the convoy, they spotted a black man standing alone on the edge of an isolated riverside plantation. Luffborough ordered his boat to the shore and began talking with the individual when about forty black and Indian musketeers, who were organized in two separate groups under the command of Garçon and an unnamed Choctaw chief, respectively, sprang from the bushes and opened fire on the Americans. Within an instant, the barrage of bullets took the lives of three sailors, Luffborough, Robert Maitland, and John Burgess. John Lopaz was also wounded in the fray but managed to swim to safety. Edward Daniels met a gruesome fate. After being taken prisoner, he was marched to the fort and summarily executed by being "tarred and burnt alive."[33]

Because Loomis's men had gotten the worst of the opening engagement of the Battle of Negro Fort, they held their positions at the mouth of the Apalachicola River while Clinch's troops followed McIntosh's warriors down the opposite end of the waterway. In the coming days, the first ever large-scale American slave-hunting expedition proved a marked success. According to army surgeon Marcus Buck, who accompanied Clinch's force, "many slaves from the United States and from the friendly settlements of Indians near the Appalachicola were apprehended."[34] Buck's estimate of several dozen black captives is plausible, yet the conspicuous absence of corroborating evidence suggests that it may have been an exaggeration. What is certain is that McIntosh's slave hunters captured some black people along the shores of the Apalachicola, including one who stood out. Bearing the scalp of navy seaman Edward Daniels, this unnamed captive was in the process of delivering the bloody relic to the Seminoles as evidence of the maroons' recent victory over the Americans.

Shortly after midnight on July 20, Clinch's soldiers and McIntosh's warriors arrived within several hundred feet of Negro Fort. Offering assistance was William Hambly. After narrowly escaping with his life several weeks earlier, the former Spanish storekeeper and British Post superintendent had moved to Fort Gaines and begun volunteering as much intelligence on the situation at Prospect Bluff as possible. With Hambly as his guide, Clinch directed his troops to remain safely ensconced behind a thicket of dense woods. At the same time, he ordered a third of McIntosh's warriors to infiltrate the forests surrounding the fort "and keep up an irregular fire."[35] For the next six days, the defenders of Negro Fort responded to the Creeks' salvo by unleashing the full power of their arsenal. With a barrage of "shot, shell, grape, and rockets" from their muskets and artillery, as well as the twenty-four-pound cannons mounted on the fort's walls, they directed most of their fire at the Indian slave catchers firing on them from the woods. They also unloaded their weapons towards the river whenever any American troops, who tried to remain concealed, "appeared in view."[36]

The effectiveness of the cannon fire from Negro Fort is a matter of some debate. According to one of the most cited reports, the gunfire was "entirely inefficient."[37] Clinch was particularly dismissive, insisting that the initial volley from McIntosh's warriors "induced the enemy to amuse us with the incessant roar of artillery, without any other effect than that of striking terror into the souls of most of our red friends."[38] Loomis, who heard the cannonade from a distance of several miles, found nothing amusing about it. Fearful of exposing his men to heavy fire, he refused to move from his position even after Clinch sent him a message instructing him to conduct the navy convoy upriver.[39]

In addition to exchanging heavy fire, McIntosh's warriors and Negro Fort's black defenders also engaged in a fierce ground war. This fact is entirely absent from the historical literature about the Battle of Negro Fort but is apparent from contemporary accounts. Citing an anonymous "informant" from Georgia, who had recently returned from the Mississippi Territory, *Niles' Weekly Register* reported that the engagement began the morning after McIntosh's warriors approached the fort and opened fire. Eager to confront their attackers, "The negroes made a sortie on the Indians," causing a violent confrontation to ensue. Rather than firearms, "The tomahawk and scalping knife (so close was the engagement) were the only weapons used." After two or three days of close hand-to-hand combat, the Indians eventually gained the upper hand, forcing the slaves to withdraw into the fort.[40]

Though easy to overlook, the use of the word "sortie" is instructive. A review of contemporary reference works indicates that the term had only recently come into use. From the French verb *"sortir,"* meaning "to issue" or "to go out," the word was defined by a British military dictionary as "the issuing out of the besieged from their works, and falling upon the besiegers to cut them off; as they often do in successful sallies, killing many men, destroying the trenches and

batteries, and nailing the cannon." Sorties did not occur when the besieged lacked men or munitions, only when forces were "strong, and
the inhabitants numerous." So when the Negro Fort maroons took
the fight to McIntosh's warriors in the woods outside their besieged
home, it was an offensive rather than a defensive maneuver.[41]

This helps explain why the American troops, who watched from
afar as the maroons retreated into their fort, suspected something
sinister was afoot. It was clear that the black soldiers and their
Choctaw allies still "wished to fight," observed Dr. Buck, "and had
gone into the Fort for no other purpose" than to regroup. The "spirited resistance" shown by the fort's defenders against McIntosh's warriors impressed the American combatants, even "though they were
Indians, negroes, and our enemies." Buck recalled that the defenders
of Negro Fort were determined to fight to the end and "never to be
taken alive."[42]

While the maroons, the Choctaws, and McIntosh's Creek warriors
engaged in mortal combat, Clinch's army troops were conspicuous
by their absence. Rather than a matter of chance, this was a part of
the plan to take the fort with minimal American casualties. Several
months before the Battle of Negro Fort, Clinch confided to William
Hambly that he never intended to put his own troops in harm's way.
Fully confident that the Creeks would "route the Negroes," he stated
that he would only send in the American detachment if McIntosh's
warriors "failed entirely." Clinch's admission is a stark reminder that
native people were not only victims of, but also important contribu-
tors to, slavery's violent expansion.[43]

As the maroons and Choctaws withdrew into the fort, McIntosh
ordered his warriors to secure the fort's perimeter and destroy all of
the fruit, corn, and other provisions growing in the adjacent fields.
He further ordered a deputation of Indian leaders to approach the
fort with a flag of truce, demanding its surrender. Instead of being
received respectfully, however, "they were abused and treated with the

utmost contempt." Besides condemning the United States for various crimes, the "Black chief" Garçon declared that "he had been left
in command of the Fort by the British Government and . . . would
sink any American vessels that should attempt to pass it, and would
blow up the Fort if he could not defend it." The Indian deputation returned to their positions convinced that the black leader's threat was
sincere, for flying above the fort was the flag of Great Britain and on
top of it a red flag, or "bloody banner," indicating that the maroons
would neither give nor take quarter from their enemy.[44]

With the Union Jack flying over their heads and red coats on
their backs, the Negro Fort maroons still identified with Great
Britain more than a year after the last British troops withdrew from
Prospect Bluff.[45] However, there is not enough evidence to prove,
as historian Nathaniel Millett surmises, that "the members of the
community acted as British subjects who were defending sovereign
territory in resisting the American invasion."[46] Given the available
evidence, the most that can be said about the Negro Fort maroons
is that some still held out hope that British troops would return to
assist them—just as Colonel Edward Nicolls had promised. Indeed,
Benjamin Hawkins claimed that there was good reason for this
belief. Just prior to his passing, the agent learned from one of his
trusted Indian informants, "There has been at intervals of a month
or so a British officer on a visit to the negro fort."[47] A month later,
Colonel Clinch wrote General Gaines from Camp Crawford, "The
rascals have sent over to England to inform them that we are coming down to take their fort as appears from a letter in my possession
written by one of them."[48]

Unfortunately, no copy of the correspondence Clinch referred to
has survived. In any case, the British had no intention of returning to America to aid the maroons, as doing so no longer served
the empire's interests. Without Great Britain's assistance, the odds
were heavily stacked against the Negro Fort maroons surviving

their battle with the United States. Those odds grew even longer when Spain's colonial government decided to launch its own pre-emptive strike against the fort.

After learning that Clinch's forces had arrived near the Florida border, Spanish officials accelerated their effort to convince the Seminoles to capture the Negro Fort maroons and return them to their owners. At an April conference at Fort St. Marks, several prominent chiefs initially rejected the offer on the grounds that they could always depend on "the assistance of the negroes" to re-sist and fight the Americans.[49] But they reconsidered several months later after learning that Clinch had already sent William McIntosh and his warriors to Negro Fort with orders to attack the "hostile Indians in Florida, the Seminoles," along the way.[50] Convinced that the Americans would use the assault on Negro Fort as an excuse to seize the Seminoles' land, chiefs Kinache, William Perryman, Yawaly, Houce Emathly, and Thlwaly, along with the mestizo Creek trader Alexander Durant, informed Pensacola governor Zúñiga that they would move on Negro Fort in return for "provisions, and a little rum." Believing that there were only sixty black soldiers at the fort, along with a similar number of women and children, the chiefs expected "to deliver the Negros without any resistance."[51]

Despite these assurances, it is, as historian Claudio Saunt sug-gests, doubtful that the Seminoles would have betrayed the Negro Fort maroons.[52] Given their longstanding alliance with fugitive slaves and their shared resentment of the United States, it is much more likely that the Seminoles were buying time, waiting to see the outcome of the American invasion. Either way, the Spaniards took the chiefs at their word. Immediately after learning of the arrange-ment, Governor Zúñiga ordered Captain Benigno Garcia Calderón to embark twenty-five black and mulatto troops aboard two gunboats for the Apalachicola River, where they would rendezvous with the Seminoles and begin the assault.[53]

The Spanish excursion emulated the one launched by the United States in several respects. While Calderón ordered his troops to destroy the fort and seize its arsenal, their "principal object" was to capture the fort's residents "in order not to cause more harm to those who have already suffered enough with the flight of their slaves." For their efforts, the Seminoles would receive fifty pesos for every adult male slave, thirty pesos for every adult female slave, and twenty pesos for every child slave they captured. If the United States had already taken possession of the fort when the Spanish and Seminole forces arrived at Prospect Bluff, Calderón was to demand that the Americans evacuate the site and "hand over the slaves in their possession."[54]

The Seminoles' apparent willingness to assist in the assault on Negro Fort marks a milestone in the history of Spain's American empire. At the opening of the nineteenth century, East and West Florida still offered opportunities to people of color that were unthinkable in the American South. Military service is one of the most frequently cited examples. Yet the use of black, mulatto, and Indian troops to assist in the killing and capturing of fugitive slaves demonstrates just how much Spanish Florida's leaders had come to share the values of their northern neighbors. Clearly, the days of Spanish Florida serving as a sanctuary for fugitive slaves were quickly coming to an end.[55]

That being said, neither the Spaniards nor the Seminoles attacked Negro Fort—because they were too late. On the same day that Calderón's party sailed out of Pensacola Bay, the unification of Clinch's army force and Loomis's navy convoy took place several miles below Prospect Bluff at another cliff on the river's eastern shore known as Dueling Bluff. Unable to transport artillery in the waterlogged terrain just south of the fort, the officers sent a small group of American troops, along with the bulk of McIntosh's warriors, to secure the fort's rear. The remainder of their force

positioned themselves on the west side of the river and began constructing a battery.[56]

At dawn the following morning, on July 27, the navy gunboats
pulled into a position alongside the battery location, which prompted
a hail of cannon fire from Negro Fort. Clinch thought the fort was
too far from the gunboats for the navy's artillery to reach and directed his troops to take cover, but Loomis insisted that they "were
within point-blank range" and ordered his sailors to open fire. For
the next hour a fierce cannonade occurred across the Apalachicola
River, with neither side gaining an advantage. Everything changed,
however, when one of the cannonballs from *Gunboat 154*, which
Sailing Master Bassett's men had heated in a makeshift furnace before firing across the river, flew over the fort's outer perimeter and
landed directly on the citadel's gunpowder magazine. The result was
a massive explosion that some claimed to hear more than one hundred miles away.[57]

Clinch's army troops and McIntosh's warriors rushed to investigate the carnage. "You cannot conceive, nor I describe the horrors
of the scene," Dr. Buck wrote his father. "In an instant, hundreds of
lifeless bodies were stretched upon the plain, buried in sand and rub-
bish, or suspended from the tops of the surrounding pines." It was
not only the corpses of men that the American troops came across
but those of women and children as well. "Piles of bodies, large heaps
of sand, broken guns, accoutrements, &c. covered the scite of the fort."
Disturbed by what they saw, Buck claimed that he and the other
soldiers checked their celebration "to drop a tear on the distressing
scene."[58] Clinch described a nearly identical situation. But instead
of suggesting any sympathy for the dead and wounded, he insisted
that his troops were grateful for the opportunity to do God's work,
inasmuch as "the great Ruler of the Universe must have used us as
his instrument in chastising the blood-thirsty & murderous wretches
that defended the fort."[59]

As for the number of casualties, there is a discrepancy among American and Spanish sources. Three Americans who participated in the Battle of Negro Fort—Clinch, Buck, and Major Daniel Hughes—asserted that the fort contained approximately three hundred slaves and twenty-five Choctaw Indians on the eve of the battle, and that no more than fifty of them survived the blast.[60] Commodore Loomis at first claimed that there were "200 men, women, and children" inside the fort, of which "about 25" survived. He later increased the estimate of fatalities to nearly three hundred with just three survivors.[61] After the navy convoy returned to New Orleans, sailors testified that while it was impossible to determine the exact number of black people killed at Negro Fort, "about 200 were buried and a great number could not be extricated from under the ruins."[62] Because "a number of" maroons fled Prospect Bluff prior to the fort's destruction, the number of deaths may have been significantly smaller than the American combatants reported.[63] Spanish sources suggest that of an estimated one hundred maroons inside the fort at the beginning of the battle, roughly half of them died as a result of the fatal explosion.[64] The figures are disparate, but as the Spanish acquired their information second-hand, the larger American estimates are more reliable.

Regardless of the actual number of losses suffered in the Battle of Negro Fort, it is worth noting that the number of fatalities increased after the magazine's explosion. This occurred for two separate reasons. First, as American and, later, Spanish eyewitnesses both testified, the "greater part" of the fort's residents who survived the explosion were "mortally wounded," having been struck down by the hailstorm of wood, metal, and flames.[65] Second, while smoke and ashes still floated in the air, McIntosh's warriors started butchering the black survivors. Members of the Fourth Infantry Regiment claimed that only Clinch's heroism stopped the killing spree. The colonel "rushed into the ruins and ascended the highest point he could find, in order that the friendly Indians might recognize him and desist from the work of pillage and slaughter."⁶⁶ While American soldiers tried to impute a noble motive to Clinch's intervention, it is worth remembering that he was saving as many of the injured as possible in order to return them to slavery.

That Garçon and the unnamed leading Choctaw chief were among those who emerged from the rubble defies explanation. That they remained defiant until their final breath was not. Though bloodied, bruised, and, in the case of the former British marine officer, blinded, the two leaders faced an ad hoc tribunal of McIntosh's mercenaries. In one last act of defiance, they accepted full responsibility for having killed the four American sailors from Loomis's naval convoy—Luffborough, Maitland, Burgess, and Daniels—ten days earlier. As a result, Negro Fort's last standing maroon commander and his unnamed Indian ally were immediately "scalped & shot" to death.⁶⁷

While burying the dead and rounding up and treating the survivors, American soldiers and sailors also collected the assortment of serviceable military and industrial materials stored throughout the fort complex and adjacent villages. Among the cache were belts, uniforms, and shoes; thousands of muskets, flints, and bayonets; hundreds of barrels of gun and cannon powder; an assortment of shovels, saws, and mills; three cannons weighing between sixteen and twenty-four pounds apiece, as well as a large mounted brass howitzer; and, for transportation, a wooden cart and a variety of boats, flats, and schooners. Clinch and Loomis estimated that the hoard was worth at least an astonishing two hundred thousand dollars (approximately three and a half million dollars in today's currency), and they agreed to divide the artillery, guns, and munitions equally between the army and navy forces. The two men disagreed over the allocation of the surplus military clothing and supplies, but in the end allowed McIntosh's warriors to take everything "except the cannon and shot."⁶⁸

Though stunningly successful as a military operation, the Battle of Negro Fort was almost a complete failure as a slave-hunting expedition. Among the hundreds of maroons who resided at the site, the American forces recovered less than two dozen, including one woman who somehow survived the blast unharmed—and may have been Garçon's wife.[69] Because the majority of survivors were "Spanish negroes," Clinch sent them to Pensacola in the custody of several of McIntosh's warriors.[70] When the group reached the West Florida capital, the city's slaveowners were dismayed, as most of the captives were "useless and of little value because of their advanced ages and other flaws."[71] Among the only five slaves returned uninjured was the forty-one-year-old shoemaker Castalio. Company owners immediately put him to work on Pensacola's public works "with a chain about his leg" as punishment for deserting Pensacola with the British two years earlier. There is no record of the fate of Castalio's wife and two daughters, who had fled to Prospect Bluff and remained at Negro Fort with their father.[72]

American slaveowners had even more reason to be disappointed than their Spanish counterparts, since Clinch's troops recovered only seven slaves from the United States or its territories. Elijah, Abraham, and Jo belonged to three Georgia frontiersmen, while Lamb's owner was none other than the recently deceased Indian agent Benjamin Hawkins.[73] Battrice and Jacob came to Florida from the Mississippi Territory after fleeing from their owner, an unnamed "Frenchman" living near Bay St. Louis. The origins of the two other captives taken by the American army are truly remarkable. Charles, who at the outbreak of war belonged to a "Gentleman in Virginia," came to Florida aboard the British frigate *Seahorse* when it joined Edward Nicolls's forces in the summer of 1814. William belonged to neither an American citizen nor a Spanish subject but rather a "Jew" in Kingston, Jamaica, named Dulendo.[74]

How did fugitive slaves from Virginia and Jamaica come to be counted among the Negro Fort maroons? The best explanation is that they served in the Colonial Marines and the British West India Regiments, respectively—which offers additional evidence of the mindset of the black veterans of His Majesty's Service both during and after the War of 1812. While their affinity for Great Britain was strong, the primary motivation for their having joined the redcoats was freedom for themselves and their families. After the war, when presented with the opportunity, they retired from the service in order to join one of the most extraordinary communities of fugitive slaves in history.

After embarking their black captives and torching what remained of Negro Fort, the American army and navy forces ran into separate dangerous situations. While ascending the Apalachicola River towards Camp Crawford, Colonel Clinch's troops learned that the Seminoles who had agreed to help the Spanish attack Negro Fort were headed in their direction. The colonel ordered the soldiers to remain in their vessels and then went ashore with two hundred of McIntosh's warriors in pursuit of the Seminoles, "but the cowardly wretches dispersed."[75] The following day, Loomis's sailors were descending the river when they met the Spanish vessels commanded by Captain Calderón. Any fear of a confrontation quickly dissipated when a Spanish messenger boarded one of the American gunboats and disclosed the Spaniards' pleasure at learning of the fort's destruction. All was not forgiven, however, as Calderón demanded a surrender of all weapons and munitions seized from the fort, which was clearly "established in the territory of S.M.C. (His Catholic Majesty)."[76] Loomis responded that because the "captured property" was found in the possession of "fugitive slaves from the U.S.," it would be delivered to the naval station at New Orleans.[77]

Loomis took the opportunity to offer a justification for the United States' destruction of Negro Fort. As a refuge for "Spanish, American, and Indian negroes," he explained, the fort and its inhabitants posed a significant threat to the peace and safety of the southern frontier. Since the late war, the English had provided the fort's maroons with money, weapons, and ammunition to resist anyone who might try to enslave them. A fugitive slave sanctuary was never acceptable to the American people, and since the Spanish government had never taken any steps to eliminate it, the United States did.[78]

Though it resulted in the reenslavement of only a small number of fugitive slaves from the United States, the Battle of Negro Fort was a major victory for American slaveowners. The elimination of this one-of-a-kind sanctuary greatly reduced the chance of enslaved people finding freedom by taking flight across the southern frontier. Just as importantly, the federal government had demonstrated an eagerness to sacrifice men and treasure on slaveowners' behalf. Though only five Americans lost their lives, the Battle of Negro Fort set a powerful precedent regarding the federal government's support of slavery and its expansion.[79]

Even with all of the benefits slaveowners derived from Negro Fort's destruction, Andrew Jackson insisted that the mission was not yet complete. In his response to Clinch's official battle summary, he wrote, "Your communication, containing an account of the complete destruction of the Negro Fort on the Appalachicola, has been received, and you will express to your officers and soldiers my approbation of their gallant conduct in this affair." However, the flight of hundreds of former slaves from the fort and surrounding villages before and after the fateful explosion required additional action. "You will demand of the Seminoles an immediate surrender of the negroes protected by them and belonging to the citizens of the United States," Jackson commanded, "and, in the event of their refusal, you will report the result to me and hold yourself in readiness to chastise them."[80]

As the order makes clear, the hunt for the Negro Fort maroons who had escaped into the East Florida wilderness was about to begin. In the meantime, citizens across the republic began learning of the assault against Negro Fort. Their reaction to the news of the nation's armed forces invading a foreign territory in order to kill or capture hundreds of fugitive slaves was of great importance. In a nation nominally dedicated to freedom, it would go a long way toward determining whether the US government would take similar actions in the future.

· 5 ·

THE BATTLE CONTINUES

"THE fort on Appalachicola bay in East Florida, where the ruffian Nicolls commanded a motley force of British, Indians and Negroes during the late war, and which has since been occupied by runaway negroes and hostile indians, was completely destroyed by our troops," the *Georgia Journal* proclaimed in the first published account of the Battle of Negro Fort. Based on the eyewitness description of the battle provided by a US Army infantryman, the article summarized the actions taken by the American troops and their Indian allies as well as the response of the fort's defenders. According to the report, the "*hot shot*" fired from the river exploded one hundred barrels of gunpowder and resulted in the death of more than one hundred of the fort's residents. "The others were taken prisoner without making further resistance."[1]

Below the article, the paper excerpted a letter from Colonel Duncan Clinch to Georgia governor David Mitchell, written after the victorious American army troops returned to Camp Crawford. "I have the honor to inform you," the colonel announced, that "the fort on the Appalachicola in East Florida, defended by one hundred Negroes and Choctaws, and containing two hundred Women and

Children, was completely destroyed." Fully aware that the governor would want to know what became of the people who survived the fort's explosion, the colonel added that he was forwarding a list of the names of all of the black captives originating from Georgia. As for any fugitive slaves who may have avoided apprehension by the American army, Clinch declared, "I have given the chiefs directions, to have every negro that comes into the nation taken and delivered up to the commanding officer at this post, or at Fort Gaines" in the Mississippi Territory.[2]

If any widespread opposition to the destruction of Negro Fort existed, it was not apparent in the press. Newspapers across the nation copied both the *Georgia Journal* article and Clinch's letter verbatim on their own pages without offering any critique or comment. In a typical example, the *New-York Columbian* placed the story on its second page, alongside accounts of the flooding of the Schuylkill River in Philadelphia and the possibility of a commercial agreement being reached between the United States and Russia.[3] An Ohio newspaper buried the story on its third page, just above the announcement of a seventy-five-year-old man marrying a woman less than half his age.[4]

Criticism of the United States' annihilation of the historic black community was also missing from accounts of the battle that soon poured from southern writers and helped shape national opinion on its outcome. Northerners and southerners consumed the exact same version of the fort's destruction, leaving no evidence of a contrasting or contradictory interpretation of the event. This does not prove that the two regions were entirely of the same mind on the matter, but it does suggest the existence of a racist pro-slavery consensus that by the second decade of the nineteenth century transcended section.

When read collectively, the earliest accounts of the Battle of Negro Fort agreed that the American victory accomplished several major objectives regarding the southern frontier. Most importantly, it closed a refuge for fugitive slaves who fled from both the United

States and Spanish Florida. A "gentleman of the first respectability at New-Orleans" celebrated the fort's eradication because "it had become a great nuisance, not only as a harbor for the hostile Indians, but for all the discontented negroes in the country, whose desertions were frequent."[5] Another Crescent City editorialist concurred. In an article that appeared in newspapers from Louisiana to the nation's capital and New York, he asserted, "It is a happy thing for the adjacent Americans, as well as for the Spanish territories, that this band of brigands has been exterminated. Appalachicola has long been a receptacle for all the run-away negroes of Georgia, Tennessee, the Mississippi Territory, and Pensacola, and for all the hostile and outcast Indians of the Creek and Seminole tribes."[6]

The destruction of Negro Fort also removed an insidious racial menace by eliminating a base from which African Americans and Native Americans preyed on the lives and property of white citizens. *Niles' Weekly Register* called Negro Fort a place "where an abominable host of Indians and negroes had collected, who were in the habit of plundering and committing depredations on all that came in their way."[7] In Georgia, the *Augusta Chronicle* hailed "the capture of the Negro and Indian Fort, on Appalachicola" by the bold and heroic actions "of our brave countrymen." Instead of lamenting the death of hundreds of people who fought and died for freedom, the editorialist expressed satisfaction that American troops had finally "relieved our southern and western frontiers from the predatory incursions of a lawless banditti; whose numbers were daily augmenting; and whose strength and resources presented a fearful aspect to our peaceful borders."[8]

Another accomplishment of the Battle of Negro Fort was to end Great Britain's influence on the southern frontier. An anonymous South Carolinian reveled in the fort's demise and the death or capture of the "horde of banditti" who resisted reenslavement, only regretting that "the British agents who planted this *virtuous community,* were not included in the explosion."[9] The sentiment was shared by a Louisiana writer who qualified the American victory with a comment on Great Britain's most notorious marine officers: "I wish Nicholls and Woodbine had been in the fort when it blew up."[10] A letter copied in *Niles' Weekly Register* declared that the fort's destruction would "strike terror into the Indians" because it was "their dernier resort in all desperate cases." This missive reminded readers that fugitive slaves were not the only target of British benevolence. The cache of weapons found in the fort was "designed as a continual supply for the Indians, or as a secure depot by the British in any future transaction against us in this quarter."[11]

As each of these examples suggests, nearly every early account of Negro Fort's destruction emphasized Great Britain's role in establishing the fortification and inspiring its inhabitants. Indeed, despite widespread use of the phrase "Negro Fort" in American print culture for more than a year, some publications now hesitated to use the term, offering the "British establishment" or the "Anglo Savage fort at Appalachicola" as alternatives.[12] Using the French word for "pupils," one writer referred to the Negro Fort maroons as "*the eleves of Colonel Nicholls*."[13] Another emphasized that during the fateful battle, these "Brigands wore the British uniform, gold epaulets, & fought under the English Jack, the bloody flag hoisted over it."[14] Other commentators stressed that the weapons and munitions inside Negro Fort were of British manufacture, as were the roughly one hundred red jackets American troops "discovered in the fort, packed up in hogsheads."[15]

By highlighting the British influence on Negro Fort, southern editorialists argued that slaves lacked both the courage and the capacity to strike for their freedom. But in an effort to justify the United States' invasion of a foreign territory, these writers unintentionally provided evidence to the contrary. One defender of the army-navy assault rejected the claim of Spanish officials that as a neutral territory Florida was immune to an American invasion, citing the fact that the fort was commanded by a fugitive slave who fought under the British flag and vowed "to let no white man approach the fort, or ascend the river, without the private signal of the British."[16] Another writer recalled how the British built the original fort according to the most modern methods and then delivered it "to the negroes and Indians, as it stood, with all its stores of artillery, arms and ammunition: col. Nichols only demanding an oath, that they would never permit a white man, except an *Englishman*, to approach it, or leave it alive." More than a year later, when the fort's defenders killed the four American sailors along the river's shore as a result of this order, the United States had no option but to retaliate. "This was an act that could not be passed over, and it was determined to destroy the fort, if possible."[17] Justifications such as these described the fort's black inhabitants as posing a serious threat, thereby undercutting the racist claim that they were unwilling and incapable of fighting for their freedom.

While citizens across the republic took satisfaction in the news of Negro Fort's demise, slaveowners along the southern frontier were thrilled at the prospect of recovering their property. Among them was William Gibson of St. Mary's, Georgia. This well-respected judge read a copy of Colonel Clinch's letter to Governor Mitchell, which mentioned the list of escaped slaves brought to Camp Crawford by the army, and requested that the governor forward a copy of the list to St. Mary's, "as there are several of our planters who have lost property of that description, and have made enquiries concerning it."[18] At Fort George Island on the East Florida coast, Zephaniah Kingsley, a former British loyalist and long-time South Carolinian, also begged the governor for assistance: "Having read in the Newspapers a communication from an Officer announcing the capture of the Runaway Negro Station at Appalachicola & securing of a good many Negros, I made no doubt but some of mine were amongst them as I have a great many with the Indians, who refuse delivering them up or allowing any one to take them." Though no longer a resident of the United States, Kingsley entreated the American governor to offer assistance in returning "the property," promising to generously compensate "those who will go and seize them & bring them out by force."[19]

At the same time southern frontiersmen openly discussed the Battle of Negro Fort and the fate of its black population, federal officials in Washington reacted with a silence that was deafening. Perhaps in an effort to avoid a conflict with the Spanish government, neither President James Madison, Secretary of State James Monroe, nor Secretary of War William Crawford offered any official comment on the battle after its conclusion. Even General Jackson at first said nothing publicly, which suggested the possibility of a cover-up.

The first to posit the existence of just such a conspiracy was Colonel Clinch. When rumors began circulating that the federal government was attempting to bury his official account of the battle, he reached out to Andrew Jackson and Edmund Gaines for support. Fearful of being scapegoated for leading an illegal invasion of a sovereign territory, the colonel notified the two generals of his fear "that my official communication of the affair that took place on the Appalachicola, would be suppressed by the W. Department." Clinch reminded his superiors of his nearly decade-long service to the republic, asserting that he would not allow his character and reputation to be "sacrificed to answer the political views of my government." To clear his name, the colonel asked Jackson to convene a court of inquiry "to inquire whether my marching a party of U. States troops, into E. Florida, & causing a fort on the Appalachicola to be destroyed, was in obedience to orders from a superior or not, & to inquire into my conduct generally in that expedition." Clinch swore that his call for an investigation had nothing to do with him wanting credit for Negro Fort's destruction. He simply wanted the record to show that his actions were proper.[20]

Without hesitating, Jackson rushed to Clinch's defense. Through one of his top aides in Nashville, the general took responsibility for the destruction of Negro Fort, insisting "that there is no room left for the existence of a doubt, but that your movement, on that occasion, was predicated upon orders received from your immediate commanding officer (Major-general Gaines) to whom instructions to that effect had been issued, the result of a previous understanding between the then commandant of Pensacola and himself." Regarding the American government's reticence to condone Clinch's actions or at least publish his report, Jackson cited fear of jeopardizing the ongoing negotiations between the United States and Spain over the future of East and West Florida. Then, in an effort to set Clinch's mind at ease, he explained that the government's silence on the matter was not a sign of disapproval. To the contrary, "Public acts, if not publicly censured, are tacitly approved."[21]

When General Gaines learned of Clinch's request for a court of inquiry and Jackson's response, he similarly defended the colonel's actions. In a brief letter forwarded from the Mississippi Territory to Clinch at Camp Crawford, Gaines wrote that he completely agreed with Jackson, whose judgment was as valuable as that of any court or committee. Regarding the expedition against Negro Fort, Gaines affirmed, "You performed the duties which I had the honor to assign to you (In conjunction with the naval force there) in a manner calculated to give you and your command high and solid claims to the approbation and confidence of your general, your government and country."[22]

Jackson and Gaines countenanced Clinch's unusual request for a public hearing because they had, after all, ordered him to destroy Negro Fort. But the reason why the generals came to Clinch's defense so quickly is that they knew he had already volunteered to lead the manhunt for the fort's black survivors and their Indian allies. Two weeks before lodging his complaint, Clinch had written

Jackson that after returning to Camp Crawford from Florida, he had arranged to send one thousand Creek warriors back into the Spanish territory. Their objective was to force the Seminoles to surrender all of the slaves among them who belonged to "Citizens of the U.S."[23]

Once again, Coweta chief William McIntosh agreed to lead the operation—but not until he returned from Washington, D.C., where he was scheduled to meet with President Madison. In the meantime, Clinch sent two other Creek chiefs to Miccosukee, just below the southern border, where they offered Chief Kinache the ultimatum "that unless the Negroes were given up immediately, that a sufficient force would be marched into his country, to drive the Seminoles into the Sea." After a two-day council, Seminole leaders indicated that they would "give up the Negroes," though Kinache prevaricated. Arguing that the Seminoles "could not take all the Negroes at once," he suggested that they wait until the "Upper Indians" recovered their own slaves before "he would have the American negroes taken and given up." Recognizing Kinache's ploy for what it was, Clinch believed that the Seminoles would "not give up the Negroes until they are compelled to do so." With an estimated four hundred Indians "& about the same number of Negroes" in opposition to the United States, he planned to send McIntosh and the Creek warriors into Florida as soon as the chief returned to the agency.[24]

Evidently, playing a decisive role in the Battle of Negro Fort did not absolve the Creeks of their obligation to serve as crack troops for the United States' southern army. It did, however, earn their representatives a trip to the White House. Accompanied by the federal Indian agent Daniel Hughes, McIntosh and several other "Chiefs and Warriors" arrived in the nation's capital in late November 1816, "with full powers to treat on all points relating to their nation." The city's *National Intelligencer* did not know the identity of any of the delegation except for McIntosh. However, the paper understood that this rare opportunity to meet with the executive was offered to the Indians because they had "marched against the Negro Fort on Apalachicola, which they united with Col. Clinch in the destruction of."[25]

While the United States and its Creek allies prepared for another Florida slave hunt, a shadowy figure emerged in East Florida, promising to finish the work left undone by Edward Nicolls, George Woodbine, and the rest of the Colonial Marines years earlier. Little is known of Alexander Arbuthnot's early life, but sometime after the Battle of Negro Fort, the elderly trader from Nassau, Bahamas, arrived in East Florida and opened several trading posts along the Gulf Coast. For the next several months, the septuagenarian took advantage of the declining fortunes of Spain's traditional trading power, John Forbes & Company. With the Spanish government's blessing, he began receiving animal pelts from the Seminoles in exchange for a variety of West Indian goods, including guns, knives, and drums painted with "the royal coat of arms."[26]

Among those welcoming Arbuthnot's arrival was Bowlegs (Boleck), a feared war chief from one of the most important and powerful families in the Seminole nation. In a letter to the governor of East Florida, the Alachua headman complained that ever since the Treaty of Ghent, his people had followed the advice of the British to avoid any conflicts with white settlers. But American citizens continually encroached on the Seminoles' land, stealing their cattle and murdering "our people." Having been victimized long enough, Bowlegs and other leaders begged King George "to fix some of his people among us," as the Spanish were too interested in the American cause "to be our friends." For the Seminoles, Arbuthnot's arrival portended additional assistance from the British in maintaining the possession of their land, even though, Bowlegs understood, "the Americans will lay hold of this as a pretext to make war on us, as they have before done, in stating we harbor their runaway slaves."[27]

If Bowlegs was the king, then Arbuthnot was a member of his royal court. Throughout the winter of 1816–1817, the Bahamian trader became a vocal advocate for the Seminoles. He was fully convinced that the Treaty of Ghent required the United States to return to its original owners all territory taken from the Indians during the War of 1812. Therefore, Arbuthnot corresponded extensively with American officials, demanding that they order all settlers to evacuate from the Seminoles' land. The actions of the aged and eccentric frontiersman were easy to ignore initially. However, after the brutal murder of several settlers by the Indians, they became an important topic of discussion among some of the republic's most prominent political and military leaders.

There is no record of the first time Andrew Jackson heard Arbuthnot's name, though it may have been in the spring of 1817, when General Gaines reported two violent incidents in southern Georgia. The first was the destruction of Camp Crawford, which the American army had recently abandoned. The second was the murder and scalping of a Camden County, Georgia, overseer named Obediah Garrett, as well as his wife and children. Gaines blamed the Seminoles for these atrocities but let Jackson know that the perpetrators had been encouraged by Arbuthnot, "one of those *self-styled Philanthropists* who have long infested our neighboring Indian villages, in the character of British Agents." Gaines asserted that while Arbuthnot claimed to be motivated by a spirit of "care and kindness," his maneuverings would inevitably lead to "the destruction of these wretched savages."[28]

When the editors of *Niles' Weekly Register* received a copy of one of Arbuthnot's letters, they offered it as proof that the destruction of Negro Fort had failed to deter the British from inciting violence along the southern frontier. The paper maintained that the "Southern Indians" had been peaceful until the British began providing them with arms and ammunition, "and a very strong fort in the *Spanish* territory, well furnished with cannon and every thing needful to its defence, was given to them as a rallying point and place of refuge." Though the fort no longer existed, little had changed because British agents like Arbuthnot continued to give the Indians hope. The solution was obvious: "Any British agent found among these Indians, within our territory, exciting them to murder, ought to be seized, and tried, and punished, with less pity than is due to a sheep-killing dog." As the Spanish government offered no assistance, it was also time for the United States to consider taking possession of East and West Florida permanently. In fact, it was a "grand mistake" that both colonies had not been seized during the last war. "It would have added nothing to the cost of the contest, and might have led to a speedy settlement of our differences with Spain."[29]

With word of Arbuthnot's activities spreading, General Gaines sent an angry letter to Kinache, demanding that he and the other Seminole chiefs fulfill a series of demands in order to avoid another American onslaught. The first was to hand over any Indians suspected of murdering American citizens, while the second was to cut all ties with their English agents, in particular Arbuthnot, "for he will be the ruin of you yet." Third and last, the Seminoles needed to betray their fugitive slave allies. "You harbor a great many of my black people among you" at the Suwannee River, Gaines explained to the Seminole chiefs before offering, "If you give me leave to go by you against them, I shall not hurt any thing belonging to you."[30]

In response, Kinache denied that the Seminoles committed any of the crimes for which they were being accused. Insisting that it was his people who had "cause to complain," he blamed the American settlers, "those lawless freebooters," for drawing first blood. On the subject of the absconded slaves Gaines referred to in his letter, the chief denied that he had anything to do with those who managed to escape into Florida from the United States, asserting, "I harbor no negroes." While some black fugitives had undoubtedly taken up with the English during the late war, Kinache declared, "It is for you white people to settle those things among yourselves, and not to trouble us with what we know nothing about."[31]

Kinache's assertion regarding fugitive slaves from the United States was disingenuous, as they continued to seek refuge among the Muscogee people following the destruction of Negro Fort. Among them was a twenty-one-year-old mulatto named Dick from South Carolina, whom slavecatchers captured in the "Creek Nation." Another was Bob, a light-skinned man with multiple facial scars who bolted from Warren County, Georgia, with a pile of homespun clothes. According to Bob's owner, Robert Lazenby, the bondsman "was in the nation in the course of last winter and may make for the Indians or for some water-craft."[32]

An advertisement placed in the *Georgia Journal* by an Indian agent working for Benjamin Hawkins's son, Philemon, revealed that despite Benjamin's passing, federal officials still shared slaveowners' interest in capturing escaped slaves. "A negro man named TOM and his wife POLLY, were apprehended (as runaways) in the Creek Nation by some Indians," the announcement read. According to the captives, they had absconded from their owners two months earlier. The ad instructed the slaves' owners "to call at the Factory of the United States at Fort-Hawkins, prove their property, pay the expence incurred by their apprehension and subsistence since received, and take them away."[33]

While some of the fugitive slaves living with the Creeks and Seminoles had come to Indian country from Negro Fort, others had not. At Fort Gaines, Indian slave catchers handed over "a negro man who calls himself JIM" who had fled from his owner near Savannah,

Georgia, "just before the negro Fort was blown up."[34] When army troops from Fort Hawkins captured a suspected escaped slave named John living among the Indians, the black man, who was "marked with cuts on each cheek," denied ever running away, insisting that he had been stolen more than a decade earlier "by some Indians." As army policy dictated, the commander at Fort Hawkins required that John's owner come to the post and pay the appropriate fees in order to take the captive away.[35]

Though American officials never acknowledged it, many of the black people living among, and in many cases claimed by, the Creeks and Seminoles belonged to Spanish subjects rather than American citizens. Following the Battle of Negro Fort, East Florida's Zephaniah Kingsley claimed to have more than "Forty Negros at Sawanee or about between there and the big Hamack and Tampa & a few about Makasukee."[36] When John Forbes & Company rehired their long-time agents William Hambly and Edmund Doyle to re-establish their Prospect Bluff store and recover any of the company's slaves who still remained at large, they soon had "seven or eight" in their possession but learned that others had joined the Seminoles.[37] "I intend to send a message to them the first opportunity," Doyle wrote his bosses, adding that once these former employees learned that the Prospect Bluff store had been reestablished, "it may have some inducement on them to return." Among the reasons for Doyle's optimism was the assistance of Colonel Clinch, who, in the months after the destruction of Negro Fort, had consistently proven himself "our friend."[38]

Besides the sanctuary Indians continued to provide fugitive slaves, it was the "predatory war" both groups were allegedly waging across the southern frontier that ignited the First Seminole War.[39] The conflict began when General Gaines ordered a surprise attack on Fowltown in November 1817. Located along the Flint River in Georgia's southwestern corner, the town was home to the Red Stick war chief Neamathla, as well as several hundred black and Indian militants, including some of the former inhabitants of Negro Fort. "They speak in the most contemptuous manner of the Americans," a Creek informant declared of Fowltown's fighters, "and threaten to have satisfaction for what has been done—meaning the destruction of the negro fort."[40] Despite the motivation of Neamathla's forces, revenge would have to wait. When Gaines's force of 250 American troops stormed into Fowltown, a brief skirmish resulted in both the Indians and the slaves retreating with their families into the woods.[41]

In his report of the Battle of Fowltown, Gaines alerted General Jackson that the alliance of Britons, Indians, and fugitive slaves across the southern frontier continued. Before burning the town, the American troops searched Neamathla's home. There they found a British red coat with gold epaulettes and a certificate signed by a British marine captain proclaiming that the chief was "a true and faithful friend to the British." Gaines learned additionally from the "friendly Indians" that George Woodbine had recently promised to return to Florida with assistance from the British government. Worst of all, there were throughout the region an estimated two thousand hostile Red Stick and Seminole warriors, "besides the blacks, amounting to near four hundred men, and increasing by runaways from Georgia."[42]

If Gaines's letter failed to attract Jackson's attention, steps taken by the Red Sticks and Seminoles in retaliation for the destruction of Fowltown did. In late November 1817, an American army supply boat with forty soldiers and several of their wives ascended the Apalachicola River under the command of Lieutenant Richard Scott. Their destination was Camp Crawford, which the Americans had recently rebuilt and renamed Fort Scott (in honor of General Winfield Scott). When a strong current forced the craft to the river's eastern shore, the vessel was attacked by as many as five hundred Indians who had been lying in wait. Within moments, all but six of the men on board the supply craft were dead. The women were "killed or taken."[43] Two weeks later, the warriors continued their brutal offensive by capturing William Hambly and Edmund Doyle, and then killing William Perryman, a Lower Creek chief who had tried to protect the two Spanish operatives.[44]

To punish Hambly and Doyle for their role in the destruction of Negro Fort a year and a half earlier, the Red Sticks and Seminoles took the two Spanish subjects on a long and difficult journey. After traveling more than 150 miles to the lower Suwannee River, some thirty miles upstream from Florida's northwestern Gulf Coast, the Indians delivered the two captives to the leaders of a burgeoning black community known as Nero's Town.[45] The arrival of Hambly and Doyle must have caused a great deal of commotion across this isolated settlement, for its population comprised "the remnant of the slaves who escaped from the negro fort previous to its capture, augmented in number since by the runaways from the Floridas and Georgia."[46]

Even before the Battle of Negro Fort, hundreds of fugitive slaves and Indians had begun to make their way to the Suwannee River. There they established the adjacent communities of Nero's Town and Bowlegs's Town, respectively. Though allied militarily, the groups did not always see eye to eye. In one instance, after a slave belonging to Alexander Durant escaped to the Suwannee, the notorious Creek trader sent seven of his men to apprehend the absconder. They promptly did so, until "the blacks rushed on them and turned him loose." To keep the conflict from escalating, or perhaps to avoid antagonizing Durant's US allies, Bowlegs intervened, demanding that the maroons surrender the man in question. But in an extraordinary display of racial solidarity with the slave, the maroons threw the eminent chief to the ground and "ordered him off."[47]

The incident was an exception to the rule. The residents of Nero's Town and Bowlegs's Town sometimes disagreed, but antipathy for the United States kept them united militarily for several years. In the words of Peter Cook, a Bahamian trader who came to Florida to assist Arbuthnot in his various business enterprises and spent months trading along the lower Suwannee River, the maroons and Indians "always said they would fight together."[48]

While little information on the size and strength of Bowlegs's Town exists, the evidence on Nero's Town suggests that it was the more formidable of the two.[49] One of the earliest accounts of the maroon community was produced by Captain Timpoochee Barnard, a "half-breed" Yuchi Creek chief and the son of one of Andrew Jackson's most trusted Indian allies. Barnard estimated the population of Nero's Town at four hundred "fit to bear arms, exclusive of the women and children," and he reported that "they are well furnished with arms and ammunition which they have received by water carriage from the mouth of the river." Though they lived apart from the Indians, Barnard learned that these former slaves still strongly identified with their Creek and Seminole allies, as they had "a red pole setup in their towns and are dancing the red stick dance."[50]

A year later, George Perryman, another pro-American Creek and a relative of the murdered William Perryman, commented on the militancy of the Nero's Town maroons. He attributed it to their having formerly defended Negro Fort: "They have chosen officers of every description, and endeavor to keep up a regular discipline, and are very strict in punishing violators of their military rules." Disappointed in their failure to stop the destruction of Negro Fort the previous summer, these black troops wanted a second chance at the American army and especially McIntosh's warriors, vowing that "they had something more to do than they had at Appalachicola."[51]

While waiting for a rematch, the residents of Nero's Town settled into a stable existence by trying "to replicate the society they had created at Prospect Bluff."[52] Besides instituting martial law, the establishment of an isolated, independent, and self-sufficient society was the most obvious trait Negro Fort and Nero's Town shared in common. The maroons along the Suwannee River "were living in quiet and plenty without a single temptation to depredate in our territory," army engineer Hugh Young later recalled. "Their distance screened them from the single efforts of their masters to recover them and the abundance of cattle and corn obviated every plea on the score of subsistence." In addition to raising corn, peas, potatoes, beans, and rice in the fertile soil surrounding their sturdily built cabins, they had fenced-in gardens, "affording good fruit and vegetables."[53]

The governance of Nero's Town by a fugitive slave also evoked Negro Fort. But the absence of substantive British support, combined with a significant Indian presence, made the Suwannee River community different.[54] George Perryman claimed that Bowlegs ruled Nero's Town and Bowlegs's Town, and that the black and Indian residents of both communities "nominated him King, and pay him all kinds of monarchical respect, almost to idolatry."[55] West Indian trader Peter Cook disagreed, swearing under oath, "Nero commanded the blacks," and "There were some negro captains who obeyed none but Nero."[56]

Though he deserves his own biography, little information exists on the namesake of Nero's Town. What is known is that he once belonged to Francis Fatio, an East Florida immigrant who established a ten-thousand-acre plantation on the St. John's River near St. Augustine.[57] In 1795, Nero fled to Indian country, where he took up with the Seminoles and years later became a familiar face among the Spanish traders at Prospect Bluff.[58] Nero's contribution to Negro Fort is unknown, but once at Suwannee he became the preeminent "negro chief."[59]

Despite the contradictory evidence, Nero and Bowlegs seem to have governed their eponymous towns collectively—the fate of Hambly and Doyle being a case in point. After arriving at the Suwannee, the two prisoners faced a tribunal of black and Indian leaders. This extraordinary trial was the suggestion of Alexander Arbuthnot, who blamed the Spanish subjects for the destruction of Negro Fort and wanted its former residents to have revenge "for the loss of their friends at that place."[60] After a brief proceeding, the court found both men guilty of various crimes and sentenced them to be tortured, presumably to death. But Nero intervened on the prisoners' behalf and for unknown reasons ordered them to be taken by a group of Indian warriors to Fort St. Marks and handed over to the Spanish authorities.[61]

The power that fugitive slaves and Seminoles continued to wield across East Florida, combined with increasing evidence that both groups were receiving arms and ammunition from British traders, eventually convinced the American government to act. In December 1817, the newly appointed secretary of war, John C. Calhoun, ordered Andrew Jackson to Fort Scott to take command of the forces in the region. Jackson was to "adopt the necessary measures to terminate a conflict which it has ever been the desire of the President, from considerations of humanity, to avoid" but that was made inevitable by the hostile actions of the Seminoles.[62] Less than a month later, Jackson left Nashville for southern Georgia, where he planned to organize more than one thousand volunteers. After gathering a sufficient supply of arms and provisions, he would initiate the third American invasion of Spanish Florida in four years.[63]

Curiously, Jackson's first stop in Florida was the ruins of Negro Fort. In March 1818, after traveling nearly the entire length of the Apalachicola River, the general ordered his troops, which included nine hundred Georgia militiamen and an unrecorded number of "friendly Creeks," to disembark at Prospect Bluff. After scaling the small cliff above the water's edge, the Americans and allied Indians saw the remnants of the once-thriving free black community all around them. "A part of the old fort still remained," army lieutenant John Banks recalled in a published memoir. "We found some of their arms and cannon ball lying in the mud," and the guns, which "had been exposed to the weather" for nearly two years, still fired.[64]

When Jackson reached the top of the bluff, he ordered his aide-de-camp, Lieutenant James Gadsden, to oversee the construction of a new fort directly atop the ruins of the old one. Less than two weeks later, the general proudly reported to Washington of his lieutenant's efforts regarding the new fortification: "His talents and indefatigable zeal displayed in the execution of this order induced me to name it Fort Gadsden, to which he is justly entitled." In addition to Prospect Bluff's natural advantages as a "depot" for military stores, the establishment of an American fort there served two important functions. By burying all traces of Negro Fort, the American army not only eliminated any possibility of its resurrection but also erased much of the evidence of its ever having existed.[65]

While stationed at the newly christened Fort Gadsden, Jackson divulged his intentions. Besides securing the southern border against hostile Indians and their foreign allies, his mission was to hunt fugitive slaves. In a letter to Captain Isaac McKeever, requesting the assistance of the US naval fleet at Apalachicola Bay, the general asserted that this effort was imperative. In the neighborhood of Fort St. Marks, Seminoles encouraged by both Red Stick chiefs Josiah Francis and Peter McQueen, as well as the British agents Alexander Arbuthnot and George Woodbine, had assembled "a motley crew of brigands—slaves enticed away from their masters, citizens of the United States, or stolen, during the late conflict with Great Britain." Convinced that these outlaws were waging a "predatory war against the United States," Jackson ordered McKeever to move his fleet along the coastline "and make prisoners of all, of every person, or description of persons, white, red or black, with all their goods," including their slaves.[66]

With that, the First Seminole War escalated dramatically in April 1818. Jackson marched eastward from Fort Gadsden with a force of

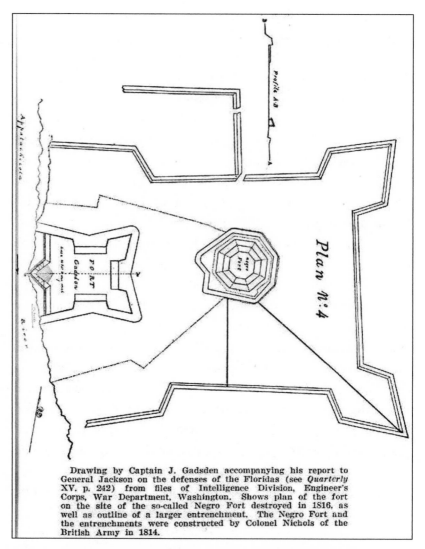

Drawing by Captain J. Gadsden accompanying his report to
General Jackson on the defenses of the Floridas (see *Quarterly*
XV. p. 242) from files of Intelligence Division, Engineer's
Corps, War Department, Washington. Shows plan of the fort
on the site of the so-called Negro Fort destroyed in 1816, as
well as outline of a larger entrenchment. The Negro Fort and
the entrenchments were constructed by Colonel Nichols of the
British Army in 1814.

FIGURE 5.1. The drawing details the smaller Fort Gadsden, which American troops
built on Prospect Bluff in 1818, while also providing a clear outline of Negro Fort's
outer perimeter and interior citadel. Courtesy of State Archives of Florida, Florida
Memory, www.floridamemory.com.

fifteen hundred militia, seven hundred army regulars, and eight hundred Creek warriors led by the newly promoted Brigadier General William McIntosh. Invading Miccosukee, they put several hundred Seminoles and maroons to flight.[67] Any satisfaction the Americans might have derived from their victory was mitigated by what they found at the council house of Chief Kinache. Suspended on a red pole were "about fifty fresh scalps, taken from the heads of extreme age, down to the tender infant, of both sexes, and in an adjacent house, near three hundred men; which bore the appearance of having been the barbarous trophies of settled hostility for three or four years past." Eager for revenge, the Americans swept across the area, killing or capturing several Indians while "leaving a tract of fertile country in ruin."[68]

Having forced the enemy to flee, the American army aimed for Fort St. Marks. After arriving at the Spanish outpost several days later, Jackson informed Commander Francisco Caso y Luengo of his reason for returning to Florida: "To chastise a savage foe, who, combined with the lawless band of negro brigands, have, for some time past, been carrying on a cruel and unprovoked war against the citizens of the United States." Jackson further explained that as "Indians and negroes" had received military supplies from the Spanish station in recent months, "the immutable principle of self-defence" required that the American troops take immediate possession of its garrison.[69] When Luengo denied having supplied any parties with weapons of war, Jackson declared that his American and Creek forces would remain in control of Fort St. Marks regardless of the thoughts of the Spanish government. He added that any further discussion of the matter would have to wait, as the war "against our common enemy should not be retarded by a tedious negotiation."[70]

In the coming days, Jackson made his authority clear in a variety of ways. He began by taking custody of Alexander Arbuthnot, who was already being held at the fort under the authority of the Spanish commandant. Jackson then ordered the arrest and execution of two Indian chiefs believed to be conspiring against the United States. Among them was the Prophet Josiah Francis, who had traveled to London with Edward Nicolls two years earlier in an effort to gain further assistance from the British government for his people. Lastly, Jackson saw to the release of William Hambly and Edmund Doyle, who almost immediately began assisting the US military with its efforts in Florida. Jackson became quite enamored of Hambly, whom he employed as an interpreter and later sent to Washington to meet with President James Monroe. From Spanish store clerk to British lieutenant, Indian captive, and American emissary, Hambly lived a more interesting and colorful life than most.[71]

With the United States in complete control of Fort St. Marks, Jackson set his sights on Nero's Town and Bowlegs's Town. Though often remembered as an effort to secure the American border, the ensuing Battle of Suwannee was essentially another federally sponsored slave-hunting expedition. Arbuthnot learned as much during his brief incarceration at Fort St. Marks. An American army deserter came to the fort and revealed that the United States' primary motivation for attacking the two settlements was not to secure the southern border but "to destroy the black population at Suwanee."[72]

As had happened before the Battle of Negro Fort, national media justified the invasion of Suwannee by depicting the community's residents as rebellious slaves and Indian savages, who, along with their foreign allies, threatened the peace and security of the southern frontier. One anonymous writer reported that George Woodbine had returned to Florida and was providing arms and ammunition to the black and Indian residents of Suwannee. As for the recipients of this materiel, a great many were Negro Fort deserters, who "joined the other banditti under Bowlegs, and now compose part of those negroes who, together with the barbarous Semmolians, have been robbing and murdering the frontier inhabitants both of Georgia and Florida indiscriminately." United by a thirst for the blood of American settlers, these enslaved and savage people were the avowed enemies of white Floridians, whose lives were consequently in grave danger.[73]

In another widely disseminated piece, a Mobile, Alabama, informer took solace in the fact that the American government had already eliminated a comparable menace in Spanish Florida and would likely do it again. While the objectives of the multiracial force gathered near the mouth of the Suwannee River were difficult to determine, he found it impossible to imagine that a small group of Spanish rebels, West Indian pirates, and a "handful of wretched Indians and negroes" would attempt to "contend against the power of the United States." Most likely, they considered that the southern border was a shield "and that under its shelter they might carry on their system of robbery and murder with impunity." But given the government's stance in this regard, "They will certainly be disappointed." With Congress back in session, it was only a matter of time before the esteemed body would arrange for the destruction of these black and Indian insurgents "and their associates."[74]

In part because of reports like these, Jackson again felt no compunction about ordering troops into Spanish territory with or without any authority to do so. On April 9, 1818, the general left Fort St. Marks with several thousand army regulars, Creek warriors, and Tennessee volunteers, whom he soon led in two "spirited engagements" with the enemy. At Econfina swamp, southeast of Tallahassee, Jackson's force won a decisive victory, killing thirty-seven Indians and capturing more than one hundred others, mostly women and children. The following day, the Americans and Creeks happened upon an isolated village and after killing two Seminoles took one warrior and two children prisoner. On April 16, the army arrived within six miles of the Suwannee River, where they were spotted by several mounted Seminoles, who immediately withdrew to warn their companions.[75]

As with the Battle of Negro Fort, the outcome of the Battle of Suwannee depended largely on the contribution of hundreds of Creek warriors who continued to serve on the front lines of the United States' southern army. Still under the command of William McIntosh, they took full advantage of their overwhelming numbers and after a brief pitched battle forced "about 300 negroes and savages" to retreat to the river.[76] Adjutant General Robert Butler recalled that after the American forces killed eleven men and took three prisoners, they drove approximately three hundred of Suwannee's residents into the water. As for the number who reached the opposite shore, the army officer assumed that most had drowned, the river "being nearly 300 yards wide." Still not satisfied, Jackson ordered his men to burn the village and then sent them across the river in pursuit of the enemy, who promptly "dispersed in every direction."[77]

Two black survivors of the Battle of Suwannee offered their own account of events. Nero did not directly participate in the battle with Jackson's forces, as he was "swimming horses across the river." Still, he knew "that a good many Indians and negroes were killed by the assailants, who were American soldiers, half-breeds, and Indians." The black chief added that as soon as the battle was over, much of Suwannee's black population had taken shelter on an island in the Suwannee River, but they were captured by the "half-breeds and Indians" and taken to the United States.[78]

John Prince, a "free colored man" from St. Augustine, offered additional details in his version of events. "There were a great many of them," he asserted of the American force, "and so strong that we stood no chance." Nevertheless, the maroons and Indians soldiering alongside him performed heroically. Among the most fearless was an East Florida fugitive named Joe, who "fought as long as he dared." Prince agreed with Nero's account of the fate of those who tried swimming across the river, adding, "The half-breeds pursued them in boats, got the other side of them, and took them all prisoners, and carried them off to the United States."[79]

The most revealing elements of Prince's testimony were his thoughts on the reasons for the United States' assault on Suwannee. When asked why the towns were targeted, he stated that the "Indians have always said that they should not have been attacked at the Suwanee, if they had not had these negroes among them." Any other alleged motivation was just an excuse for southern slaveowners to regain their valuable property. The Americans' "hope of getting possession of them (the negroes) invited the attack and proved the destruction of the town."[80]

During the hunt for fugitive slaves near the mouth of the Suwannee River, Jackson's troops seized a schooner believed to belong to Alexander Arbuthnot, causing the general to nearly instigate an international incident. As the vessel purportedly "brought supplies of powder and lead to the Indians and negroes," the sentinels arrested the three passengers and promptly delivered them to Fort St. Marks.[81] Among the prisoners were two Bahamian backwoodsmen. While Peter Cook had come to East Florida to help Alexander Arbuthnot establish his trading posts, Robert Christie Ambrister had joined George Woodbine's effort to "see the negroes righted."[82] A former lieutenant in the Corps of Colonial Marines, Ambrister had not only served with Nicolls and Woodbine at the British Post but had also assisted in its construction and design.[83]

Upon Jackson's return to Fort St. Marks on April 25, he ordered Arbuthnot and Ambrister to face a special military tribunal on three separate charges. The most serious of these was exciting "the Indians and negroes to acts of hostility against the United States."[84] The trial focused largely on the testimony of Peter Cook and several other witnesses, as well as a cache of documents seized from Arbuthnot's schooner. After two days of deliberation, the court found both men guilty of most of the charges and sentenced them to death by hanging.

When the court reduced Ambrister's punishment to "fifty stripes on his bare back" and twelve months of hard labor, Jackson intervened and immediately carried out the execution of both British subjects.[85]

The third man taken prisoner aboard Arbuthnot's ship was Fernando, a multilingual and literate fugitive slave from St. Augustine. This man's story is almost impossible to believe. He belonged to an East Florida official until the War of 1812, when he absconded and enlisted in the Corps of Colonial Marines. He served briefly at the British Post and stayed on for an undetermined length of time at Negro Fort. After the Battle of Negro Fort, Fernando made his way to Suwannee, where he lived as a free man until being arrested "with arms in his hands, under the character of a British soldier." Something about Fernando must have impressed Jackson, for the general resisted his initial urge to execute the black rebel and instead ordered him to be taken, along with some of Jackson's other belongings, to Nashville.[86]

Once a Negro Fort maroon, Fernando would spend the remainder of his life as Jackson's slave—a sadistic souvenir of the general's efforts to capture fugitive slaves across the southern frontier. But it is hard to imagine that the former redcoat ever suffered his fate with resignation. "One can only wonder," Jane Landers writes in her study of the revolutionary Atlantic world, "what the other slaves at the Hermitage learned from the multilingual and literate man who had once lived among the Seminoles and stood, gun in hand, against their 'master.'"[87]

After executing Arbuthnot and Ambrister, Jackson led twelve hundred army regulars, Tennessee volunteers, and "friendly Indian warriors" westward and conquered Pensacola for the second time in four years, effectively bringing the First Seminole War to an end.[88] In the coming weeks, Jackson boasted that the conquest of Florida marked "an end to all Indian wars." But he made no such claim regarding the problem of fugitive slaves. Indeed, in a confidential letter to President Monroe, the general confessed that although building Fort Gadsden atop the ruins of Negro Fort, capturing Fort St. Marks in East Florida, and seizing Fort Barrancas in West Florida were signal achievements, the peace and security of the southern frontier remained in peril. Though the Indians were defeated, "the hords of negro Brigands" from Negro Fort and Suwannee had now taken refuge at Tampa Bay on the west coast of the Florida peninsula, where under "foreign influence" they remained in opposition to the United States.[89]

Though anxious to lead another slave-hunting expedition into Spanish Florida, Jackson decided to wait. Desperate to recover from a number of physical ailments, the fifty-one-year-old general informed Monroe before returning to his Nashville plantation, "I must have rest, it is uncertain whether my constitution can be restored to stand the fatigues of another campaign."[90] Besides health, there was another variable that would determine whether Jackson would return to Florida. Throughout the summer and fall of 1818, government leaders began to openly question the legality of Jackson's actions in the Spanish territories. As a result, the US House of Representatives launched one of the first and most important investigations in its short history.

• 6 •

SLAVERY OR FREEDOM

O N December 30, 1818, just days before the US Congress opened its investigation of Andrew Jackson's Florida campaign, the *National Intelligencer*, a pro-administration daily published several blocks away from the US Capitol, printed a letter intended to sway public and congressional opinion in the general's favor. Written by Secretary of State John Quincy Adams to the US minister to Spain, George Erving, the lengthy communication was a response to the chorus of complaints from both home and abroad about Jackson's conduct. By providing a cursory account of the "late Seminole War," Adams endeavored "to justify the measures of this Government relating to it, and as far as possible the proceedings of General Jackson."[1]

According to the secretary of state, the trouble began with the arrival of British forces on Florida's Gulf Coast during the War of 1812. After disembarking on the eastern shores of the Apalachicola River, Colonel Edward Nicolls invited "all the runaway negroes—all the savage Indians—all the pirates, and all the traitors to their country" to wage a war of extermination against the United States. Following the ratification of the Treaty of Ghent, the colonel withdrew "the

white portion of his force" from the Spanish territory, but he left
the British Post on Prospect Bluff "amply supplied with military
stores and ammunition, to the Negro department of his allies." In
the coming months, this "Negro Fort" served as a base for a series
of "depredations, outrages, and murders" against American citizens.
In July 1816, the fort's inhabitants opened fire on US gunboats, and
in an obvious act of self-defense, the navy's sailors reduced the fort
to rubble. Negro Fort was gone, but many of its inhabitants had escaped to East Florida, where they joined the Seminoles and "*stuck to
the cause*"—that is, "the savage, servile, exterminating war against the
United States."[2]

Adams's letter is remarkable on two separate accounts. First, it
marked an important milestone in the history of American slavery.[3]
Instead of taking a bold stand against the institution or its violent
expansion, this internationally regarded New England intellectual—
the son of a northern antislavery president, no less—renounced the
sentiments of his father and his section and embraced a pro-Jackson,
pro-slavery, pro-southern point of view. To defend an emerging slave-
expansion-at-all-costs policy, Adams applauded both the destruction
of Negro Fort and the death of hundreds of its defenders. Given the
bigoted and biased tone of Adams's famous public correspondence, it
is worth considering whether the many actions he took later in life as
an ardent antislavery activist were in some part a result of—or pen-
ance for—his having repudiated Negro Fort so strongly.[4]

Second, the letter provided the blueprint for Jackson's defenders in
the congressional hearings that followed. Though historians have long
analyzed these hearings in relation to Jacksonian imperialism, Indian
removal, and, most recently, nation building, they have generally over-
looked the role Negro Fort played in them.[5] The omission is notable
because from the opening days of the investigation, the fugitive slave
community was an important touchstone of the defense fashioned
by Jackson's defenders. By borrowing Adams's strategy and depicting

Negro Fort as a base of both slave rebellion and Indian revolt, pro-Jackson congressmen exploited two of American citizens' greatest fears. In so doing, they made Negro Fort a pretext for American involvement in Spanish Florida and the First Seminole War.

The House of Representatives' investigation of Jackson's 1818 Florida invasion began in January 1819, when members considered four resolutions calling for Jackson's censure. Among the crimes the general stood accused of committing were the unlawful executions of Alexander Arbuthnot and Robert Ambrister, as well as the capture of Fort St. Marks and Pensacola. To disprove these charges, Jackson's supporters modeled their own arguments on the secretary of state's, insisting that US military intervention in Spanish Florida became necessary the moment Negro Fort came into existence.

Portraying the fort as a base for Indians, fugitive slaves, and their foreign allies, who wantonly committed murderous depredations across the southern frontier, as Adams had done, helped immensely in this regard. John Holmes, a Democratic-Republican from Massachusetts, condemned Colonel Nicolls and the British marines for building the infamous fort, which became an asylum for the frontier's most desperate people: "All vagrant Indians, fugitive negroes, Spanish renegadoes, British malefactors, outlaws, and pirates, were associated here, to ferment and breed plots of blood, and torture, and murder, and treason." John Rhea of Tennessee was somewhat less hyperbolic, accusing Nicolls of erecting Negro Fort "for the reception of hostile Indians and Negroes, from whence he might sally out, with his motley crew of black, white, and red combatants, and annoy the defenceless frontiers of the United States." No congressman was as certain as Mississippi's George Poindexter that Negro Fort was the "*nucleus*" of years of frontier violence that Jackson was duty-bound to avenge. The Natchez lawyer declared, "The negro fort was erected on the Appalachicola, with the avowed intention of war with the United States."[6]

Pro-Jackson congressmen also repeated Adams's claim that the torture and killing of navy seaman Edward Daniels forced Jackson to order the fort's destruction. Though Daniels would still have been alive if Jackson had never ordered more than one hundred sailors and soldiers to Prospect Bluff, Representative George Strother declared that the American sailors headed to Negro Fort "could not have produced an attack, unless the hostile temper pre-existed" among the "outlaw Indians and runaway negroes" inhabiting the compound. Referring to the deceased Daniels, the Virginia congressman beseeched his chamber mates to remember how his murderers "had stuck a sailor full of splinters and burnt him to death." It was a heinous crime, an "outrage against humanity" perpetrated on a sailor "who had borne the 'star-spangled banner in triumph over the wave.'" Fortunately, the death cries of this American patriot were not made in vain as "this horde of brigands was given to the winds!"[7]

Several of Jackson's defenders copied Adams by painting Indians and slaves with the same brush, yet some drew a sharp distinction between the groups. While ignoring the plight of Negro Fort's African American population, House Speaker Henry Clay, who delivered the most memorable speech during the investigation, offered a spirited defense of Native American people and culture. Denouncing the Treaty of Fort Jackson for impoverishing the Creeks and robbing them of their land, he excused the tribes' warriors for the frontier violence they perpetrated as a result. "A truce thus patched up with an unfortunate people, without the means of existence, without bread, is no real peace," Clay explained about the failed treaty. "The instant there is the slightest prospect of relief, from such harsh and severe conditions, the conquered party will fly to arms, and spend the last drop of blood rather than live in such degraded bondage."[8]

Pennsylvania's Henry Baldwin did not go so far as to justify violence against the American people, but he explained the reason for the government's contrasting views on Indians and slaves. According to the Yale-educated lawyer, although the black and Indian inhabitants of Negro Fort shared similar ambitions—namely, the "butchery and murder" of American citizens—the law viewed them differently. The legal status of Indians was ambiguous given their long history on the land, Baldwin confessed, "but, as to negroes, there can be but one opinion"—they were property. According to the "rules of civilized warfare," the soldiers and sailors sent to destroy Negro Fort were not required to offer its black population any protections, because "they were, in fact, suppressing an insurrection of slaves, aided by an Indian force, all assembled and armed for purposes hostile to the country."[9]

The congressmen's inability to depict the Negro Fort maroons as anything other than rebellious slaves deserving of whatever misfortune befell them is easily explained. In her examination of the congressional investigation, legal scholar Deborah Rosen concludes, "Many white Americans were accustomed to the violence and extraterritorial practices that underlay the institution of slavery." In an era of violent slave expansion, killing and capturing fugitive slaves and destroying their sanctuaries was "an essential goal that could not be derailed by abstract territorial legal principles."[10]

In the end, the emotional appeals to white Americans' fears of a southern frontier menaced by rebel slaves and savage Indians were successful. After nearly a month of debate beneath galleries that were "crowded almost to suffocation," Jackson won the day.[11] In a series of one-sided votes that were both bipartisan and cross-sectional, the House of Representatives rejected the four proposed resolutions. Compelled by the mutually reinforcing ideologies of nationalism and racism, they refused to censure the general despite strong evidence that he acted improperly.[12] Still, Jackson was not quite in the clear.

Two weeks after the House of Representatives' investigation concluded, a Senate select committee completed its own inquiry—and it went in a different direction. In its scathing summary report, the five-member group condemned Jackson for unlawfully invading Florida and killing Indians and slaves, who were woefully outnumbered. The committee members also excoriated the general for executing Arbuthnot and Ambrister. Expertly researched and written, the report had the potential to undercut Jackson's rising political career and the pro-slavery imperialism he espoused. However, the Senate refused to discuss the committee's findings. Even if it had addressed them, the result might have been negligible. For on the same day the Senate released its report, the esteemed body ratified the Adams-Onís Treaty, which permanently transferred control of East and West Florida to the United States.[13]

The acquisition of Florida was an extraordinary achievement for Jackson. According to biographer Robert Remini, it brought the general closer to accomplishing his lifelong objective: protecting the lives of American citizens across the southern frontier by eradicating "the foreign presence in the south" and removing "the southern tribes west of the Mississippi River."[14] Remini's assertion is impossible to deny; the removal of foreign agents and Indians in the name of national security motivated Jackson throughout his military career. But by accepting the general's own claims unequivocally, Remini ignores Jackson's obsession with eliminating the problem of fugitive slaves—an obsession that had not been satisfied by the victories in the Battle of Negro Fort and the First Seminole War.

Jackson's fixation on fugitive slaves was apparent in the weeks before the congressional investigation, when he called for an American invasion of Tampa Bay, where African Americans from the United States and Spanish Florida had again found sanctuary. Though the fact was widely unknown at the time, there were several black communities near the expansive harbor on south Florida's western coast. Little evidence survives of the people who resided at places like "Sarrazota" and "Angola," located near present-day Sarasota and

Bradenton, respectively—but it is clear that a significant number were Negro Fort maroons.[15] According to a British eyewitness, they were "the remnant of the black and colored people who had served with colonel Nichols during the late war, fugitive slaves from all the southern section of the union, as well as from the Spanish plantations in Florida and from St. Augustine."[16]

Benjamin Hawkins had first brought the existence of the Tampa Bay communities to the attention of the American government during the War of 1812. However, it was a letter Jackson received from Florida's Gabriel Perpall in the summer of 1818 that seems to have piqued his interest in the area. Hoping to persuade the general to return to Florida to continue hunting fugitive slaves, the spokesman for some of St. Augustine's most prominent residents explained that "near three hundred" escaped slaves had relocated from the Suwannee River to Tampa Bay. To convince Jackson that intervention was necessary, Perpall emphasized the great threat this new sanctuary posed to American slaveowners. "Their combination is dangerous not only to the subjects of this province, but the Citizens of Georgia, as they offer great inducements for Slaves to run from their masters." Hopeful that Jackson's past actions in Florida were a prologue, Perpall closed deferentially, "We anxiously wish their whole establishment destroyed and the negroes brought into a state of subjugation, but we regret we have not the ability or means of effecting it."[17]

Several weeks after reading Perpall's letter, Jackson received a report from James Gadsden, who had just finished a brief tour of central and south Florida. In "The Defences of Florida," the army captain described Tampa Bay as "one of the finest harbors in the gulf." He went on to note that it had become "the last rallying spot of the disaffected negroes and Indians and the only favorable point from whence a communication can be had with Spanish and European emissaries." Gadsden further revealed that the British still operated a store "in that neighborhood and the negroes and Indians driven from Micosukey and Suwaney towns have directed their march to that quarter."[18]

Having been thus informed, Jackson became fully convinced that Tampa Bay had become yet another haven for "the savages and negroes who have not submitted to our authority." In November 1818, he forwarded to Washington a plan for an invasion of the secluded Gulf Coast harbor. While admitting that the combined force of Indians and slaves was insufficient "to create any serious disturbances with this country," Jackson nonetheless believed that "they should be persued, before they recover from the panic of our last operations." The invasion would begin the following spring with seven hundred army regulars marching toward Tampa Bay, where they would build a defensive fortification, obliterate the "negro establishment," and then head in an eastwardly direction towards the St. John's River, "deviating only where Indian villages or settlements (if there are any in the country) invite their attention." The cost of the expedition would be minimal, Jackson insisted, but its benefits were extraordinary, including the final end of "hostilities in the South."[19]

Regardless of the merits of Jackson's plan, the American government had no appetite for another invasion of Florida. There were two separate reasons for this. First was the fallout from both the congressional and the Senate investigations. Though neither body disciplined Jackson for his actions, their deliberations exposed the general's penchant for violence as well as a blatant disregard for the law. For the time being at least, he could not be trusted. Second, a combination of Spanish ineptitude and imposition kept the Adams-Onís Treaty from taking effect for two years. Fearful of doing anything that might threaten the United States' long-sought acquisition of Florida, President James Monroe and his administration resisted taking any further action in the Spanish territories for the time being.

While American and Spanish officials wrangled over Florida's future, the black communities near Tampa Bay prepared to defend themselves against an inevitable American invasion. Horatio Dexter, a British-born colonist familiar with the Florida peninsula, claimed that the "refugee Negroes" inhabited a series of islands from the bay along the coast to Charlotte Harbor, more than fifty miles to the south. Though unsure of their numbers, Dexter believed they were a force to be reckoned with. By carrying on an extensive trade with ship wreckers, pirates, and other "white persons who resorted to these places in armed vessels," they were "completely armed with Spanish musquets, Bayonets & Cartouche boxes."[20]

Extensive interaction with coastal traders led some of Tampa Bay's black and Indian leaders to reach out for additional help in staving off the expected assault. In the fall of 1819, Miccosukee Chief Kinache led a small delegation to the Bahamas seeking the assistance of the colonial government. "The Indians, who arrived here on Wednesday last from Florida," the *Nassau Royal Gazette* announced, "are come to solicit some supplies." Carrying a copy of one of Alexander Cochrane's proclamations from the War of 1812, and a certificate of faithful service to Great Britain, the Indians expected a warm reception from sympathetic island officials. They were mistaken. Fearful of endangering the peace between Great Britain and the United States, Bahamian leaders refused the delegation's request for supplies and ordered the chiefs to return to Florida and fend for themselves.[21]

While Tampa Bay's maroon and Indian communities were momentarily safe from an American invasion, that would soon change. In January 1821, William McIntosh and more than twenty other opportunistic Creek chiefs agreed to the First Treaty of Indian Springs. This treaty resulted in the cession of nearly five million additional acres of land in southwestern Georgia to the United States. While the treaty is remembered for the generous annuities provided to the signatories, the issue of fugitive slaves also played a significant part in the negotiations.[22]

During the conversations leading up to the agreement, a dispute emerged between the two parties when American treaty commissioners accused the Creeks of failing to fulfill their historical obligations to the United States as slave catchers. McIntosh responded by citing the leading role his people had played in the Battle of Negro Fort. It was "his warriors," he informed the negotiators, who "attacked the fort and blew it up," and then rounded up the survivors and delivered them to their owners. McIntosh conceded that many fugitive slaves remained in Florida with the Seminoles and thus proposed a deal: "If the President admits that country to belong to the Creek nation, he will take his warriors down, and bring all he can get, and deliver them up."[23]

Despite McIntosh's and the Creeks' lengthy record of service to the United States' southern army, the commissioners rejected the chief's proposal outright. "As to the negroes now remaining among the Seminoles," they countered, "we consider those people (the Seminoles) a part of the Creek nation." Therefore, McIntosh and the Creeks needed to capture and return the Seminoles' slaves who belonged to American citizens—and they were to receive absolutely nothing in return.[24] The dismissal of McIntosh's request for land in Florida explains why, when two hundred Coweta warriors raided Tampa Bay and surrounding areas several months later, McIntosh stayed home.

Andrew Jackson did not participate in the Creek raid on Tampa Bay either. Furthermore, his role in organizing the attack—if any—remains uncertain. After spending much of the two years since the congressional investigation defending his name and reputation, the general reluctantly accepted an offer from President Monroe to serve as the first governor of the territories of East and West Florida.[25] Even before arriving in Pensacola to assume his post in the spring of 1821, Jackson contacted Washington about removing the remaining Indian population from the new territories. In a tone suggesting that the congressional investigations into his character may have taken a toll, he promised obsequiously, "Whatever may be the Presidents Instructions upon this subject shall be strictly obeyed and likewise in relation to the negroes who have run away from the States & inhabit this country and are protected by the Indians."[26] Given Governor Jackson's record and reputation, it is hard to imagine that the Creeks marched hundreds of warriors into Florida without his permission. Nevertheless, there is no evidence that he ordered the Tampa Bay raid, as some historians have suggested.[27]

About the only thing certain about the Creek raid on Tampa Bay is that rather than a government-sponsored military operation, it was a private business venture initiated by, and for the benefit of, slave owners and traders.[28] Indeed, evidence suggests that the Indians attacked Tampa Bay at the behest of a group of frontier traffickers looking "to obtain Slaves for a trifle." In April 1821, the unnamed "men of influence" ordered the Indians to march towards Tampa Bay "and there take, in the name of the United States, and make prisoners, of all the men of colour, including women and children, they would be able to find." They were then to deliver their bounty to a secret location.[29]

In McIntosh's absence, several "half breed Indians" agreed to the mission. While some of them, including the Coweta chief Captain William Miller, were relatively unknown to American officials, the mestizo war chief William Weatherford was not. Following the Fort Mims Massacre, white settlers had regarded this former Red Stick leader as a "red-skinned, bloody-handed savage." However, he eventually rejected much of his Indianness, becoming a successful planter and slaveowner as well as one of Andrew Jackson's fast friends. As much as any other individual, Weatherford's personal transformation signaled a fundamental shift in the cultural practices of indigenous peoples across the southern frontier due to American expansion.[30]

When Captain Miller and a force of two hundred Creek warriors finally reached Tampa Bay early in the summer of 1821, they zeroed in on the maroon community near present-day Sarasota.[31] After taking three hundred black people captive, they "plundered their plantations, set on fire all their houses, and then proceeding Southerly captured several others." By the middle of June, the warriors had made their way more than fifty miles south of Tampa Bay to San Carlos Bay, where they robbed local fishermen of thousands of dollars' worth of property. Having blazed a long and bloody trail along East Florida's western coast, the Creeks "broke all the establishments of both black and Indians, who fled in great consternation."[32]

Of the hundreds of fugitive slaves believed to have been apprehended by Miller's warriors, seventy-nine were taken to a small army camp on the Apalachicola River. There, US Army colonel Matthew Arbuckle recorded their names, heights, skin colors, owners, and former places of residence. Ranging in age from one to seventy, nearly every captive named on the hand-written list belonged to Spanish colonists in St. Augustine, St. Marks, and Pensacola. Some belonged to prominent Creek and Seminole chiefs, including Bowlegs, William McIntosh, and Peter McQueen. Though it did not matter to their captors, several of the people on Arbuckle's list do not appear to have been slaves at all: a light-skinned thirty-year-old named John insisted that he was "Born free," while seven other men claimed they were free black soldiers who came to Tampa Bay after deserting from the Spanish garrison at Fort St. Marks.[33]

One prisoner's story was truly extraordinary. Jim, a short, dark-skinned forty-year-old captive from St. Augustine, belonged to "the estate of George Washington" prior to his enslavement in East Florida. How a man owned by the first president of the United States became the property of a Spanish colonist is fascinating to

consider. It testifies to two important developments in the early decades of the American republic: both the long-distance forced migration of hundreds of thousands of slaves from the Upper South to
the Lower South and the determination of those who survived this
Second Middle Passage to be free.[34]

After determining the identities of these captives, US Indian agent
John Crowell allowed the Creeks to take twenty of them into their
possession and ordered the others to be moved to Fort Mitchell on
the Alabama-Georgia border. Through an announcement published
in newspapers in Florida, Alabama, and Georgia, Crowell instructed
slaveowners across the region to attend a public sale near the fort on
the first Monday of November "and prove their property, otherwise
they will be sold for the benefit of their captors."[35] Apparently, the
threatened sale never took place, for three months later Crowell reported the "disposition" of all remaining slaves to their Spanish or
Indian owners. In the end, only ten of the absconders captured at
Tampa Bay managed to avoid reenslavement, having, in Crowell's
words, "escaped since my last return."[36]

The conspicuous absence of any slaves from the United States on
Arbuckle's list led some to believe that most of the captives from
Tampa Bay were sold away from their owners to the highest bid-
der. "If I am not greatly misinformed the negroes lately taken by
the Cowetas, as fugitives from the United States from the Bay of
Tampa have in many instances been carried to the Creek nation &
there disposed of," Horatio Dexter complained to Captain John Bell,
the US Army commander at St. Augustine. "If this be the fact," the
St. John's River resident asked on behalf of slaveowners across the
southern frontier, "how are the proprietors to recover them or their
proceeds?"[37]

While most slaveowners who had lost slaves to the Florida wilderness were disappointed or even distraught by the outcome of the
Tampa Bay raid, some were not. A number of prominent men in St.

Augustine were "highly gratified with the expedition" as it resulted in their recovery of dozens of slaves. According to agent Crowell, "The owners of the negroes had given up all hope of recovering them as their situation rendered it impracticable for any but an Indian force to operate successfully."[38] After traveling hundreds of miles to and from Fort Mitchell, East Floridians James Darley and Francis Sanchez published "A CARD" on the front page of the *St. Augustine Florida Gazette* in December 1821. Having recovered twenty-nine slaves belonging to themselves or their associates, the two men thanked Crowell and the Creek chiefs for helping in "the recovery of said property."[39] The unusual thank-you card aside, Florida's slaveowners were not the only beneficiaries of the Tampa Bay raid.

Hundreds of fugitive slaves took advantage of the chaos the assault unleashed to make their way from the United States to the Bahamas. According to an eyewitness, they floated aboard canoes in small groups from the Florida shore to a number of West Indian salvaging vessels working along the coast. After boarding the wreckers, they sailed southward until they were "carried to Nassau and clandestinely landed." Initially, as many as 250 former slaves made the one-hundred-mile journey to the small West Indian colony. An estimated forty "stragglers" completed the voyage several weeks later.[40] The Bahamas was a crown jewel in Great Britain's growing antislavery empire, because the archipelago had recently welcomed thousands of African slaves liberated from captured slave ships by the British Navy's West Africa Squadron; consequently, the Tampa Bay refugees must have looked forward to arriving at their destination with great anticipation.[41]

That being said, despite the humanitarian policies of imperial officials back in London, colonial leaders often resisted the immigration of free black people. Fearful that the immigrants would subvert the colony's enslaved population, they protested the arrival of any former slaves, regardless of their origins. One Nassau editorialist complained of the recent arrivals from Tampa Bay, "Such persons are not wanted here, and the country would be better rid of them."[42] Because of such opposition in the densely populated colonial capital, the black Floridians avoided landing at Nassau and instead disembarked in "the remoter islands."[43]

Fugitive slaves put to flight by the Creek raid on Tampa Bay disembarked at the northern tip of Andros Island, where they hoped their long and desperate struggle for freedom had finally come to an end. Within several years of their landing, these well-traveled black migrants, as they had done before, established several independent and relatively isolated communities where they lived "peacefully and quietly." Taking advantage of the skills learned while surviving in the Florida forests, they caught fish and crabs on the water and inland grew corn, yams, plantains, potatoes, and peas.[44] That they named one of their settlements "Nicholls Town" suggests that a significant portion of them had served in the British marines on Prospect Bluff during the War of 1812, as well as at the subsequent garrison at Negro Fort.[45]

The British Empire had abolished the Atlantic slave trade in 1808 but still allowed slavery in its West Indian colonies. Therefore, the status of black Bahamians who escaped to the islands from Florida was often ambiguous. In 1828, reports surfaced that Spanish traffickers had smuggled black captives into the colony and intended to forward them to Cuba for sale. Because some officials suspected that the settlers on Andros Island were among those brought to the Bahamas "in a clandestine manner" and against the law, an investigation into their origins ensued.[46]

Among the first to assert the freedom of these black islanders was British Army major general Lewis Grant. In a letter to London, the recently appointed Bahamian governor summarized the events that led these people to take up residency in the Bahamas. In the process, he offered an insightful account of the American army's motivations

for its multiple invasions of Spanish Florida. Shortly after the War of
1812, when Andrew Jackson ordered troops across the southern border,
he did so "under the pretence" that fugitive slaves, including those
who had served in the British marines, "in conjunction with some
of the Indian Tribes, had committed aggression upon the settlers
within the boundaries of the United States or threatened to do so."
Although these charges were untrue, the Americans destroyed Negro
Fort and Suwannee, causing the inhabitants of both communities to
remove further south, where after meeting with salvagers along the
coast, "they easily reached the Bahamas and settled afterwards."[47]

After a lengthy inquiry lasting almost three years, the British government determined that the Tampa Bay refugees were free people
and thus allowed them to remain on Andros Island as full subjects
of the king. J. Carmichael Smyth, Grant's successor in the governor's
office, summarized the findings of the colonial investigators when
he asserted that rather than being the victims of human trafficking,
the "negroes in question" came to the Bahamas voluntarily, including
a great number who had served in the Corps of Colonial Marines.
For that reason alone, they were as deserving of the protection of the
British government "as any other free person."[48]

Besides oral testimony, Smyth believed that the most convincing
evidence of the freedom of these "poor people" was the freedom
certificates some of them possessed. They had received these from
Colonel Nicolls upon their discharge from the Colonial Marines
some sixteen years earlier. The governor stated that he had no choice
but to believe the assertions of those black men claiming military service, "as many of them still have their discharges from His
Majesty's service."[49] The governor's statement evoked the words of
a US agent in Florida. After learning of the departure of hundreds
of black people from Tampa Bay in the summer of 1821, the agent
reported that "there were many runaway negroes among them having free passes."[50]

In subsequent decades, free black Bahamians continued to insist that they had come to the islands from Florida after serving in the British Marines. This was evident during a dispute over the eligibility of black voters in an 1844 election on Andros Island. A writer in the *Nassau Guardian* observed that a dozen "Americans" who took to the polls were entitled to the rights of all British subjects, regardless of their race, for they "had served as soldiers in the British Army, under colonel Edward Nicolls in Florida and had been regularly discharged therefrom at the conclusion of the late war."[51]

Several years later, a black Andros Island shipwright named Mitchell Roberts swore before a Bahamian court that he had served with the Colonial Marines in Spanish Florida. Roberts appeared in a case concerning a Cuban slave named Ben who claimed to be a free man. Roberts testified that he had known Ben's family decades earlier in Spanish Florida, where they all lived freely "among the Indians" before eventually finding their way to the Bahamas. When pressed to explain his own origins, Roberts swore that "he was born in Florida, and served in the Royal Colonial Marines there stationed during the American War, at a fort called Prospect Bluff."[52]

While an undeterminable number of Negro Fort maroons found freedom in the Bahamas, others remained in Florida. There, along-side the Seminoles, they continued to resist American expansion. During his extensive tour, Horatio Dexter counted 1,395 Indians and 430 "Refugee Negroes" dispersed throughout more than a dozen central and south Florida towns.[53] Though the Tampa Bay raid wreaked havoc on many of these communities, neither the Seminoles nor their black allies showed any signs of backing down from the United States. Dexter noted that after an American Indian agent requested a meeting with Seminole leaders at St. Augustine, an emerging Alachua headman known as Micanopy responded that he "was assembling his warriors & negroes & was determined to fight in defence of his home & his property."[54]

Throughout the 1820s, American slaveowners continued lobby-
ing the federal government for assistance in recovering their slaves
who remained at large in Florida and the Bahamas—but to no
avail.[55] With Florida firmly in the possession of the United States,
officials decided that the cost of a second war with the Seminoles
outweighed its benefits and decided to postpone another violent
confrontation in its newly acquired territories. As for the Bahamas,
these same American officials refused to press the issue of fugitive
slaves with their British counterparts for fear that doing so would
upset negotiations over the money owed to American slaveowners
for the thousands of slaves lost to Great Britain during the War
of 1812. It was, in the end, a wise decision, as the British government eventually agreed to pay more than one million dollars in
compensation.[56]

While the American government was making these decisions regarding the recovery of hundreds of fugitive slaves in Florida and the
Bahamas, Governor Jackson resigned his position in Pensacola and
returned to Nashville, where his focus soon shifted to national politics. In 1824, the retired general made history by becoming the first
presidential candidate to win the popular and electoral votes yet lose
the election. Because Jackson failed to win a majority of Electoral
College votes, the decision went to the House of Representatives,
which selected John Quincy Adams for the position. The "corrupt
bargain" allegedly struck between Adams and House Speaker Henry
Clay infuriated Jackson's supporters, who launched a successful political revolution to see their candidate elevated to the presidency four
years later.

During his White House tenure, Jackson spent eight years cham-
pioning the cause of democracy on behalf of the nation's white
male population. His symbolic empowerment of the common man
through the elimination of the elite-owned Second Bank of the
United States, along with the passage and early implementation of

the Indian Removal Act of 1830, further helped establish a white republic in which the benefits of citizenship were extended to all white men regardless of class or ethnicity. Yet trouble remained. The continued refusal of Seminoles and maroons to forfeit their land to white settlers meant that before Jackson left office, the United States would embark on another Florida war.[57]

Though several decades in the making, the Second Seminole War arose immediately out of one of the greatest defeats in the history of the US Army. On the morning of December 28, 1835, more than one hundred troops led by Brevet Major Francis Langhorne Dade crossed an open field in central Florida, about fifty miles west of present-day Orlando. They were ambushed and "slaughtered by a remorseless and savage foe" that outnumbered them by as many as two to one.[58] In fact, the numbers may have been even more lopsided than that. According to Private Ransom Clarke, one of only two American survivors, "The Indians are supposed to have been 800 strong with 100 negroes, who were more savage than the Seminoles."[59]

Even though the Dade Massacre provided a legitimate cause for war, white southerners resurrected the same arguments used two decades earlier to justify American involvement in both the Battle of Negro Fort and the First Seminole War. Just days after the ambush of Dade's forces, the *Washington Globe* reiterated the necessity of removing every last Indian from Florida, "as they would unquestionably become a lawless banditti, committing depredations upon the inhabitants." By resorting to the territory's marshes and swamps, they would inevitably, "joined by runaway negroes, do much mischief in the country."[60] At a public gathering in Charleston, South Carolina, community leaders called on local residents to provide both money and volunteers to help their "fellow-citizens" in Florida. According to a published account of the meeting, "The negroes, in considerable numbers, are leagued with the savages, and to the horrors of an Indian war will probably be added those of a servile revolt."[61]

Of course, no call for American military intervention in Florida would have been complete without the accusation that foreign emissaries provided means and materiel to Florida's maroon and Indian populations. An Alabama reporter declared that "immediate measures" were necessary to protect southern citizens from the Seminoles and slaves who murdered Dade's men "with arms and ammunition from the West India Islands." While southern writers once held British subjects responsible for supplying the necessities of war, this journalist suspected that the guilty parties were Spanish fishermen from Cuba, "who swarm uninterruptedly along the coasts."[62]

While there is no evidence proving the assistance of Cuban subversives, it is certain that some of the vanquishers of Dade's force were Negro Fort maroons. The most famous was Abraham, a Pensacola shipwright owned by John Forbes & Company, who in 1814 fled the city with the British marines and disembarked at Prospect Bluff when he was twenty-four years old. Subsequent to abandoning Negro Fort some time later, he fled eastward, and after adopting the language and culture of the region's native people, became known as Souanaffe Tustennuggee, meaning "Suwanee Warrior."[63] By the 1830s, Abraham served as an interpreter and adviser to Chief Micanopy and was a powerful leader in his own right, ruling over "about five hundred negroes, of whom he is legislator, judge, and executioner." By the outbreak of the Second Seminole War, Abraham had also become an effective recruiter of black soldiers. Secretly visiting plantations across East Florida to speak with slaves, he "endeavored to seduce them from their allegiance to their owners, with promises of liberty and plunder."[64]

Harry was another black Seminole who participated in the assault against Dade and in all likelihood fought in the Battle of Negro Fort. Once considered the most valuable slave in Spanish Pensacola, the former master ship carpenter, who also had belonged to John Forbes & Company, could read and write and "knew something about

FIGURE 6.1. After escaping from Pensacola with the British forces during the War of 1812, Abraham resided at Negro Fort before joining the Seminoles. From Joshua R. Giddings, *The Exiles of Florida* (1858). Special Collections, University of Houston Libraries.

sailing."[65] After fleeing with Abraham and the Colonial Marines to the British Post, Harry was among those who met with the Spanish delegation and refused their offer to return to Pensacola. Following the destruction of Negro Fort, he lived among the Seminoles and long remained one of Abraham's closest associates. By the 1830s, Harry commanded "about a hundred warriors" from the Seminole town of Tolokchopko in central Florida. The Americans regarded Harry's warriors as primary instigators of the Dade Massacre.[66]

Given the part Negro Fort maroons played in killing Dade's men, it is not surprising that when President Jackson learned of the army's defeat, he called on two of the men most responsible for the victory in the Battle of Negro Fort to exact revenge.[67] In January 1836, Edmund Gaines reunited with Duncan Clinch in Florida, and the two generals, with a force of fifteen hundred men, began scouring the forests and swamps of the peninsula for Seminoles and maroons.[68] Over the course of the next seven years, Gaines, Clinch, and the southern army embarked on the most expensive war in the history of the United States to that point. By the time it was finished, they had accomplished the removal of most of the Seminoles still in Florida to the Indian Territory, in present-day Oklahoma. While an estimated five hundred maroons earned their freedom by making the grueling long-distance trek alongside the Seminoles, several hundred others remained in Florida at the mercy of the American government. Most are believed to have been sold into slavery.[69]

Generals Gaines and Clinch were not the only veterans of the Battle of Negro Fort who became part of the national conversation on the Second Seminole War during the 1830s. For more than two decades, the US Congress had considered a bill to provide financial compensation to sailing masters Jarius Loomis and James Bassett for commanding *Gunboat 149* and *Gunboat 154* during the navy's assault on Negro Fort. According to the text of the proposed legislation, the officers were attempting to deliver supplies up the Apalachicola River

when they were savagely attacked by a fort "occupied by a number
of fugitive negroes and Indians." In a heroic act of self-defense, they
"blew up and destroyed said fort, with the greatest part of those by
whom it was occupied." At the height of the Second Seminole War,
congressmen proved their support for the current conflict by turn-
ing the bill into a law. In March 1839, the Twenty-fifth Congress
appropriated $5,465 as "prize money" to be divided among Loomis,
Bassett, and the rest of the officers and crew (or their heirs) of the
two gunboats.[70]

More than a patriotic effort to secure the United States' southern-
most territories, the Second Seminole War was the culmination of an
imperialistic pro-slavery public policy adopted more than a quarter-
century earlier with the Battle of Negro Fort. As white settlers poured
into Florida, carrying their dreams of cotton and slaves along with
them, the American government could claim an important victory.
It was not a total one, however, as fugitive slaves across the South
continued to take flight. By the middle of the nineteenth century, the
abolitionist movement gave rise to the Underground Railroad, which
by multiplying the number of escaped people increased slaveowners' demand for federal protections. The US Congress's subsequent
passage of the Fugitive Slave Act in 1850 prompted more than a decade of violent antislavery resistance by southern slaves and northern
abolitionists alike. Ultimately, it would take a terrible civil war to
determine just how long the institution of slavery—and the Slave
Power—would last.

EPILOGUE

IN the decades after the Battle of Negro Fort, knowledge of the largest independent community of fugitive slaves in the history of the present-day United States survived mainly in histories and biographies written for a popular audience. Based largely on the correspondence of Andrew Jackson, John Quincy Adams, and other government officials, which told the history of the battle from a pro-slavery southern point of view, these publications celebrated the battle's outcome and reveled in the community's demise. As a result, generations of Americans learned that rather than a beacon of freedom in a sea of slavery, Negro Fort was "a receptacle for fugitive slaves and other malefactors" who waged a relentless and savage war against the United States.[1]

Among the most influential books in shaping public opinion on Negro Fort was James Parton's *Life of Andrew Jackson*, a three-volume literary tour-de-force that devoted an entire chapter to the fort's rise and fall.[2] Parton referred to Negro Fort as "the strongest and most unassailable place in all the southeastern country." He explained that the "existence of such a place, so near the borders of slave States, was looked upon as an evil of the first magnitude by the planters of the extreme south, whose slaves, in a few hours or days, could reach the negro settlements in the vicinity of the fort, and place themselves beyond pursuit." When American armed forces approached the fort in July 1816 in a peaceful attempt to move supplies up the Apalachicola River, "The negroes, unfortunately for themselves, had resolved on war." The result was a "red-hot shot" from one of the American gunboats that exploded the entire complex, eliminating "not the Negro Fort only, but the growing negro power of Florida."[3] Like other popular accounts of the Battle of Negro Fort written before the Civil War, Parton's portrayed the destruction of Negro Fort as a triumph of both the American nation and the white race.

However, that point of view was challenged by the convergence of two separate events in the 1830s. The first was the advent of the American abolitionist movement. While a significant number of American citizens had always opposed slavery, the publication of William Lloyd Garrison's *Liberator* beginning in 1831 marked the beginning of an egalitarian crusade to destroy the institution along with the white supremacy that sustained it. Led by men and women of various races, ethnicities, and classes, it was a radical social movement unprecedented in the history of the republic.[4] The second event was the Second Seminole War, which confirmed the government's increasingly pro-slavery stance. "This is a southern war," Garrison's *Liberator* raged. "Its origin was in slavery: the money and the lives which have been spent, have been sacrificed in defence of our 'southern brethren,' and the management of it has been committed to southern hands."[5]

Abolitionists' opposition to the Second Seminole War sparked renewed interest in the history of Negro Fort. In 1838, while explaining the root causes of the "Florida war," George Ratrie Parburt offered the fort's destruction as evidence that the nation had lost its way. According to the New England preacher, the republic began to drift away from its founding ideals during the War of 1812, when fugitives

from the "slaveholding states" escaped to Spanish Florida and established a defensive fortification on the shores of the Apalachicola
River. To secure these slaves, "and to prevent the escape of any more
oppressed Americans in that section of the country," the American
government ordered the invasion of Spanish Florida and the destruction of the fort and its community. Borrowing imagery from one of
his Sunday sermons, Parburt professed that the annihilation of this
"altar of liberty and the worshippers thereat," demonstrated how the
republic had abandoned its sacred principles of freedom and equality.[6]

Though it took nearly a quarter of a century, an American writer
had finally taken pen to paper and produced an earnest and impas-
sioned defense of Negro Fort—and he would not be the last. In the
coming decades, abolitionists would repeatedly invoke the fort's
destruction and the murder or reenslavement of its defenders as
evidence of a Slave Power that trampled on the rights of enslaved
black southerners and free white northerners alike. In fact, just a few
months after Parburt's essay appeared in the American Anti-Slavery
Society's *New York Emancipator*, the same publication introduced the
word "slavocracy" into the American lexicon. Referring to the federal
government's dominance by a small but powerful class of southern
slaveowners and their northern allies, the word quickly became a
touchstone of abolitionists' rhetorical war against slavery.[7]

While Parburt's essay found a limited audience, William Jay's
View of the Action of the Federal Government, in Behalf of Slavery
reached a wide abolitionist readership. Published for the first time in
March 1839, the two-hundred-plus-page, fifty-cent book was heavily promoted by the American Anti-Slavery Society. After quickly
selling out, it went through two new editions in the next five years.[8]
New York abolitionist J. C. Jackson implored all who shared his hatred of slavery to read and disseminate the volume, calling it "the
most elaborate and finely written work which has ever been issued on
the connection of our Government with slavery." Through a detailed

analysis of American domestic and foreign policy, "It introduces the reader into the secret doings of the Government, and shows him that our resources, our politics, our powder and ball, our votes, our diplomacy, have been used by the Slave Power, to prostrate the North, and elevate the South."[9]

Among dozens of other examples, Jay cited the Battle of Negro Fort as proof of the existence of slavocracy. He began by referring to William Crawford's letter to Andrew Jackson in March 1816, in which the secretary of war informed the general that the president would investigate whether an assault on Negro Fort required congressional approval. Before the inquiry could be completed, however, Jackson ordered Gaines to destroy the fort, capture as many fugitive slaves as possible, and return these captives to their owners. Jay then quoted navy commodore Daniel Patterson. Just days after the Battle of Negro Fort, Patterson revealed that the greatest significance of the fort's destruction was neither national security nor any other government interest—but rather its effect on slaves across the southern frontier. "This hold being destroyed," Patterson noted approvingly, "they have no longer a place to fly to, and will not be so liable to *abscond*."[10]

Jay closed his discussion indignantly. Aware of recent developments in Congress, he rebuked lawmakers for granting a reward to the officers and crew of US *Gunboat 149* and *Gunboat 154* for their role in the destruction of Negro Fort. Because the spread of abolitionism would discourage soldiers and sailors from participating in future "kidnapping expeditions" like the one that targeted and eliminated Negro Fort, Jay considered the bonus a blatant attempt by proslavery legislators to bribe America's volunteers into maintaining the Slave Power.[11]

Given the success of Jay's work, it is worth considering the author's background and upbringing. Born into one of New York's prominent families, the Yale-educated judge and social reformer inherited much more than wealth from his famous father, the first chief justice of the United States, John Jay. As the Federalist governor of New York, the elder Jay played a key role in founding the New York Manumission Society. He also signed the 1799 emancipation law that gradually abolished slavery statewide. The Founding Father instilled his staunch antislavery attitude in both of his sons, who, in the words of a noted legal scholar, "viewed their opposition to slavery as a continuation of Chief Justice Jay's federalist ideology."[12] Taking this context into account, William Jay's literary assault on the Slave Power provided abolitionists an important reminder that even some of the most eminent Founding Fathers once imagined the federal government as a bulwark against—rather than a buttress for—slavery.

With Jay's volume circulating widely, "Negro Fort" could again be heard echoing in the halls of Congress. It was most frequently invoked in opposition to Manifest Destiny. Angered by the United States' role in the Mexican-American War (1846–1848), Amos Tuck reminded his colleagues in the House of Representatives that slaveowners had appropriated "the national purse and army to subserve slavery." For evidence, the New Hampshire educator cited the destruction of Negro Fort by American soldiers and sailors, who "in obedience to the request of slaveholders, attacked that fort, blew up the magazine, destroyed three hundred negroes on the spot, and returned several hundred more to bondage."[13] In the debate over the Compromise of 1850 two years later, Indiana's George Washington Julian also invoked the Battle of Negro Fort to make a similar point. He argued that the United States' involvement in two separate wars with the Seminoles only occurred "because it was demanded by the slaveholding interest," who also demanded the deaths of hundreds of black men, women, and children who resided peacefully at Negro Fort. "Certainly," the Quaker congressman declared, "the Government was under no obligation to commit this wholesale murder, merely because the slaveholders of Florida desired it."[14]

Julian's argument borrowed much of the language used by his famous father-in-law, Joshua Giddings. Giddings staked a claim to
being one of the most radical abolitionists in the United States by,
among other things, continually invoking Negro Fort.[15] Shortly after
taking his seat in the US Congress in 1844, the Ohio representative
published a sixteen-page pamphlet that enumerated some of the instances when the federal government acted solely on behalf of slavery.
The Battle of Negro Fort appeared in a section on the use of the
armed forces. Regarding the hundreds of slaves believed to have died
in the conflict, Giddings pointed out, "No act or offence against the
United states is alleged against these people, except that they fled
from slavery." Then, in an unapologetic and confrontational tone that
would become his hallmark, he exclaimed, "For that alone they were
thus murdered by the Federal Government."[16]

A decade later, Giddings published an essay on the Battle of Negro
Fort called "Massacre at Blount's Fort." Despite an abundance of errors, including misnaming the fort after the Creek chief John Blount,
the essay proved the government's strong pro-slavery stance. The
story began with a description of the Negro Fort maroons, who for
years enjoyed peace and prosperity at their isolated compound until
American slaveowners requested federal assistance in regaining possession of their property. As a southerner, President James Madison
"entertained no doubt of the right of one man to enslave another," so
he instinctively ordered the fort's destruction and the reenslavement
of its inhabitants. The joint army-navy assault then commenced. But
instead of a quick and easy victory, the maroons rose to the challenge,
proclaiming defiantly, "*Give me liberty or give me death!*"[17]

To underscore the atrocity that followed, Giddings graphically
described the effects of the fort's obliteration. Hundreds of burned,
crushed, mutilated, and mangled bodies greeted the first group of
Americans to enter the exploded complex. This group included sixty
sailors, who despite their familiarity with the carnage of war were

"horror-stricken" by what they saw. By contrast, the slaveowners who accompanied them ignored the dead and dying so they could refasten the chains of bondage on the limbs of the living. Recognizing that some readers might doubt the veracity of Giddings's incredible story, he referred them to a rich source of documentary evidence officials had stored in the nation's archives for decades. "But no historian has been willing to collect and publish them, in consequence of the deep disgrace which they reflect upon the American arms, and upon those who then controlled the government."[18]

In the end, the historicity of Giddings's essay mattered less than its reach. The British abolitionist Julia Griffiths, who had immigrated to the United States to assist in the fight against slavery, first published "Massacre at Blount's Fort" in 1854 as part of a collection of antislavery articles, editorials, and poems called *Autographs for Freedom*. Within weeks of the book's publication, the essay appeared in abolitionist newspapers across the country, including on the front page of William Lloyd Garrison's *Liberator*.[19] A year later, William Cooper Nell copied "Massacre at Blount's Fort" in *The Colored Patriots of the American Revolution*, the first book-length treatment of black military service in the United States written by an African American.[20] Giddings expanded his essay in the summer of 1858 when he published a devastating three-hundred-plus-page attack on the Slave Power. In *The Exiles of Florida: or, The Crimes Committed by Our Government against the Maroons, Who Fled From South Carolina and Other Slave States, Seeking Protection under Spanish Law*, Giddings described the shame the American government's actions in Florida had brought upon the United States, calling the destruction of Negro Fort "one of the darkest crimes which stains the history of any civilized nation."[21]

Not every abolitionist agreed with Giddings's harsh indictment— but John Brown did. In 1859, the aging white abolitionist was planning to spark a southern slave insurrection by seizing the US armory and arsenal at Harpers Ferry, Virginia, some fifty miles outside of the nation's capital. On the Fourth of July, he wrote a statement of the rights and obligations of enslaved people that he called "A Declaration of Liberty by the Representatives of the Slave Population of the United States of America." Modeled on the list of grievances against King George III provided in the Declaration of Independence, the document catalogued the various injustices committed against slaves over the course of American history. For Brown, the federal government was the perpetrator of many of these crimes, both in the United States and in adjacent territories. An obvious example was the destruction of "Blount's Fort" in Spanish Florida, when the US government acted exclusively "under the Jurisdiction & guidance of Slave holding Authority, & in strict accordance with Slaveholding rules."[22]

With the Slave Power firmly and permanently entrenched since the days of Negro Fort, Brown saw no alternative but to pursue the violent overthrow of slavery. Three months after drafting his declaration, he led a small army of twenty-one black and white abolitionists into Harpers Ferry for that purpose. Though a failure as a slave revolt, the raid succeeded in bringing the sectional crisis to a head. In the coming months, northerners, troubled by the idea that their democracy had given way to slavocracy, elected a president from a new antislavery Republican Party that was deeply committed to halting slavery's expansion. White southerners considered Abraham Lincoln's ascendency to the White House an unacceptable reversal of the status quo and immediately began the process of secession.

In the civil war that followed, slaves across the South rushed to join the Union Army just as they had done with the British when the redcoats came ashore a half-century earlier. Only this time they came by the tens and eventually hundreds of thousands. By undermining the Confederate cause and supporting and sustaining the Union war effort, fugitive slaves—or, as they became known, contrabands—helped transform the bloody conflict between the North and South from a limited conflict over the fate of the union into a total war over freedom. Like the Battle of Negro Fort, the Civil War centered on slavery. Because of the contributions of enslaved people and their allies, the American government was forced to take a stand on the institution and the racism that supported and sustained it.

ACKNOWLEDGMENTS

ISTORIANS stand on the shoulders of those who wrote before them. I first learned about Negro Fort in graduate school after reading Herbert Aptheker, followed quickly in succession by Jane Landers and Claudio Saunt. Instantly, I was inspired to share the fort's story with as large an audience of students, teachers, scholars, and general readers as possible. Now, as this book finally comes to fruition, I hope it in some way reflects well on the efforts of these pioneering historians and the wealth of scholarship they have since inspired.

While traversing much of the United States and crossing the Atlantic Ocean to complete the research for this project, I became indebted to a great number of people and organizations. Acknowledgment is owed to the staffs of the Houston Public Library; Library of Congress; Mobile Public Library; National Archives and Records Administration, Washington, D.C., and College Park, MD; National Archives, London; New York Public Library; and in particular, Bobby Ticknor at the Historic New Orleans Collections in the French Quarter; Jim Cusick at the P.K. Yonge Library of Florida History in Gainesville; and Stephanie Johnson at the University

Archives and West Florida History Center in Pensacola. I also owe special thanks to Steve Belko, Jane Landers, and Scott Satterwhite for early conversations on Negro Fort—including several at the site of the former fort—which further fueled my desire to initiate this project and ultimately see it to the end.

In this limited space, it is hard to convey how fortunate I have been to work with NYU Press. My editor, Clara Platter, not only demonstrated great enthusiasm for the project from our first conversation but ushered the book to the finish line in record-breaking time. Emily Wright's copyediting saved me from a series of errors and helped make the book much clearer and more accessible. I want to acknowledge Beverly Tomek and several anonymous readers who at various stages of the publication process offered important comments and critiques. I also want to thank Richard Blackett, Graham Russell Gao Hodges, Manisha Sinha, and Phillip Troutman for their comments on a related conference paper.

This book would not have been possible without the support of the University of Houston. Travel grants from the College of Liberal Arts and Social Sciences and the Division of Research funded research trips, while the university's Interlibrary Loan staff amazed me with their ability to acquire rare and obscure items in a timely fashion. In the Department of History, Karl Ittmann and Kirsten Hilson helped me track down several hard-to-find documents, while Phil Howard was first among a group of extraordinary people on the fifth floor of Agnes Arnold Hall who never failed to take the time to listen to my questions, ideas, and concerns. For the students who sat up at attention every time my lectures veered into a discussion of Negro Fort and demanded to know why they had never learned about the subject before, it is important that they know that this book would not exist without them.

Most importantly, I want to thank Gladys, Maddie, Joey, and Josh for making the entire journey worthwhile.

ABBREVIATIONS

ACP Alexander Cochrane Papers, Williams Research Center, The
    Historic New Orleans Collection, New Orleans, Louisiana
ADM Admiralty Papers, National Archives, Kew, London
AJP Andrew Jackson Papers, Library of Congress, Washington, D.C.
ASP: FR *American State Papers: Foreign Relations*, Washington, D.C.
ASP: IA *American State Papers: Indian Affairs*, Washington, D.C.
ASP: MA *American State Papers: Military Affairs*, Washington, D.C.
CAJ John Spencer Bassett, ed., *Correspondence of Andrew Jackson*, 7 vols.
    (Washington, DC: Carnegie Institution of Washington, 1926–1935)
CO Colonial Office Papers, National Archives, Kew, London
DNI *Daily National Intelligencer* (Washington, D.C.)
FHQ *Florida Historical Quarterly*
GJ *Georgia Journal* (Milledgeville, GA)
GP Marie Taylor Greenslade Papers, P.K. Yonge Library of Florida
    History, University of Florida, Gainesville
HCP Heloise H. Cruzat Papers, P.K. Yonge Library of Florida
    History, University of Florida, Gainesville
JFP John Forbes & Company Papers, Mobile Public Library,
    Mobile, Alabama

JMP James Madison Papers, Library of Congress, Washington, D.C.

LJWBH Benjamin Hawkins, *Letters, Journals, and Writings of Benjamin Hawkins*, 2 vols., ed. C. L. Grant (Savannah, GA: Beehive Press, 1980)

LP Joseph Byrne Lockey Papers, P.K. Yonge Library of Florida History, University of Florida, Gainesville

LRSW Letters Received by the Secretary of War: Registered Series, 1801–1870, RG107, M221, National Archives and Records Administration, Washington, D.C., and College Park, MD

LRSWIA Letters Received by the Office of the Secretary of War relating to Indian Affairs, 1800–1823, RG75, M271, National Archives and Records Administration, Washington, D.C., and College Park, MD

LRSWU Letters Received by the Secretary of War: Unregistered Series, 1789–1861, RG107, M222, National Archives and Records Administration, Washington, D.C, and College Park, MD

NWR *Niles' Weekly Register* (Baltimore, MD)

PAJ Harold D. Moser, David R. Hoth, George H. Hoemann, eds., *Papers of Andrew Jackson*, 5 vols. (Knoxville: University of Tennessee Press, 1980–1996)

PC: LOC *Papeles de Cuba* (Archivo General de Indias), Library of Congress, Washington, DC

PC: UF *Papeles de Cuba* (Archivo General de Indias), P.K. Yonge Library of Florida History, University of Florida, Gainesville

SNAD Southeastern Native American Documents, 1730–1842, Telamon Cuyler Collection, Hargrett Rare Book and Manuscript Library, The University of Georgia Libraries, presented in the Digital Library of Georgia

VSP Vicente Sebastián Pintado Papers, Library of Congress, Washington, D.C.

WO War Office Papers, National Archives, Kew, London

NOTES

INTRODUCTION

1 Andrew Jackson to Mauricio de Zuñiga, April 23, 1816, *CAJ*, 2:241.

2 Andrew Jackson to Edmund Gaines, April, 8, 1816, *CAJ*, 2:239.

3 David Waldstreicher, *Slavery's Constitution: From Revolution to Ratification* (New York: Hill and Wang, 2009), 3.

4 For a recent assertion of slavery as a constitutional paradox, see Sean Wilentz, *No Property in Man: Slavery and Antislavery at the Nation's Founding* (Cambridge, MA: Harvard University Press, 2018).

5 Max Farand, ed., *The Records of the Federal Convention of 1787* (New Haven, CT: Yale University Press, 1911), 2:417. In her examination of Madison's quotation, Mary Sarah Bilder suggests that the founding father never made the statement at the Constitutional Convention and only later inserted it in his revised notes; still, it is worth noting that the quotation closely resembles that made at the convention by another southern delegate, Maryland's Luther Martin. *Madison's Hand: Revising the Constitutional Convention* (Cambridge, MA: Harvard University Press, 2015), 188–89. Important studies of slavery, the Constitution, and the early American government include Paul Finkelman, *Slavery and the Founders: Race and Liberty in the Age of Jefferson*, 3d ed. (New York: Routledge, 2015); David F. Ericson, *Slavery in the Early American Republic: Developing the Federal Government, 1791–1861* (Lawrence: University Press of Kansas, 2011); Don E. Fehrenbacher, *The Slaveholding Republic: An Account of the United States Government's Relations to Slavery*, ed. Ward M. McAfee (New York: Oxford University Press, 2001).

6 George Washington to Robert Morris, April 12, 1786, W.W. Abbott and Dorothy Twohig, eds., *The Papers of George Washington: Confederation Series* (Charlottesville: University Press of Virginia, 1995), 4:16.

7   Eric Armstrong Dunbar, *Never Caught: The Washingtons' Relentless Pursuit of Their Runaway Slave, Ona Judge* (New York: Atria, 2017); Philip Morgan, "'To Get Quit of Negroes': George Washington and Slavery," *Journal of American Studies* 39, no. 3 (December 2005): 403–29; Henry Wiencek, *An Imperfect God: George Washington, His Slaves, and the Creation of America* (New York: Farrar, Straus and Giroux, 2003).

8   Thomas Jefferson, *Notes on the State of Virginia, by Thomas Jefferson: Illustrated with a Map, including the States of Virginia, Maryland, Delaware, and Pennsylvania. A New Edition, Prepared by the Author, Containing Notes and Plates Never Before Published* (Richmond, VA: J. W. Randolph, 1853), 155.

9   Thomas Jefferson, *The Works of Thomas Jefferson*, ed. Paul Leister Ford (New York: Putnam's, 1904), 1:210.

10 The literature on Jefferson's view on slavery is extensive. See Henry Wiencek, *Master of the Mountain: Thomas Jefferson and His Slaves* (New York: Farrar, Straus and Giroux, 2012): Peter S. Onuf, *The Mind of Thomas Jefferson* (Charlottesville: University of Virginia Press, 2005); Joseph J. Ellis, *American Sphinx: The Character of Thomas Jefferson* (New York: Vintage, 1998); John Chester Miller, *The Wolf by the Ears: Thomas Jefferson and Slavery* (Charlottesville: University Press of Virginia, 1991); Robert McColley, *Slavery and Jeffersonian Virginia* (Urbana: University of Illinois Press, 1964). The best accounts of Jefferson's relationship with Sally Hemings are Annette Gordon-Reed's *Hemingses of Monticello: An American Family* (New York: Norton, 2008), and *Thomas Jefferson and Sally Hemings: An American Controversy* (Charlottesville: University Press of Virginia, 1997).

11 Beverly C. Tomek, *Colonization and Its Discontents: Emancipation, Emigration, and Antislavery in Antebellum Pennsylvania* (New York: NYU Press, 2011); Ousmane K. Power-Greene, *Against the Wind and Tide: The African American Struggle against the Colonization Movement* (New York: NYU Press, 2014); David Brion Davis, *The Problem of Slavery in the Age of Emancipation* (New York: Knopf, 2014); James Sidbury, *Becoming African in America: Race and Nation in the Early Black Atlantic* (New York: Oxford University Press, 2007); Eric Burin, *Slavery and the Peculiar Solution: A History of the American Colonization Society* (Gainesville: University Press of Florida, 2005); Claude Andrew Clegg, *The Price of Liberty: African Americans and the Making of Liberia* (Chapel Hill: University of North Carolina Press, 2004); David Kazanjian, *The Colonizing Trick: National Culture and Imperial Citizenship in Early America* (Minneapolis: University of Minnesota Press, 2003); P. J. Staudenraus, *The African Colonization Movement, 1816–1865* (New York: Columbia University Press, 1961).

12 Thomas Jefferson to John Holmes, April 22, 1820, *The Works of Thomas Jefferson*, 12:210. In the original letter, Jefferson uses the singular "ear" instead of "ears": www.monticello.org.

13 For the long process of northern abolition, see Ira Berlin, *The Long Emancipation: The Demise of Slavery in the United States* (Cambridge, MA: Harvard University Press, 2015); Patrick Rael, *Eighty-Eight Years: The Long Death of Slavery in the United States, 1777–1865* (Athens: University of Georgia Press, 2015); Leon Litwack, *North of Slavery: The Negro in the Free States, 1790–1860* (Chicago: University of Chicago Press, 1961).

14 For slavery's westward expansion, see Edward E. Baptist, *The Half Has Never Been Told: Slavery and the Making of American Capitalism* (New York: Basic Books, 2014); Walter Johnson, *River of Dark Dreams: Slavery and Empire in the Cotton Kingdom* (Cambridge, MA: Harvard University Press, 2013); Adam Rothman, *Slave Country: American Expansion and the Origins of the Deep South* (Cambridge, MA: Harvard University Press, 2005).

15 Despite the best efforts of generations of white settlers, antebellum Florida struggled to replicate the South meaningfully. Edward E. Baptist, *Creating an Old South: Middle Florida's Plantation Frontier before the Civil War* (Chapel Hill: University of North Carolina Press, 2002).

16 Virginia Meacham Gould, "The Free Creoles of the Antebellum Gulf Ports of Mobile and Pensacola: A Struggle for the Middle Ground," in James H. Dorman, ed., *Creoles of Color of the Gulf South* (Knoxville: University of Tennessee Press, 1996), 28–50; C. C. Robin, *Voyage to Louisiana by C. C. Robin, 1803–1806, an Abridged Translation from the Original French by Stuart O. Landry, Jr.* (New Orleans: Pelican, 1966), 4.

17 James Adair, *The History of the American Indians* (London: Edward and Charles Dilly, 1775), 258. The word "Creek" initially referred to the "Ochese Creek Indians" but later denoted the Muscogee-speaking Indians of present-day Georgia and Alabama, whose lands were traversed by multiple waterways. Verner W. Crane, "Notes and Documents: The Origin of the Name of the Creek Indians," *Mississippi Valley Historical Review* 5, no. 3 (December 1918): 339–42.

18 Claudio Saunt, *A New Order of Things: Property, Power, and the Transformation of the Creek Indians, 1733–1816* (Cambridge: Cambridge University Press, 1999). For the Creek people generally, see also Angela Pulley Hudson, *Creek Paths and Federal Roads: Indians, Settlers, and Slaves and the Making of the South* (Chapel Hill: University of North Carolina Press, 2010); Joshua Piker, *Okfuskee: A Creek Indian Town in Colonial America* (Cambridge, MA: Harvard University Press, 2006); Steven C. Hahn, *The Invention of the Creek Nation, 1670–1763* (Lincoln: University of Nebraska Press, 2004); Kathryn E. Holland Braund, *Deerskins and Duffels: The Creek Indian Trade with Anglo-America, 1685–1815* (Lincoln: University of Nebraska Press, 1996).

19 There are several possible derivations of the term "Seminole," including the Creek terms, "*isti semole*," for "wild men," or "*simaló-li*," for "wild." The Spanish

term *"cimarrón,"* meaning "wild" or "runaway," is also a possible source of the term. See Christine Snyder, *Slavery in Indian Country: The Changing Face of Captivity in Early America* (Cambridge, MA: Harvard University Press, 2010), 214; Kevin Mulroy, *Freedom on the Border: The Seminole Maroons in Florida, the Indian Territory, Coahuila, and Texas* (Lubbock: Texas Tech University Press, 1993), 5; J. Leitch Wright, *Creeks and Seminoles: The Destruction and Regeneration of the Muscogulge People* (Lincoln: University of Nebraska Press, 1986), 4–5.

20 "Milledgeville," *NWR*, January 7, 1815, 303. For the changing concept of Spanish borderlands, see David J. Weber, "The Spanish Borderlands, Historiography Redux," *History Teacher* 39, no. 1 (November 2005): 43–56; David J. Weber, ed., *The Idea of Spanish Borderlands* (New York: Garland, 1991); Herbert Bolton, *The Spanish Borderlands: A Chronicle of Old Florida and the Southwest* (New Haven, CT: Yale University Press, 1921). For the history of the Seminoles, see Daniel F. Littlefield, *Africans and Seminoles: From Removal to Emancipation* (Jackson: University Press of Mississippi, 2001); Brent Richards Weisman, *Unconquered People: Florida's Seminole and Miccosukee Indians* (Gainesville: University Press of Florida, 1999); James W. Covington, *The Seminoles of Florida* (Gainesville: University Press of Florida, 1993); Mulroy, *Freedom on the Border.*

21 For Spain's liberal policy towards fugitive slaves in colonial Florida and the reversal of this policy in part due to pressure from the United States government in 1790, see Jane Landers, *Black Society in Spanish Florida* (Urbana: University of Illinois Press, 1999), 1–81 (quotation on 79). John Paul Nuño addresses the significance of this reversal in "'República de Bandidos': The Prospect Bluff Fort's Challenge to the Spanish Slave System," *FHQ* 94, no. 2 (Fall 2015): 192–221.

22 Kenneth W. Porter, *The Black Seminoles: History of a Freedom-Seeking People* (Gainesville: University Press of Florida, 2013); Jane Landers, "Blood Seminoles and Black Seminoles on the Florida Frontier," in Richmond F. Brown, ed., *Coastal Encounters: The Transformation of the Gulf South in the Eighteenth Century* (Lincoln: University of Nebraska Press, 2007), 99–116; Mulroy, *Freedom on the Border.*

23 Maya Jasanoff, *Liberty's Exiles: American Loyalists in the Revolutionary World* (New York: Knopf, 2011); Thomas B. Allen, *Tories: Fighting for the King in America's First Civil War* (New York: Harper, 2010); Linda Williams, "East Florida as a Loyalist Haven," *FHQ* 54 (1976): 465–78.

24 William S. Coker and Thomas D. Watson, *Indian Traders of the Southeastern Borderlands: Panton, Leslie & Company, and John Forbes & Company, 1783–1847* (Gainesville: University Presses of Florida, 1986).

25 Thomas Jefferson to George Washington, April 2, 1791, *The Writings of Thomas Jefferson: Being His Autobiography, Correspondence, Reports, Messages,*

Addresses, and Other Writings, Official and Private, ed. H. W. Washington (Washington, DC: Taylor & Maury, 1853), 3:235.

26 For Manifest Destiny generally, see Amy S. Greenberg, *A Wicked War: Polk, Clay, Lincoln, and the 1846 U.S. Invasion of Mexico* (New York: Vintage, 2013); Greenberg, *Manifest Manhood and the Antebellum American Empire* (Cambridge: Cambridge University Press, 2005); Robert W. Johannsen, John M. Belohlavek, Thomas R. Hietala, Samuel J. Watson, Sam W. Haynes, and Robert E. May, *Manifest Destiny and Empire: American Antebellum Expansionism*, ed. Sam W. Haynes and Christopher Morris (College Station: Texas A&M University Press, 1997); Reginald Horsman, *Race and Manifest Destiny: The Origins of American Racial Anglo-Saxonism* (Cambridge, MA: Harvard University Press, 1986); Thomas R. Hietala, *Manifest Design: Anxious Aggrandizement in Late Jacksonian America* (Ithaca, NY: Cornell University Press, 1985); Frederick Merk, *Manifest Destiny and Mission in American History: A Reinterpretation* (New York: Knopf, 1963).

27 Reliable accounts of Jackson's actions along the southern frontier during the War of 1812 include Robert Remini, *Andrew Jackson and His Indians Wars* (New York: Viking, 2001) and *Andrew Jackson and the Course of American Empire, 1767–1821* (New York: Harper & Row, 1977).

28 Referring to the Creek's defeat during the War of 1812, Daniel Richter concludes, "The east at last ceased to be Indian country." *Facing East from Indian Country: A Native History of Early America* (Cambridge, MA: Harvard University Press, 2001), 236.

29 Mark R. Cheathem, *Andrew Jackson, Southerner* (Baton Rouge: Louisiana State University Press, 2013), 4.

30 "Jackson Consistency," *Chillicothe (OH) Scioto Gazette*, October 18, 1827, 2. Biographer Sean Wilentz writes of Jackson, "He came of age just as the questioning of human bondage by liberal, Enlightenment-influenced planters was fading. . . . Unlike his political hero Thomas Jefferson, he appears never to have doubted the morality of slavery." Sean Wilentz, *Andrew Jackson* (New York: Times Books, 2005), 121.

31 For one of the earliest uses of the nickname see "Washington," *DNI*, November 4, 1815, 2. For Jackson's southern identity and his appeal to southern voters especially, see Cheathem, *Andrew Jackson, Southerner*, and William J. Cooper Jr., *The South and the Politics of Slavery* (Baton Rouge: Louisiana State University Press, 1978), 5–22.

32 Eugene D. Genovese, *From Rebellion to Revolution: Afro-American Slave Revolts in the Making of the Modern World* (Baton Rouge: Louisiana State University Press, 1979).

33 Sylviane A. Diouf, *Slavery's Exiles: The Story of the American Maroons* (New York: NYU Press, 2014), 310.

34 Historians examining the impact of the early American government's commit-
    ment to slavery on foreign policy generally focus on the antebellum era.
    Matthew Karp, *This Vast Southern Empire: Slaveholders at the Helm of American
    Foreign Policy* (Cambridge, MA: Harvard University Press, 2016); Edward
    Bartlett Rugemer, *The Problem of Emancipation: The Caribbean Roots of the
    American Civil War* (Baton Rouge: Louisiana State University Press, 2009);
    Brian Schoen, *The Fragile Fabric of Union: Cotton, Federal Politics, and the
    Global Origins of the Civil War* (Baltimore, MD: Johns Hopkins University
    Press, 2009); Matthew Pratt Guterl, *American Mediterranean: Southern
    Slaveholders in the Age of Emancipation* (Cambridge, MA: Harvard University
    Press, 2008); Gerald Horne, *The Deepest South: The United States, Brazil, and
    the African Slave Trade* (New York: NYU Press, 2007). An exception is
    Deborah A. Rosen, *Border Law: The First Seminole War and American
    Nationhood* (Cambridge, MA: Harvard University Press, 2015).

35 The quotation is from US Senator William Plumer in 1803. Lynn W. Turner,
    William Plumer of New Hampshire, 1759–1850 (Chapel Hill: University of
    North Carolina Press for the Institute of Early American History and Culture,
    1962), 137. For one of the first published discourses against the Slave Power, see
    Sereno Edwards Dwight, *Slave Representation, by Boreas. Awake! O Spirit of
    the North!* (New Haven, CT: n.p., 1812). The controversy over slave representa-
    tion in the election of 1800 is described in Garry Wills, *"Negro President":
    Jefferson and the Slave Power* (Boston: Houghton Mifflin, 2003).

36 David Brion Davis famously called the Slave Power a "conspiracy," compar-
    ing it to those "of the French Illuminati, of Federalist oligarchs, of
    Freemasons, of the money power, of the Catholic Church . . . of foreign
    anarchists, of Wall Street bankers, of Bolsheviks, of internationalist Jews, of
    Fascists, of Communists, and of Black Power," in *The Slave Power
    Conspiracy and the Paranoid Style* (Baton Rouge: Louisiana State University
    Press, 1969), 3–4. More recent historians, including Leonard L. Richards,
    accept the existence of the Slave Power unequivocally. *The Slave Power: The
    Free North and Southern Domination, 1780–1860* (Baton Rouge: Louisiana
    State University Press, 2000). See also Wills, *"Negro President"*;
    Fehrenbacher, *The Slaveholding Republic*; Finkelman, *Slavery and the
    Founders*; and William W. Freehling, *The Road to Disunion*. Vol. 1,
    Secessionists at Bay, 1776–1854 (New York: Oxford University Press, 1990). For
    other important interpretations, see Eric Foner, *Free Soil, Free Labor, Free
    Men: The Ideology of the Republican Party before the Civil War* (New York:
    Oxford University Press, 1995); William E. Gienapp, "The Republican Party
    and the Slave Power," in *New Perspectives on Race and Slavery in America*, ed.
    Robert H. Abzug and Stephen F. Maizlish (Lexington: University Press of
    Kentucky, 1986), 51–78; Michael F. Holt, *The Political Crisis of the 1850s* (New

York: Wiley, 1978); Larry Gara, "Slavery and the Slave Power: A Crucial Distinction," *Civil War History* 15, no. 1 (March 1969): 5–18; and Russel B. Nye, *Fettered Freedom: Civil Liberties and the Slavery Controversy, 1830–1860* (East Lansing: Michigan State College Press, 1949). Contemporary accounts of the Slave Power include J. E. Cairnes, *The Slave Power: Its Character, Career, and Probable Designs: Being an Attempt to Explain the Real Issues Involved in the American Contest* (New York: Carleton, 1862); Henry Wilson, *History of the Rise and Fall of the Slave Power in America*, 3 vols. (Boston: Houghton Mifflin, 1872–1877); and Theodore Parker, "The Slave Power," in *The Slave Power* (Boston: American Unitarian Association, 1910), 248–86.

CHAPTER 1. WAR AND RESISTANCE

1 "Milledgeville," *NWR*, January 7, 1815, 303.

2 Michael J. Crawford, Christine F. Hughes, Charles E. Brodine Jr., and Carolyn M. Stallings, eds., *The Naval War of 1812: A Documentary History* (Washington, DC: Naval Historical Center, Department of the Navy, 2002), 3:38.

3 "Indian War," *NWR*, March 7, 1812, 5. For the clash of people and cultures along the United States–Canadian border, see Alan Taylor, *The Civil War of 1812: American Citizens, British Subjects, Irish Rebels, and Indian Allies* (New York: Vintage, 2011).

4 Stephen Warren, *The Worlds the Shawnees Made: Migration and Violence in Early America* (Chapel Hill: University of North Carolina Press, 2014); Colin Calloway, *The Shawnees and the War for America* (New York: Viking, 2007); R. David Edmunds, *The Shawnee Prophet* (Lincoln: University of Nebraska Press, 1983).

5 John Francis Hamtramck Claiborne, *Mississippi as a Province, Territory, and State, with Biographical Notices of Eminent Citizens*, vol. 1 (Jackson, MS: Power & Barksdale, 1880), 317.

6 Alan Taylor, *The Internal Enemy: Slavery and War in Virginia, 1772–1832* (New York: Norton, 2013). See also Gene Allen Smith, *The Slaves' Gamble: Choosing Sides in the War of 1812* (New York: St. Martin's, 2013) and Thomas Malcolmson, "Freedom by Reaching the Wooden World: American Slaves and the British Navy during the War of 1812," *Northern Mariner/marin du nord* 22, no. 4 (October 2012): 361–92.

7 Captain John Barrie, R.N., to Admiral Sir John B. Warren, November 14, 1813, ADM 1/505, 131–33. See also Christopher T. George, "Mirage of Freedom: African Americans in the War of 1812," *Maryland Historical Magazine* 91, no. 4 (Winter 1996): 427–50.

8 Charles Ball, *Slavery in the United States: A Narrative of the Life and Adventures of Charles Ball* (New York: John S. Taylor, 1837), 469 (first and second quotation), 471 (third and fourth quotation), 472 (fifth quotation).

9   "Proclamation of Vice Admiral Sir Alexander F. I. Cochrane, R.N.," April 2,
    1814, ADM 1:508, 579.

10 James A. Henretta, Rebecca Edwards, and Robert O. Self, *Documents for
    American History*. Vol. 1, *To 1877* (New York: Bedford/St. Martins, 2011), 129.

11 Douglas R. Egerton, *Death or Liberty: African Americans and Revolutionary
    America* (New York: Oxford University Press, 2009); Cassandra Pybus, *Epic
    Journeys: Runaway Slaves of the American Revolution and Their Global Quest for
    Liberty* (Boston: Beacon, 2006); Sylvia R. Frey, *Water from the Rock: Black
    Resistance in a Revolutionary Age* (Princeton, NJ: Princeton University Press,
    1991); Benjamin Quarles, *The Negro in the American Revolution* (Chapel Hill:
    University of North Carolina Press, 1961).

12 Taylor, *The Internal Enemy*, 441–42.

13 Gerald Horne, *Negro Comrades of the Crown: African Americans and the British
    Empire Fight the U.S. before Emancipation* (New York: NYU Press, 2012), 5.
    Horne traced the origins of the relationship between the British Empire and
    black soldiers and sailors in *The Counter-Revolution of 1766: Slave Resistance
    and the Origins of the United States of America* (New York: NYU Press, 2014).

14 "A Sailor's Epistle," *National Weekly Intelligencer*, April 6, 1813, 3. Alan Taylor
    asserts that the War of 1812 provided Great Britain "a chance to highlight
    American hypocrisy about liberty." Taylor, *The Internal Enemy*, 213. Matthew
    Mason also addresses the issue in "The Battle of the Slaveholding Liberators:
    Great Britain, the United States, and Slavery in the Early Nineteenth
    Century," *William and Mary Quarterly*, 3d ser., 59, no. 3 (July 2002): 665–96.

15 George Cockburn to Alexander Cochrane, April 2, 1814, in Crawford et al.,
    The Naval War of 1812, 3:44.

16 George Cockburn to Alexander Cochrane, May 10, 1814, Crawford et al., *The
    Naval War of 1812*, 3:65.

17 George Cockburn to Alexander Cochrane, June 25, 1814, Crawford et al., *The
    Naval War of 1812*, 3:116.

18 "An Exposition: of the Causes and Character of the Late War with Great
    Britain," *NWR*, April 8, 1815. For the Haitian Revolution, see Philippe R.
    Girard, *The Slaves Who Defeated Napoleon: Toussaint Louverture and the
    Haitian War of Independence, 1801–1804* (Tuscaloosa: University of Alabama
    Press, 2011); Laurent Dubois, *Avengers of the New World: The Story of the
    Haitian Revolution* (Cambridge, MA: Harvard University Press, 2014); C. L. R.
    James, *The Black Jacobins: Toussaint L'Ouverture and the San Domingo
    Revolution* (New York: Vintage, 1989).

19 Alexander Cochrane to Earl Bathurst, July 14, 1814, in Crawford et al., *The
    Naval War of 1812*, 3:132.

20 Vicente Sebastian Pintado to José de Soto, April 29, 1815, PC: LOC, Box 3069,
    Legajo 1796, 592 ("la loma de Buena vista ó Prospect Bluff"). See also map

enclosed in John Innerarity to Vicente Folch, June 7, 1811, Panton, Leslie & Company Collection, M1986–10, University Archives and West Florida History Center, Pensacola.

21 George Woodbine to Hugh Pigot, May 25, 1814, ACP, MS2328, 15, reel 3. According to Edmund Gaines, the perimeter of the entire compound was "nearly square and extends over near two acres of ground," though the site was actually more than twice that size. Edmund Gaines to Andrew Jackson, May 14, 1816, *PAJ*, 4:31.

22 Vicente Sebastian Pintado to José de Soto, 599–600; George Woodbine to Hugh Pigot, May 25, 1814, ACP, MS2328, 15, reel 3. See also Stephen R. Poe, "Archeological Excavations at Fort Gadsden, Florida," *Notes in Anthropology* 8 (1963): 1–35; John W. Griffin, "An Archeologist at Fort Gadsden," *FHQ* 28, no. 4 (April 1950): 254–61.

23 Map Showing the Course of the Apalachicola River from Its Mouth to the Junction with the Flint River, MPI (Maps and Plans) 1/266, enclosed in Alexander Cochrane to John Wilson Croker, June 20, 1814, ADM 1/506, 390–93.

24 Hugh Pigot to Alexander Cochrane, June 8, 1814, ADM 1/506, 394–97 (first quotation on 395, second quotation on 396). See also Alexander Cochrane to John Wilson Croker, June 20, 1814, ADM 1/506, 390–93.

25 "To the Great and Illustrious Chiefs of the Indian Nations," June 29, 1814, ADM 1/505, 163–65.

26 Response of the "Great and Illustrious," [undated], ADM 1/505, 166.

27 George Woodbine to Hugh Pigot, May 25, 1814, ACP, MS2328, 15 (first quotation), 14 (third quotation), reel 3; George Woodbine to Hugh Pigot, May 31, 1814, ACP, MS2328, 16, reel 3 (second quotation).

28 Nathaniel Millett, *The Maroons of Prospect Bluff and Their Quest for Freedom in the Atlantic World* (Gainesville: University Press of Florida, 2013), 19.

29 Alexander Cochrane to Edward Nicolls, July 4, 1814, ADM 1/506, 480–85.

30 For the British occupation of Pensacola, see: Nathaniel Millett, "Britain's 1814 Occupation of Pensacola and America's Response: An Episode of the War of 1812 in the Southeastern Borderlands," *FHQ* 84, no. 2 (Fall 2005): 229–55; Frank Lawrence Owsley Jr., *Struggle for the Gulf Borderlands: The Creek War and the Battle of New Orleans, 1812–1815* (Gainesville: University Presses of Florida, 1981), 95–119.

31 "From the Mobile," *DNI*, September 12, 1814, 2.

32 Affidavit of Captain Parker McCobb, August 19, 1814, enclosed in Abraham Bessent to Peter Early, August 20, 1814, SNAD.

33 Benjamin Hawkins, *The Collected Works of Benjamin Hawkins, 1796–1810*, ed. Thomas Foster (Tuscaloosa: University of Alabama Press, 2003), 9. For Hawkins's life and career, see *LJWBH* 1: ix–xxxiii; Historical Society, *Letters of*

Benjamin Hawkins, 1796–1806, Collections of the Georgia Historical Society, vol. 9 (Savannah, GA: Morning News, 1916), 3–12; Florette Henri, *The Southern Indians and Benjamin Hawkins, 1796–1816* (Norman: University of Oklahoma Press, 1986); Merritt B. Pound, *Benjamin Hawkins—Indian Agent* (Athens: University of Georgia Press, 1951).

34 Merritt B. Pound, *Benjamin Hawkins,* 103 (quotation), 138–54. For "A Sketch of the Creek Country in the Years 1798 and 1799" see *LJWBH,* 1:284–327. For another abridged version of the "Sketch" see the enclosure in Benjamin Hawkins to Thomas Jefferson, March 1, 1801, 351–56.

35 Hawkins owned seventy-five slaves when he died in June 1816. Carl Mauelshagen and Gerald H. Davis, trans. and ed., *Partners in the Lord's Work: The Diary of Two Moravian Missionaries in the Creek Indian Country, 1807–1813* (Atlanta: Georgia State College, 1969), 52; Pound, *Benjamin Hawkins,* 174–75; Benjamin Hawkins to James Jackson, February 18, 1798, *LJWBH,* 1:174; Benjamin Hawkins to James Jackson, August 2, 1798, *LJWBH,* 1:213.

36 Benjamin Hawkins to John Armstrong, *LJWBH,* August 16, 1814, 2:693.

37 Benjamin Hawkins to Tustunnuggee Hopoie, Speaker for the Lower Creeks, and Tustunnuggee Thlucco, Speaker for the Upper Creeks, enclosed in Benjamin Hawkins to Andrew Jackson, August 30, 1814, *LJWBH,* 2:694–95.

38 Andrew F. Frank, "The Rise and Fall of William McIntosh: Authority and Identity on the Early American Frontier," *Georgia Historical Quarterly* 87, no. 1 (Spring 2002): 28.

39 The role of mestizo chiefs in the transformation of the Creeks is traced in Claudio Saunt, *A New Order of Things: Property, Power, and the Transformation of the Creek Indians, 1733–1816* (Cambridge: Cambridge University Press, 1999) and Kathryn E. Holland Braund, *Deerskins and Duffels: The Creek Indian Trade with Anglo-America, 1685–1815* (Lincoln: University of Nebraska Press, 1993). Andrew F. Frank also addresses the place of mestizos in Creek society in *Creeks and Southerners: Biculturalism on the Early American Frontier* (Lincoln: University of Nebraska Press, 2005). For an illuminating historiographical debate on the role of multiracial chiefs in southern history, see Theda Perdue, "Race and Culture: Writing the Ethnohistory of the Early South," *Ethnohistory* 51, no. 4 (Fall 2004): 701–23; Claudio Saunt, Barbara Krauthamer, Tiya Miles, Celia E. Naylor, and Circe Sturm, "Rethinking Race and Culture in the Early South," *Ethnohistory* 53, no. 2 (Spring 2006): 399–405; Theda Purdue, "A Reply to Saunt et al.," *Ethnohistory* 53, no. 2 (Spring 2006): 406.

40 For McIntosh's biography, see Benjamin W. Griffith Jr., *McIntosh and Weatherford: Creek Indian Leaders* (Tuscaloosa: University of Alabama Press, 1998) and George Chapman, *Chief William McIntosh: A Man of Two Worlds* (Atlanta: Cherokee Publishing Company, 1988).

41 H. W. Brands, *Andrew Jackson: His Life and Times* (New York: Anchor Books, 2006); Andrew Burstein, *The Passions of Andrew Jackson* (New York: Knopf, 2003); Robert Remini, *The Life of Andrew Jackson* (New York: Harper & Row, 1988).

42 James Parton, *Life of Andrew Jackson* (Boston: Houghton, Mifflin, 1859), 1:110–12 (quotation on 111); John Henry Eaton, *The Life of Andrew Jackson, Major-General in the Service of the United States: Comprising a History of the War in the South, from the Commencement of the Creek Campaign, to the Termination of Hostilities before New Orleans* (Cincinnati, OH: Hatch & Nichols, 1817), 392–93.

43 Kenneth S. Greenberg, *Honor and Slavery: Lies, Duels, Noses, Masks, Dressing as a Woman, Gifts, Strangers, Humanitarianism, Death, Slave Rebellions, the Proslavery Argument, Baseball, Hunting, and Gambling in the Old South* (Princeton, NJ: Princeton University Press, 1996); John Hope Franklin, *The Militant South, 1800–1861* (Urbana: University of Illinois Press, 2002); Bertram Wyatt-Brown, *Southern Honor: Ethics and Behavior in the Old South* (New York: Oxford University Press, 1982).

44 Record of Slave Sale, November 17, 1788, *PAJ*, 1:15.

45 For Jackson's slave dealings, see: Mark R. Cheathem, *Andrew Jackson: Southerner* (Baton Rouge: Louisiana State University Press, 2013); Cheathem, "Andrew Jackson, Slavery, and Historians," *History Compass* 9, no. 4 (2011): 326–38; Whitney Adrienne Snow, "Slave Owner, Slave Trader, Gentleman: Slavery and the Rise of Andrew Jackson," *Journal of East Tennessee History* 80 (2008): 47–59; Matthew Warshauer, "Andrew Jackson: Chivalric Slave Master," *Tennessee Historical Quarterly* 65 (Fall 2006): 203–28; Robert V. Remini, *The Legacy of Andrew Jackson: Essays on Democracy, Indian Removal, and Slavery* (Baton Rouge: Louisiana State University Press, 1988), chapter 3.

46 "Advertisement for Runaway Slave," September 26, 1804, *PAJ*, 2:40–41.

47 Because of widespread illegal slave trading, the law required slaveowners to carry passports for their slaves. The episode is related in Parton, *Life of Andrew Jackson*, 1:353–54.

48 Andrew Jackson to William Charles Cole Claiborne, January 5, 1813, *PAJ*, 2:352.

49 Adam Rothman, *Slave Country: American Expansion and the Origins of the Deep South* (Cambridge, MA: Harvard University Press, 2005), 122.

50 "From the Citizens of Greene County Georgia," August 13, 1812, in J. C. A. Stagg, Martha King, Ellen J. Barber, Anne Mandeville Colony, Angela Kreider, and Jewel L. Spangler, *The Papers of James Madison: Presidential Series* (Charlottesville: University of Virginia Press, 2004), 5:153 (first and second quotations), 154 (third quotation), 155 (fourth quotation). The settlers' petition came as a rebellion of frontier nationalists to conquer East Florida entered its fifth month. For the East Florida invasion, see J. C. A. Stagg, "George

Mathews and John McKee: Revolutionizing East Florida, Mobile, and Pensacola in 1812," *FHQ* 85, no. 3 (Winter 2007): 269–96; James G. Cusick, *The Other War of 1812: The Patriot War and the American Invasion of Spanish East Florida* (Gainesville: University Press of Florida, 2003).

51 Harry Toulmin to James Madison, Stagg et al., *The Papers of James Madison*, 6:616. In another letter, Toulmin reported the deaths of more than one hundred American soldiers additionally. "Indian Warfare," *DNI*, October 12, 1813. See also Gregory A. Waselkov, *A Conquering Spirit: Fort Mims and the Redstick War of 1813–1814* (Tuscaloosa: University of Alabama Press, 2006); Robert V. Remini, *Andrew Jackson and His Indian Wars* (New York: Viking, 2001), 50–93.

52 Andrew Jackson to the Tennessee Volunteers, *PAJ*, 2:428.

53 Andrew Jackson, "Battle of Tehopiska, or the Horse Shoe," March 31, 1814, *CAJ*, 1:489–92 (quotation on 492).

54 *Indian Treaties, and Laws and Regulation relating to Indian Affairs* (Washington City [DC]: Way & Gideon, 1826), 207–11.

55 Andrew Jackson to John Reid, August 27, 1814, *PAJ*, 3:124–25.

56 John Smith to Andrew Jackson, August 30, 1814, AJP, reel 11.

57 Willie Blount to James Monroe, November 18, 1814, B-193, LRSW, reel 59.

58 According to Nathaniel Millett, "Nicolls saw himself leading both a military expedition and an anti-slavery experiment." The statement is apt, though Nicolls's actions more broadly evoke the idea of interracial contact, cooperation, and collaboration known as interracialism. *The Maroons of Prospect Bluff*, 52. For examples and discussion of early American interracialism, see Matthew J. Clavin, *Aiming for Pensacola: Fugitive Slaves on the Atlantic and Southern Frontiers* (Cambridge, MA: Harvard University Press, 2015); Melvin Patrick Ely, *Israel on the Appomattox: A Southern Experiment in Black Freedom from the 1790s through the Civil War* (New York: Random House, 2004); David S. Cecelski, *The Waterman's Song: Slavery and Freedom in Maritime North Carolina* (Chapel Hill: University of North Carolina Press, 2001); John Stauffer, *The Black Hearts of Men: Radical Abolitionists and the Transformation of Race* (Cambridge, MA: Harvard University Press, 2001); Martha Hodes, ed., *Sex, Love, Race: Crossing Boundaries in North American History* (New York: NYU Press, 1999); Paul Goodman, *Of One Blood: Abolitionism and the Origins of Racial Equality* (Berkeley: University of California Press, 1998).

59 George Woodbine to Alexander Cochrane, August 9, 1814, ACP, MS2328, 57, reel 3.

60 Willie Blount to Harry Toulmin, October 26, 1814, *Territorial Papers of the United States Senate*, National Archives and Records Administration, Record Group 46, M2000, reel 9.

61 Edward Nicolls, "Orders for the First Battalion of Royal Colonial Marines," [August 26, 1814], LP, 1–3.

62 Millett, *The Maroons of Prospect Bluff*, 55.

63 "British Proclamations, &c.," *NWR*, November 5, 1814, 133–35.

64 Following Nicolls's death in 1865, London's popular *Gentleman's Magazine* read, "In his early days he was commonly known as 'Fighting Nicolls,' and no wonder, for he was almost constantly employed in boat and battery actions, and in desperate 'cutting-out' affairs." *Gentleman's Magazine*, May 1865, 644.

65 Thomas Hart Benton to Andrew Jackson, September 11, 1814, *PAJ*, 3:132. Nicolls recalled the deployment of sixty Royal Marines, twelve marine artillery, and 180 Indians. Jackson put the numbers of the British land forces slightly lower at 110 marines and two hundred Creek Indians. Edward Nicolls to Alexander Cochrane, August 12, 1814–November 17, 1814, ACP, MS2328, 59, reel 3; Edward Nicolls, "Memorial to Lord Melville," May 5, 1817, LP, 1–5. See also Andrew Jackson to Secretary Monroe, September 17, 1814, Bassett, *CAJ*, 2:50–51, and Willie Blount to Harry Toulmin, October 26, 1814.

66 Andrew Jackson to David Holmes, September 14, 1814, *CAJ*, 2:49.

67 For the battle of Fort Bowyer, see: William Lawrence to Andrew Jackson, September 15, 1814, *PAJ*, 3:137–39; Owsley Jr., *Struggle for the Gulf Borderlands*, 106–19.

68 Edward Nicolls, "Memorial to Lord Melville," May 5, 1817, LP, 2–4.

69 John Innerarity, "Narrative of the Operations of the British in the Floridas," [January] 1815, HCP. John Innerarity and his brother James Innerarity, along with John Forbes, were partners in the Gulf Coast trading firm of John Forbes & Company, a successor to Panton, Leslie & Company.

70 "Citizens of Pensacola to the Governor of West Florida," March 8, 1815, ACP, MS2328, 149, reel 3; William H. Robinson and Charles Muir to Andrew Jackson, July 28, 1814, *CAJ*, 2:21–22; Andrew Jackson to Secretary Armstrong, August 5, 1814, *CAJ*, 2:30–31.

71 John Forbes & Co. to Lord Viscount Castlereagh, May 20, 1815, JFP, reel 2.

72 William Lawrence to John Forbes, February 25, 1816, HCP (first quotation); William H. Robertson to Harry Toulmin, October 26, 1814, accompanying a letter from William Blount to the Secretary of War, November 18, 1814, *Territorial Papers of the United States Senate, 1789–1873*, RG46, NARA, M200, reel 9 (second quotation). See also "Pensacola," *NWR*, Supplement to Volume 7 (September 1814–March 1815), 165–67.

73 William Lawrence to John Forbes, February 25, 1816, HCP.

74 "Pensacola," *NWR*, Supplement to Volume 7 (September 1814–March 1815), 166.

75 William Lawrence to John Forbes, February 25, 1816, HCP; "Bill of Indictment against John Bennett," August 3, 1816, JFP, reel 2. In August 1816,

Bennett under oath denied having served in the Colonial Marines and associating with Woodbine, but a Bahamian court found him guilty of perjury.

76 "Indictment of George Woodbine for Theft of Slaves," August 3, 1816, HCP; John Innerarity, "Narrative of the Operations of the British in the Floridas"; "Relacion de nombre de los esclavos de la propiedad de las vecinos de Panzacola que se hallan en Apalachicola," May 8, 1815, PC: LOC, Box 3070, Legajo 1796, 771.

77 In 1805, after a surge of immigration as a result of the Louisiana Purchase two years earlier, Pensacola's total population was 1,398, including 449 slaves, roughly one-third of the total number of residents. William S. Coker and G. Douglas Inglis, *The Spanish Censuses of Pensacola, 1784–1820* (Pensacola, FL: Perdido Bay Press, 1980), 90.

78 "Citizens of Pensacola to the Governor of West Florida," March 8, 1815, ACP, MS2328, 149, reel 3.

79 Andrew Jackson to James Monroe, October 10, 1814, *PAJ*, 3:155.

80 James Monroe to Andrew Jackson, October 21, 1814, *PAJ*, 3:171.

81 Andrew Jackson to James Monroe, November 14, 1814, *CAJ*, 2:97. First-hand accounts of the American invasion and British evacuation include Andrew Jackson to Willie Blount, November 14, 1814, *PAJ*, 3:184–86; Arsène Lacarrière Latour, *Historical Memoir of the War of West Florida and Louisiana in 1814–1815* (Gainesville: University Press of Florida, 1964), 44–51; John Innerarity to James Innerarity, November 10th/11th, 1814, in "Letters of John Innerarity," *FHQ* 9, no. 3 (January 1931): 127–30. For the removal and eventual return of seventy black Spanish troops to Pensacola who were originally from Havana, Cuba, see "Citizens of Pensacola to the Governor of West Florida," March 8, 1815, ACP, MS2328, 150, reel 3.

82 "Important," *GJ*, December 21, 1814, 3.

CHAPTER 2. THE BRITISH POST ON PROSPECT BLUFF

1 George Woodbine to Pigot, May 25, 1814, ACP, MS2328, 15, reel 3.

2 Edward Nicolls to Sir John Barrow, September 11, 1843, *Correspondence on the Slave Trade with Foreign Powers, Parties to Treaties, under Which Captured Vessels Are to Be Tried by Mixed Tribunals. From January 1 to December 31, 1844, Inclusive* (London: William Clowes and Sons, 1844), 13. Alexander Durant claimed that the citadel's walls were "25 or 30 feet high," while the free black informant Ned added that they were "about thirteen foot through." See Kendal Lewis and William Hardridge, "Confidential Report of Occurrences at Apalachicola," August 6, 1815, H-191, LRSW, reel 62; and "Statement of Ned, a Free Man of Colour," attached to Edmund Gaines to William H. Crawford, February 20, 1816, G-22, LRSW, reel 69. The numerous accounts of

the fort's dimensions are often contradictory and at times confuse or conflate the dimensions of the inner and outer structures; nevertheless, they collectively allow a fair representation of the fort's overall size and appearance. See Edward Nicolls to Alexander Cochrane, December 3, 1814, ACP, MS2328, 118, reel 3; Benjamin Hawkins to Peter Early, February 15, 1815, *LJWBH*, 3:717; Report of William McGirt to Christian Limbaugh, July 20, 1815, LRSW, H-185, reel 62; Vicente Sebastian Pintado to José de Soto, April 29, 1815, PC: LOC, Box 3069, Legajo 1796, 599–600; Stephen R. Poe, "Archeological Excavations at Fort Gadsden, Florida," *Notes in Anthropology* 8 (1963): 1–35; John W. Griffin, "An Archeologist at Fort Gadsden," *FHQ* 28, no. 4 (April 1950): 254–61.

3 *To the Great and Illustrious Chiefs of the Creek and Other Indian Nations*, December 5, 1814, WO, 1/141, 113, NAGB.

4 Captain Robert Henry to Captain William Rawlins, December 18, 1814, ACP, MS2328, 125, reel 3.

5 Edward Nicolls to Alexander Cochrane, December 3, 1814, ACP, MS2328, 117, reel 3. See also "Statement of Indian Chiefs and Warriors Entertained by Major Nicolls, Commanding a Detachment of Royal Marines—at the Bluff," January 4, 1815, ACP, MS2328, 131, reel 3.

6 George Woodbine to Edward Nicolls, October 27, 1814, ACP, MS2328, 99, reel 3.

7 Edward Nicolls to Alexander Cochrane, August 12, 1814–November 17, 1814, ACP, MS2328, 60–61, reel 3.

8 Benjamin Hawkins to Edward Nicolls, May 24, 1815, *LJWBH*, 2:728.

9 For some of the varieties and complexities of Native American slavery, see Tiya Miles, *Ties That Bind: The Story of an Afro-Cherokee Family in Slavery and Freedom* (Oakland: University of California Press, 2015); Miles, *The House on Diamond Hill: A Cherokee Plantation Story* (Chapel Hill: University of North Carolina Press, 2010); Barbara Krauthamer, *Black Slaves, Indian Masters: Slavery, Emancipation, and Citizenship in the Native American South* (Chapel Hill: University of North Carolina Press, 2013): Christine Snyder, *Slavery in Indian Country: The Changing Face of Captivity in Early America* (Cambridge, MA: Harvard University Press, 2012); Claudio Saunt, *A New Order of Things* (Cambridge: Cambridge University Press, 1999).

10 "Indian Annuities, &c.," June 3, 1836, *Register of Debates*, House of Rep., 24th Cong., 1st sess., 4145.

11 Kevin Mulroy, *Freedom on the Border: The Seminole Maroons in Florida, the Indian Territory, Coahuila, and Texas* (Lubbock: Texas Tech University Press, 1993).

12 Edward Nicolls to Alexander Cochrane, August 12, 1814–November 17, 1814, ACP, MS2328, 62, reel 3.

13 George Stiggins, *Creek Indian History: A Historical Narrative of the Genealogy, Traditions, and Downfall of the Ispocoga or Creek Indian Tribe of Indians*, ed. Virginia Pounds Brown (Tuscaloosa: University of Alabama Press, 1989), 120.

14 Edward Nicolls to Alexander Cochrane, August 12, 1814–November 17, 1814, ACP, MS2328, 59, reel 3.

15 Ibid.

16 Adam Rothman, *Slave Country: American Expansion and the Origins of the Deep South* (Cambridge, MA: Harvard University Press, 2005), 106–16 (quotation on 106); Junius P. Rodriguez, "Rebellion on the River Road: The Ideology and Influence of Louisiana's German Coast Slave Insurrection of 1811," in John R. McKivigan and Stanley Harrold, eds., *Antislavery Violence: Sectional, Racial, and Cultural Conflict in Antebellum America* (Knoxville: University of Tennessee Press, 1999), 65–88.

17 Patterson to Jones, July 8, 1814, United States Department of the Navy, Area File of the Naval Records Collection, 1775–1910, MF625, reel #200, 608.

18 Arsène Lacarrière Latour, *Historical Memoir of the War in West Florida and Louisiana in 1814–1815, with an Atlas* (Philadelphia: John Conrad, 1816), 20.

19 Andrew Jackson to William C. C. Claiborne, July 21, 1814, *PAJ*, 3:91.

20 William C. C. Claiborne to Andrew Jackson, September 20, 1814, *PAJ*, 3:143.

21 For accounts of the Battle of New Orleans that explore the African American experience, see Gene Allen Smith, *The Slaves' Gamble: Choosing Sides in the War of 1812* (New York: Palgrave Macmillan, 2013), 159–73; and Rothman, *Slave Country*, 139–62. A reliable general history is Robert V. Remini's *Battle of New Orleans: Andrew Jackson and America's First Military Victory* (London: Pimlico, 2001).

22 "The Memorial of Edward Nicolls Major by Brevet in the Royal Marines," May 5, 1817, LP.

23 Remini, *The Battle of New Orleans*, 152–53.

24 For the number of black soldiers, see Roland McDonnell, *Negro Troops of Antebellum Louisiana: A History of the Battalion of Free Men of Color* (Baton Rouge: Louisiana State University Press, 1968), 67–90, and "Troop Roster: Tennessee Volunteers & Militia, Kentucky Volunteers & Militia, Battalion of Free Men of Color, Louisiana Volunteers & Militia," National Park Service, www.nps.gov, 1, 112–17. For the democratic narrative, see: Caryn Cossé Bell, *Revolution, Romanticism, and the Afro-Creole Protest Tradition in Louisiana, 1718–1868* (Baton Rouge: Louisiana State University Press, 1997), 48–64.

25 Latour, *Historical Memoir*, 111.

26 Rothman, *Slave Country*, 113.

27 James Roberts, *The Narrative of James Roberts, a Soldier under Gen. Washington in the Revolutionary War, and under Gen. Jackson at the Battle of New Orleans, in*

the War of 1812: "A Battle Which Cost Me a Limb, Some Blood, and Almost My Life." (Chicago: James Roberts, 1858), 13, 15, 17, 31.

28 "Indemnities Due under the Award of the Emperor of Russia, for Slaves and Other Private Property Carried Away by the British Forces in Violation of the Treaty of Ghent," *ASP: FR*, 5:801. Latour provided a list of 199 slaves from "the shores of the Mississippi." *Historical Memoir*, clxxxi.

29 Latour, *Historical Memoir*, 202.

30 Andrew Jackson to Hughes Lavergne, February 20, 1815, *PAJ*, 3:283.

31 "Depositions concerning Slaves Liberated by British Forces after the Battle of New Orleans," Historic New Orleans Collection, New Orleans, Louisiana, MSS199, 1. See also John Lambert to Andrew Jackson, February 27, 1815, *PAJ*, 3:290.

32 "Depositions concerning Slaves Liberated by British Forces."

33 Rothman, *Slave Country*, 160. After years of negotiation, the British eventually paid $1,204,960 to the United States for 3,601 American slaves liberated from the Atlantic and Gulf Coasts during the War of 1812. Of this sum, slaveowners in Louisiana and Mississippi received approximately $156,000 to compensate for the loss of 259 and 22 slaves, respectively. John Bassett Moore, *History and Digest of the International Arbitrations to Which the United States Has Been a Party* (Washington, DC: Government Printing Office, 1898), 1:350–90; "Indemnities Due under the Award of the Emperor of Russia," 5:800–829. For the slaves' removal to the Bahamas and Trinidad, see Thomas Malcolmson, "Freedom by Reaching the Wooden World: American Slaves and the British Navy during the War of 1812," *Northern Mariner/le marin du nord* 22, no. 4 (October 2012): 361–92, and Latour, *Historical Memoir*, 221–22.

34 Latour, *Historical Memoir*, cxxi.

35 "Depositions concerning Slaves Liberated by British Forces."

36 Smith, *The Slaves' Gamble*.

37 Historians who have studied the rare phenomenon of African Americans choosing to become or remain slaves in the late antebellum era find that the decision was a difficult one aimed primarily at retaining close family and community ties. Ted Maris-Wolf, *Family Bonds: Free Blacks and Re-Enslavement Law in Antebellum Virginia* (Chapel Hill: University of North Carolina Press, 2015); Emily West, *Family or Freedom: People of Color in the Antebellum South* (Lexington: University Press of Kentucky, 2012).

38 Gene Dattel, *Cotton and Race in the Making of America: The Human Costs of Economic Power* (Lanham, MD: Ivan R. Dee, 2009), 81. See also Sven Beckert, *Empire of Cotton: A Global History* (New York: Knopf, 2015).

39   Robert Henry to Mateo González Manrique, January 12, 1815, HCP.

40   For the first historical appraisal of these lists and their significance, see Jane Landers, *Black Society in Spanish Florida* (Urbana: University of Illinois Press, 1999), 231–33.

41   Robert Henry to Mateo González Manrique; Report of Lieutenant Don José Urcullo, January 23, 1815, JFP, reel 2.

42   Mateo González Manrique, "Relacion delos Negros pertenecientes á los habitants de la Plaza Panzacola que se ha fugado y llevado los Ingleses á Apalachicola," March 4, 1815, ACP, MS2328, 176, reel 3.

43   Report of Lieutenant Don José Urcullo, January 23, 1815, JFP, reel 2.

44   "Return of Muscogee or Creek Indians under the Command of Lieut. Col. Nicolls," February 1815, WO, 1/144, 68–69.

45   Edward Nicolls to Alexander Cochrane, March 1, 1815, WO, 1/144, 67.

46   Alexander Cochrane to John Lambert, February 3, 1815, WO, 1/143, 23–27; Alexander Cochrane to John Lambert, February 17, 1815, WO, 1/143, 27–28.

47   Vicente Sebastian Pintado to Antonio Ventura Bocatro, February 9, 1816, VSP, 863–64, reel 3 ("Blancos, Indios, Mulatos y Negros libres y Esclavos, al mando del Teniente Colonel Don Eduardo Nicolls" and "el estado y clase de establecimientos que habian formado en aquel Rio, las obras de fortifications que habian hecho, la Artillerra, pertrechos, municiones &c. que allí tenian y dar cuenta exācta de todo").

48   John Innerarity to John Forbes, May 22, 1815, JFP, reel 2.

49   Vicente Sebastián Pintado to José de Soto, 590–95 (quotation on 592, "sin la presencia de los otros negros"); John Innerarity to John Forbes, May 22, 1815, JFP, reel 2.

50   Robert Spencer to Vicente Sebastián Pintado, March 30, 1815, VSP, reel 4.

51   Alexander Cochrane to Mateo González Manrique, February 10, 1815, HCP.

52   Vicente Sebastián Pintado to José de Soto, 593.

53   John Innerarity to John Forbes, May 22, 1815, JFP, reel 2.

54   Vicente Sebastián Pintado to José de Soto, 593 ("quando los Americans ocupaban esta con su exercito al mando del general Jackson"); "Relacion de los Esclavos pertenecientes á los vecinos de Panzacola que se pudieron hallan con los Ingleses en Apalachicola," May 6, 1815, PC: LOC, Legajo 1796, Box 3069, 666 ("los embarcaria para las Colonias Inglesas.")

55   "Relacion de los Esclavos," 665–67 (quotation on 667, "Pais Americano"); Robert Spencer to Vicente Sebastián Pintado, April 4, 1815, VSP.

56   Vicente Sebastián Pintado to José de Soto, 593 ("se dixe son Americanos y tomaron nombres de tales").

57   John Wilson Croker to William Hamilton, April 7, 1818, LP.

58   "Relacion de los Esclavos," 662–65 ("no quiso venir" and "no quisieron venir").

59 Ibid., 663 ("lo matarián si venia"). See also "Relacion de nombre de los esclavos de la propiedad de las vecinos de Panzacola que se hallan en Apalachicola," May 8, 1815, PC: LOC, Legajo 1796, Box 3070, 772.

60 "Relacion de los Esclavos," 662. See also "Relacion de nombre de los esclavos," 768, 771.

61 "Relacion de los Esclavos," 664–65 (quotation on 665, "lo llevaran por fuerza y amarrado los Indios"); see also "Relacion de nombre de los esclavos," 770, 773.

62 "Relacion de los Esclavos," 663 (first quotation, "presentó algunos papeles tendentes á probarlo aunque indirectamente"); 662 (second and third quotations, "Este se quizo hacer libre en virtud de una certificacion firmado por un Juez de Paz, y despachada en la Secretaria de Pazacola en la idioma Igles, lo que me parecio burlesco"); 665 (fourth and fifth quotations, "dijo son libre y que solo trabajaba á jornal"). See also "Relacion de nombre de los esclavos," 768–69, 771.

63 "Relacion de los Esclavos," 664 ("le otorgase entera libertad"). See also "Relacion de nombre de los esclavos," 769.

64 Millett, *The Maroons of Prospect Bluff*, 115.

65 Vicente Sebastián Pintado to José de Soto, 594 ("sus haberes como soldados," "esta licencias era una carta de libertad," "en qualquir passage que se presentarán con esto documento").

66 Discharge Certificate of Private Parish Lane, March 31, 1815, AJP, reel 17. Nathaniel Millett copies the papers of another volunteer, José Hambroso, in *The Maroons of Prospect Bluff*, 115.

67 Memorandum of a gentleman of respectability at Bermuda, May 21, 1815, *ASP: FR*, 4:552.

68 Vicente Sebastián Pintado to José de Soto, 594 ("unos voluntariamente, y otros ganados por la persuacion").

69 Edward Nicolls to Juan Ruiz Apodaca, November 9, 1814, LP, 3. See also John Innerarity, "Narrative of the Operations of the British in the Floridas," [January] 1815, HCP; Mateo Gonzáles Manrique to Alexander Cochrane, January 25, 1815, HCP; Alexander Cochrane to Mateo Gonzáles Manrique, February 10, 1815, HCP; "Citizens of Pensacola to the Governor of West Florida," March 8, 1815, ACP, MS2328, 150, reel 3; Vicente Sebastián Pintado to José de Soto, 594.

70 Vicente Sebastián Pintado to José de Soto, 599 ("sesenta toesas"), 600 ("un foso de poco profundidand," "un numero considerable de cabañas"), 599 ("cajónes de metralla y polvora"), 595 ("de los establecimientos Americanos ó Indios," "tienen formado el projecta de ir establecer se en la bahio del Tampa").

71 John Innerarity to John Forbes, May 22, 1815, JFP, reel 2.

72 Benjamin Hawkins to Peter Early, April 21, 1815, *LJWBH*, 2:724–25.

73 Deposition of Samuel Jervais, May 9, 1815, *ASP: FR*, 4:551.

74 Edmund Gaines to A. J. Dallas, May 14, 1815, *ASP: FR*, 4:551 (first, second, and
    third quotations); Edmund Gaines to Andrew Jackson, May 14, 1815, *PAJ*,
    3:355–56 (fourth and fifth quotations on 356). For Gaines's biography, see
    James W. Silver, *Edmund Pendleton Gaines: Frontier General* (Baton Rouge:
    Louisiana State University Press, 1949), 3–7; Ward Hartzell, "Brigadier
    General Edmund Pendleton Gaines" (M.A. thesis, University of Wisconsin–
    Madison, 1930), 1–2.

75 "War Events; or, Things Incidental to the Late War," *NWR*, June 10, 1815, 261.

76 Treaty of peace and amity between His Britannic Majesty and the United
    States of America, *ASP: FR*, 4:747–48.

77 "Indian Affairs: From the *Georgia Journal*," *NWR*, June 24, 1815, 286.

78 Ibid., 287.

79 "War Events," 261.

80 "Indian Affairs: From the *Georgia Journal*," 285.

81 James Monroe to Anthony St. John Baker, July 10, 1815, *British and Foreign
    State Papers: 1818–1819* (London: James Ridgway, 1835), 367.

82 John Quincy Adams to James Monroe, September 19, 1815, *British and Foreign
    State Papers: 1818–1819* (London: James Ridgway, 1835), 368.

83 Ibid., 368. While in London, Francis received a gilded ceremonial tomahawk as
    well as a new commission as brigadier general in His Majesty's Service, yet
    these tokens of appreciation and support proved illusory as the British
    government promptly withdrew its support of the Indians' cause. For the
    journey to England and Francis's reception see "June 10," *NWR*, July 15, 1815,
    347; "The Navy," *NWR*, March 15, 1817, 46; "Milledgeville," *NWR*, June 13, 1818,
    269; "From the Augusta Chronicle," *NWR*, August 8, 1818, 399.

84 Alan Taylor, *The Internal Enemy: Slavery and War in Virginia, 1772–1832* (New
    York: Norton, 2013), 441–42.

85 "Col. Nicolls," *NWR*, July 1, 1815, 311; Memorandum of a gentleman of
    respectability at Bermuda.

86 Edward Nicolls to Sir John Barrow, September 11, 1843, *Correspondence on the
    Slave Trade with Foreign Powers*, 13. In stressing Nicolls's achievements, Millett
    accepts the colonel's words uncritically; however, the likelihood that at least
    some of the maroons—like the Indians who had recently abandoned the
    post—had by the summer of 1815 lost faith in their British allies remains a
    possibility. Millett, *The Maroons of Prospect Bluff*, 116–17.

87 Andrew Kinsman to James Cockburn, August 10, 1815, ADM, 37/73, 58–59
    (quotation). For Colonial Marines' fears of relocating to the British West
    Indies and serving in the West India Regiments, see Alexander Cochrane to
    James Cockburn, April 6, 1815, CO, 37/73, 143–44, and George Cockburn to Sir
    Henry Torrens, August 23, 1815, CO, 37/73, 52–55. A hint of Hambly's biogra-
    phy can be gleaned from the following: Daniel J. J. Ross and Bruce S.

Chappell, eds., "Visit to the Indian Nations: The Diary of John Hambly," *FHQ* 55, no. 1 (July 1976): 60–73; John H. Goff, "Across Georgia with LaFayette," *Georgia Review* 17, no. 2 (Summer 1963): 202; Richard K. Murdoch, "A Voyage to the Miami Region in 1793," *FHQ* 31, no. 1 (July 1952): 16–32.

88 "The Creek Country," *DNI*, July 6, 1815, 3.

CHAPTER 3. A FREE BLACK COMMUNITY

1 There are some reports that Hambly was one of two white officers remaining at the fort, though evidence on this second individual is wanting. For example, see Benjamin Hawkins to Edmund Gaines, June 14, 1815, *LJWBH*, 2:736.

2 Report of William McGirt to Christian Limbaugh, July 20, 1815, H-185, LRSW, reel 62.

3 Ibid.

4 Benjamin Hawkins to Edmund Gaines, October 17, 1815, *LJWBH*, 2:764.

5 Harry Toulmin to Andrew Jackson, July 3, 1815, AJP, reel 18.

6 Benjamin Hawkins to Andrew Jackson, August 4, 1815, LRSW, H-191, reel 62.

7 For Hambly's commission see "Memorial of Major Edward Nicolls," ACP, MS2338, 121, reel 3.

8 "Journal," *GJ*, June 14, 1815, 3. Benjamin Hawkins also reported Nicolls's promise to return to Prospect Bluff in six months. Benjamin Hawkins to Edmund Gaines, June 14, 1815, *LJWBH*, 2:736, and Benjamin Hawkins to Alexander Dallas, July 8, 1815, *LJWBH*, 2:739–40.

9 Kendal Lewis and William Hardridge, "Confidential Report of Occurrences at Apalachicola," August 6, 1815, H-191, LRSW, reel 62.

10 Ibid.

11 William S. Willis, "Divide and Rule: Red, White, and Black in the Southeast," *Journal of Negro History* 48, no. 3 (July 1963): 158.

12 For the employment of Native Americans, and in particular Creeks, as slave catchers, see Kathryn E. Holland Braund, "The Creek Indians, Blacks, and Slavery," *Journal of Southern History* 57, no. 4 (November 1991): 601–36.

13 Kendal Lewis and William Hardridge, "Confidential Report of Occurrences at Apalachicola." See also Benjamin Hawkins to George Graham, August 11, 1815, *LJWBH*, 2:747–48.

14 For maroons in the early United States and adjacent territories, see Sylviane A. Diouf, *Liberty's Exiles: The Story of the American Maroons* (New York: NYU Press, 2014); Gwendolyn Midlo Hall, *Africans in Colonial Louisiana: The Development of Afro-Creole Culture in the Eighteenth Century* (Baton Rouge: Louisiana State University Press, 1992); Herbert Aptheker, *American Negro Slave Revolts* (New York: Columbia University Press, 1943); Aptheker, "Maroons within the Present Limits of the United States,"

Journal of Negro History 24, no. 2 (April 1939): 167–84. For the examination of marronage in the Americas more generally, see Michael Craton, *Testing the Chains: Resistance to Slavery in the British West Indies* (Ithaca, NY: Cornell University Press, 2009); Alvin O. Thompson, *Flight to Freedom: African Runaways and Maroons in the Americas* (Mona, Jamaica: University of the West Indies Press, 2006); John K. Thornton, *Africa and Africans in the Making of the Atlantic World, 1400–1800* (Cambridge: Cambridge University Press, 1998); Bonham C. Richardson, *The Caribbean in the Wider World, 1492–1992: A Regional Biography* (Cambridge: Cambridge University Press, 1992); Gad Heuman, ed., *Out of the House of Bondage: Runaways, Resistance, and Marronage in Africa and the New World* (London: Frank Cass, 1986); Richard Price, *The Guiana Maroons: A Historical and Bibliographical Introduction* (Baltimore, MD: Johns Hopkins University Press, 1996); Eugene Genovese, *From Rebellion to Revolution: Afro-American Slave Revolts in the Making of the New World* (Baton Rouge: Louisiana State University Press, 1979); Richard Price, ed., *Maroon Societies: Rebel Slave Communities in the Americas* (Garden City, NY: Anchor Press, 1973).

15 Nathaniel Millett, *The Maroons of Prospect Bluff and Their Quest for Freedom in the Atlantic World* (Gainesville: University Press of Florida, 2013), 30.

16 "Relacion de nombre de los esclavos de la propiedad de las vecinos de Panzacola que se hallan en Apalachicola," May 8, 1815, PC: LOC, Legajo 1796, Box 3070, 768–76; Mateo González Manrique, "Relacion delos Negros pertenecientes á los vecinos de esta Plaza de Panzacola que se han fugado y llevado los Ingleses á Apalachicola," March 4, 1815, ACP, MS2328, 172–73, reel 3. Jane Landers first posited the ethnicity of these West Florida fugitives in *Black Society in Spanish Florida* (Urbana: University of Illinois Press, 1999), 232.

17 "Relacion de nombre de los esclavos," 768–76.

18 Jane Landers, *Black Society in Spanish Florida*, 233.

19 Duncan L. Clinch to Robert Butler, August 2, 1816, JMP, reel 18, 3839–40. The large cache led Millett to conclude that Negro Fort was "materially the wealthiest maroon settlement in the history of the Western Hemisphere." *The Maroons of Prospect Bluff*, 175.

20 Marcus Buck to his father, August 4, 1816, in "Gen. Clinch and the Indians," *Army and Navy Chronicle*, February 25, 1836, 116. See also Henry Wilson and James Basket, "Inventory of Military Stores Captured at the Negro Fort East Florida," enclosed with Duncan L. Clinch to Robert Butler, August 2, 1816, JMP, reel 18, 3839–40.

21 Nathaniel Millett found that as a result of several natural advantages, Negro Fort's maroons were "well fed," adding, "Much of the population may well

have been better fed and healthier than they had been while enslaved." *The Maroons of Prospect Bluff*, 179.

22 *Record in the Case of Colin Mitchell and Others, versus the United States* (Washington, DC: Duff Green, 1831), 432, 619. Alexander Cochrane wrote of the area around the British Post, "The Country abounds in Cattle." Alexander Cochrane to Pulteney Malcolm, February 17, 1815, WO, 1/143, 19.

23 Mateo González Manrique, "Relacion delos Negros," 175–78, reel 3.

24 Robert Henry to Alexander Cochrane, December 22, 1814, ACP, MS 2328, 126, reel 3.

25 David Ewen Bartholomew to Alexander Cochrane, January 31, 1815, ACP, MS 2328, 126, reel 3. See also William Rawlins to Alexander Cochrane, January 16, 1815, ACP, MS 2328, 136–37, reel 3. One report circulated among American officials claimed that as a result of starvation, "an Indian woman ate her own child." There is, however, no evidence to support the claim. Benjamin Hawkins to Peter Early, April 21, 1815, *LJWBH*, 2:724.

26 Daniel T. Patterson to Benjamin W. Crowninshield, August 15, 1816, *ASP: FR*, 4:561.

27 "General Clinch and the Indians," *Army and Navy Chronicle*, February 25, 1836, 116; Report of William to Christian Limbaugh, July 20, 1815, H-185, LRSW, reel 62.

28 Duncan L. Clinch to Robert Butler, August 2, 1816, JMP, reel 18, 3834.

29 Benigno García Calderon to Mauricío de Zuñiga, August 8, 1816, PC: LOC, Box 3090, Legajo 1873, 111 ("sembrados de todo especíe de viveres").

30 Benjamin Hawkins to Peter Early, April 21, 1815, *LJWBH*, 2:724; Edward Nicolls to Alexander Cochrane, August 24, 1814, ACP, MS2328, 60. For a comparison of the Negro Fort food supply with that of other maroon communities, see Millett, *The Maroons of Prospect Bluff*, 177–80.

31 Edward Nicolls to Sir John Barrow, September 11, 1843, *Correspondence on the Slave Trade with Foreign Powers*, 13.

32 For an example, see Duncan Clinch to Edmund Gaines, May 7, 1816, G-55, LRSW, reel 69.

33 "Statement of Ned, a Free Man of Colour," attached to Edmund Gaines to William H. Crawford, February 20, 1816, G-22, LRSW, reel 69.

34 Francisco Caso y Luengo to Don Jose Masot, May 14, 1818, *ASP: FR*, 4:567.

35 [George Robert Gleig], *Narrative of the Campaigns of the British Army at Washington and New Orleans, under Generals Ross, Pakenham, and Lambert, in the Years 1814 and 1815* (London: John Murray, 1821), 264–69.

36 Early accounts of the Choctaws' recruitment and their eventual commitment to the United States include John Peirce to Harry Toulmin, July 18, 1813, B-289, LRSW, reel 50; George Gaines to Willie Blount, July 23, 1813, B-289, LRSW, reel 50; Harry Toulmin to Willie Blount, July 23, 1813,

B-289, LRSW, reel 50; Moshulatubbee to George Gaines, August 8, 1813, B-317, LRSW, reel 50; John Pitchlynn to Willie Blount, August 18, 1813, P-1813, LRSWU, reel 9; John Sibly to John Armstrong, October 3, 1813, S-329, LRSW, reel 57; John Pitchlynn to Willie Blount, December 9, 1813, P-1813, LRSWU, reel 9. John Sugden summarizes this correspondence and Tecumseh's efforts to recruit the Choctaws in *Tecumseh: A Life* (New York: Holt, 1997), 241–49. For a more detailed albeit dated account of Tecumseh's time among the Choctaws, see also H. S. Halbert and T. H. Ball, *The Creek War of 1813 and 1814* (Chicago: Donohue & Henneberry, 1895), 40–57.

37 George Gaines to John Mason, July 22, 1813, B-289, LRSW, reel 50. For additional reports of Choctaws joining the Creeks in preparation for war against American settlements, see Moshulatubbee to George Gaines, July 15, 1813, B-289, LRSW, reel 50; and John Peirce to Harry Toulmin, July 18, 1813, B-289, LRSW, reel 50. See also Sugden, *Tecumseh*, 351–52.

38 George Woodbine to Hugh Pigot, May 31, 1814, ACP, MS2328, 16, reel 3.

39 "Return of Muscogee or Creek Indians under the Command of Lieut. Col. Nicolls," February 1815, WO, 1/144, 68–69. Claudio Saunt shares the belief of other historians of Negro Fort that the Choctaws resided inside the fort alongside the maroons; however, this does not appear to be the case. *A New Order of Things: Property, Power, and the Transformation of the Creek Indians, 1733–1816* (Cambridge: Cambridge University Press, 1999), 282.

40 Vicente Sebastián Pintado, *Plano Borrador del Rio y Bahia de Apalachicola Para Mejor Inteligencia de los Partes Dados en 29 de Abril 6 y 8 de Mayo de Este Año* (1815), and *Plano del Rio Apalachicola, Territorio é Yslas Adyacentes* (1815), Library of Congress Geography and Map Division, Washington, DC.

41 Benjamin Hawkins to Andrew Jackson, August 12, 1815, *LJWBH*, 2:748 (first quotation); Francisco Caso y Luengo to José de Soto, September 18, 1815, PC: UF, Legajo 147B, folio 568, reel 479 (second quotation). For a contemporary description of Fort San Marcos de Apalache, see "Florida," *Pensacola Floridian*, January 7, 1822, 3.

42 "Indictment of George Woodbine for Theft of Slaves," August 3, 1816, HCP. See also John Innerarity, "Narrative of the Operations of the British in the Floridas," [January] 1815, HCP. For the ages and occupations of Cyrus, Prince, and Garçon, see "Relacion de nombre de los esclavos," 770–71.

43 "Statement of Ned, a Free Man of Colour." For fears of a repetition of the Haitian Revolution in the southern United States, see Matthew J. Clavin, *Toussaint Louverture and the American Civil War: The Promise and*

Peril of a Second Haitian Revolution (Philadelphia: University of Pennsylvania Press, 2011); Alfred N. Hunt, *Haiti's Influence on Antebellum America: Slumbering Volcano in the Caribbean* (Baton Rouge: Louisiana State University Press, 2006).

44 Millett, *The Maroons of Prospect Bluff,* 201 (first quotation), 207 (second and third quotations). In one example, Millett cites the activities of some of the Negro Fort maroons in other parts of Florida the year after the fort's destruction to prove the existence of "formalized law" and "a high degree of political sophistication" at Negro Fort, 208–9.

45 William Hayne Simmons, *Notices of East Florida, with an Account of the Seminole Nation of Indians* (Charleston, SC: A. E. Miller, 1822), 75.

46 Vicente Sebastián Pintado to Robert Spencer, March 30, 1815, VSP, reel 3 ("una nueva republica de Bandidos"). For a discussion of the meaning of Pintado's expression, see John Paul Nuño, "'República de Bandidos': The Prospect Bluff Fort's Challenge to the Spanish Slave System," *FHQ* 94, no. 2 (Fall 2015): 192–221.

47 Millett, *The Maroons of Prospect Bluff,* 208.

48 "Statement of Ned, a Free Man of Colour" (quotation); Report of William McGirt to Christian Limbaugh, July 20, 1815, H-185, LRSW, reel 62. Andrew Jackson complained that the Negro Fort maroons were "well clothed and disciplined." Andrew Jackson to Mauricio de Zuñiga, April 23, 1816, *CAJ*, 2:241.

49 "Indictment of George Woodbine for Theft of Slaves."

50 John Innerarity, "Narrative of the Operations of the British in the Floridas."

51 Ibid.

52 Kendal Lewis and William Hardridge, "Confidential Report of Occurrences at Apalachicola."

53 John Innerarity to John Forbes, November 1815, GP.

54 "Twenty Dollars Reward," *GJ*, September 6, 1815, 4.

55 "Ranaway," *GJ*, May 17, 1815, 3.

56 "150 Dollars Reward," *GJ*, December 6, 1815, 3 (quotations). For Carter's service as an army contractor, refer to "Wanted," *GJ*, April 27, 1814, 1, and "Cash Notice," *GJ*, November 16, 1814, 1.

57 "10 Dollars Reward," *GJ*, February 7, 1816, 1.

58 Benjamin Hawkins to William Crawford, February 3, 1816, *LJWBJ*, 2:771; Benjamin Hawkins to William Crawford, February 9, 1816, *LJWBJ*, 2:773.

59 Benjamin Hawkins to William Crawford, February 16, 1816, *LJWBH*, 2:774.

60 Benjamin Hawkins to Peter Early, October 26, 1814, *LJWBH*, 2:698.

61 Benjamin Hawkins to Thomas Pinckney, May 12, 1815, *LJWBH*, 2:726.

62 Edward Nicolls to Alexander Cochrane, November 17, 1814, ACP, MS2328, 61, reel 3. See also Benjamin Hawkins to John Houston McIntosh, November 26,

1814, *LJWBH*, 2:707, and Benjamin Hawkins to Thomas Pinckney, May 12, 1815, *LJWBH*, 2:726.

63 Johann Christian Burckhard, *Partners in the Lord's Work: The Diary of Two Moravian Missionaries in the Creek Indian Country, 1807–1813*, trans. and ed. Carl Mauelshagen and Gerald H. Davis (Atlanta: Georgia State College, 1969), 36–39, 52–61 (first quotation on 52, second quotation on 59). The murderer was "a white man turned Indian," Kendal Lewis, who later worked as one of Hawkins's trusted spies. Traylor Russell, "Kendall Lewis," *Texana* 9, no. 1 (1971): 17.

64 Christian Limbaugh to Benjamin Hawkins, July 25, 1815, and Timothy Barnard to Benjamin Hawkins, July 25, 1815, H-185, LRSW, reel 62. The agent may have been referring to Phil's initial escape to Prospect Bluff, but the date of his comment suggests he was referring to Phil's joining the British evacuation from the site. Christian Limbaugh to Benjamin Hawkins, July 25, 1815, H-185, LRSW, reel 62.

65 "Shred of the Late War," *NWR*, August 31, 1816 (quotation). See also Vicente Sebastián Pintado to José de Soto, April 29, 1815, PC: LOC, Box 3069, Legajo 1796, 595; "Deposition of Samuel Jervais," May 9, 1815, *ASP: FR*, 4:551; Edmund Gaines to A. J. Dallas, May 22, 1815, *ASP: FR*, 4:552; Report of Captain Amelung to General Jackson, June 4, 1816, *ASP: FR*, 4:557; Jarius Loomis to Commodore Daniel T. Patterson, August 13, 1816, *ASP: FR*, 4:559–60; "Statement of Ned, a Free Man of Colour"; Duncan L. Clinch to Robert Butler, August 2, 1816, JMP, reel 18, 3832. William Harris Crawford to Andrew Jackson, March 15, 1816, *PAJ*, 4:15–16; Edmund Gaines to Andrew Jackson, May 14, 1816, *PAJ*, 4:31.

66 Edward Nicolls to Alexander Cochrane, August 24, 1814, ACP, MS2328, 60, reel 3.

67 Mateo Gonzalez Manrique, "Relacion delos Negros," 175–78, reel 3; Henry Wilson and James Basket, "Inventory of Military Stores Captured at the Negro Fort East Florida," 3839.

68 Francisco Caso y Luengo to José de Soto, July 5, 1815, PC: LOC, Box 3070, Legajo 1796, 1058 ("los Negros tienen armadas con su Cañon, la una muy regular, y la otra poco mas que una Bercha").

69 Ibid., 1058–59 (quotation on 1058, "á apresar todo barco, que no sea Ingles"). See also Francisco Caso y Luengo to José de Soto, July 14, 1815, PC: LOC, Box 3070, Legajo 1796, 1061–63.

70 John Innerarity to John Forbes, August 12, 1815, *FHQ* 12, no. 3 (January 1934): 128–29.

71 Vicente Sebastián Pintado to José de Soto, 599 ("con una tronera á cada lado en situacion de poder batir la subida y baxada del Rio").

72 Edmund Gaines to Andrew Jackson, *PAJ*, 4:31.

73 Felipe Prieto to Francisco Caso y Luengo, June 17, 1815, JFP, reel 2 ("dispuestos á executar qualquier").

74 Still, it is important not to dismiss the degree to which Negro Fort "presented an affront that even a racially fluid Spanish hierarchy could not abide." John Paul Nuño, "República de Bandidos,'" 194.

75 José de Soto to Juan Ruiz Apodaca, July 15, 1815, PC: LOC, Legajo 1796, Box 3070, 960–63 ("perfectamente armado," "malvados de todas clases y Nacion," "dueño del Comercio").

76 One report put the fort "about a mile" from the original trading post, or "factory," though a contemporary British map clearly shows the company store at the same location on Prospect Bluff. William H. Robertson to Thomas Flournoy, June 17, 1814, *ASP: IA*, 1:859; Map Showing the Course of the Apalachicola River from Its Mouth to the Junction with the Flint River, MPI (Maps and Plans) 1/266, enclosed in Alexander Cochrane to John Wilson Croker, June 20, 1814, ADM 1/506, 390–93.

77 John Innerarity to John Forbes, 128–29.

78 "Milledgeville, May 24," *DNI*, June 6, 1815, 3.

79 "Florida," *GJ*, June 21, 1815, 3. See also "Milledgeville, June 14," *GJ*, June 14, 1815, 3. For the rumors of Great Britain acquiring the Floridas in 1815, see Rembert W. Patrick, *Florida Fiasco: Rampant Rebels on the Georgia-Florida Border, 1810–1815* (Athens: University of Georgia Press, 2010), 296–99.

80 "The Journal," *GJ*, November 29, 1815, 3.

81 "Of the Floridas, &c.," *DNI*, February 12, 1816, 2.

82 "British Papers," *DNI*, November 18, 1815, 2.

83 The idea is discussed further in Matthew J. Clavin, "'It is a negro, not an Indian war': Southampton, St. Domingo, and the Second Seminole War," in William S. Belko, ed., *America's Hundred Years' War: U.S. Expansion to the Gulf Coast and the Fate of the Seminole, 1763–1858* (Gainesville: University Press of Florida, 2011), 181–208.

84 "Milledgeville, June 21," *NWR*, July 15, 1815, 347.

85 "Extract of a Letter from a Gentleman on St. Simon's Island to Another in This City, dated 18th June, 1815," *DNI*, July 8, 1815, 2. The *Georgia Journal* began the tradition of replacing the words "blacks" and "negroes" with asterisks the previous summer when copying a letter from Benjamin Hawkins to Florida governor Peter Early and US secretary of war John Armstrong. "Copy of a Letter from Col. Hawkins, Agent for Indian Affairs, to His Excellency the Governor, Dated Creek-Agency, August 23, 1814," *GJ*, August 31, 1814, 2.

86 See also Robert Remini, *Andrew Jackson and His Indian Wars* (New York: Viking, 2001), 98–107.

87 "Chronicle," November 11, 1815, *NWR*, 188.

88 Andrew Jackson to Creek Chiefs, September 4, 1815, *PAJ*, 3:382 (first quotation), 383 (second quotation).

89 Andrew Jackson to Edmund Gaines, September 30, 1815, *PAJ*, 3:386.

CHAPTER 4. FIGHTING TO THE DEATH

1 Edmund Gaines to William Crawford, February 20, 1816, G-22, LRSW, reel 69. For a contemporary account of the ambush, see "Reported Indian Murders," *GJ*, February 28, 1816, 3.

2 "Statement of Ned, a Free Man of Colour," attached to Edmund Gaines to William Crawford, February 20, 1816, G-22, LRSW, reel 69.

3 For Gaines's views on race and slavery, see James W. Silver, *Edmund Pendleton Gaines: Frontier General* (Baton Rouge: Louisiana State University Press, 1949); Edmund Gaines, *Memorial of Edmund Pendleton Gaines, to the Senate and House of Representatives of the United States, in Congress Assembled* (Memphis, TN: Enquirer Office, 1840), 27–29.

4 Benjamin Hawkins to William Crawford, February 16, 1816, *LJWBH*, 2:773–74 (quotations on 773).

5 Benjamin Hawkins to Andrew Jackson, March 21, 1816, *LJWBH*, 2:778. See also Benjamin Hawkins to William Crawford, March 29, 1860, H-53, LRSW, reel 69.

6 Benjamin Hawkins to William Crawford, April 2, 1816, *LJWBH*, 2:780.

7 Ibid., 2:780–81.

8 James G. Cusick, *The Other War of 1812: The Patriot War and the American Invasion of Spanish East Florida* (Gainesville: University Press of Florida, 2003), 7. See also William C. Davis, *The Rogue Republic: How Would-Be Patriots Waged the Shortest Revolution in American History* (New York: Houghton Mifflin Harcourt, 2011); J. C. A. Stagg, "George Mathews and John McKee: Revolutionizing East Florida, Mobile, and Pensacola in 1812," *FHQ* 85, no. 3 (Winter 2007): 269–96; Frank Lawrence Owsley Jr. and Gene A. Smith, *Filibusters and Expansionists: Jeffersonian Manifest Destiny, 1800–1821* (Tuscaloosa: University of Alabama Press, 1997); Rembert W. Patrick, *Florida Fiasco: Rampant Rebels on the Georgia-Florida Border, 1810–1815* (Athens: University of Georgia Press, 1954).

9 William Crawford to Andrew Jackson, March 15, 1816, *CAJ*, 2:236–37.

10 Even before receiving the president's directive, Jackson ordered General Gaines to move the US Army's Fourth and Seventh Infantry Regiments to the southern border and construct two forts at the junctions of the Escambia and Apalachicola Rivers. Jackson also ordered Major Joseph Pulaski Kennedy and the Creek chief and former Red Stick warrior William Weatherford to pursue the murderers of Johnston and

McGaskey. Andrew Jackson to William Crawford, March 15, 1816, J-64, LRSW, reel 70.

11 Andrew Jackson to Edmund Gaines, April 8, 1816, *CAJ*, 2:238 (first quotation), 239 (second, third, and fourth quotations).

12 Ibid., 2:239.

13 Andrew Jackson to William Crawford, April 24, 1816, *PAJ*, 4:25–26. Jackson's unilateralism is further demonstrated by the fact that he waited more than a month after his communication with Gaines to forward copies of the correspondence to the secretary of war. Jackson wrote in a cover letter, "I trust you will be satisfied with the order I have taken with regard to the Negro Fort. You find by my letter to Genl Gaines of the 8th ult. accompanying this—that even before the receipt of your letter of the 15 March that officer was vested by me with full discretionary powers to act on this subject." Andrew Jackson to William Crawford, May 12, 1816, J-92, LRSW, reel 70.

14 Edmund Gaines to Andrew Jackson, April 18, 1816, AJP, reel 20.

15 Benjamin Hawkins to Andrew Jackson, April 21, 1816, *PAJ*, 4:21.

16 Talk from the Little Prince, Tustunnuggee Hopoy, to the Commander of the United States Forces in the Indian Nation, April 26, 1816, *ASP: FR*, 4:558.

17 Benjamin Hawkins to Tustunnuggee Hopoie, April 30, 1816, *LJWBH*, 2:784–85. See also Benjamin Hawkins to Mauricio de Zúñiga, May 24, 1816, *LJWBH*, 2:789.

18 Duncan Clinch to Edmund Gaines, May 9, 1816, G-55, LRSW, reel 69. See also Duncan Clinch to Benjamin Hawkins, May 3, 1816, H-79, LRSW, reel 69; Duncan Clinch to Edmund Gaines, May 7, 1816, G-55, LRSW, reel 69; Benjamin Hawkins to William Crawford, May 24, 1816, *LJWBH*, 2:788. Kendal Lewis reported that the Fowltown Creeks initially agreed to the slave hunting expedition but changed their minds after two hundred of Kinache's Seminole warriors converged on the town. Kendal Lewis to Benjamin Hawkins, May 4, 1816, H-79, LRSW, reel 69.

19 Benjamin Hawkins to Edmund Gaines, May 3, 1816, *LJWBH*, 2:785.

20 Benjamin Hawkins to Mauricio Zúñiga, May 24, 1816, *LJWBH*, 2:789–90. The standard work on Bowles and his rebellion is J. Leitch Wright, *William Augustus Bowles, Director General of the Creek Nation* (Athens: University of Georgia Press, 1967). For a more recent portrayal, see Gilbert C. Din, *War on the Gulf Coast: The Spanish Fight against William Augustus Bowles* (Gainesville: University Press of Florida, 2012).

21 Edmund Gaines to Andrew Jackson, May 14, 1816, *PAJ*, 4:31.

22 Edmund Gaines to Duncan Clinch, May 23, 1816, *ASP: FR*, 4:558. See also Edmund Gaines to Daniel Patterson, May 22, 1816, *ASP: FR*, 4:558–59.

23 Edmund Gaines to Daniel Patterson, May 22, 1816, *ASP: FR*, 4:559.

24 Andrew Jackson to Mauricio de Zúñiga, April 23, 1816, *CAJ*, 2:241–42.

25 Mauricio de Zuñiga to Andrew Jackson, May 26, 1816, *PAJ*, 4:41–43 (quota-
    tions on 42). For Amelung's account of the conversation with Zúñiga, see
    Report of Captain Amelung to Andrew Jackson, June 4, 1816, *ASP: FR*, 4:557.
26 Andrew Jackson to William Crawford, June 15, 1816, *ASP: FR*, 4:557.
27 "The Journal," *GJ*, June 26, 1816, 3. As a mouthpiece of American expansionists,
    the Milledgeville paper provided frequent updates on Negro Fort and
    Indian-American relations across the southern frontier. Among the newspa-
    pers that reprinted part or all of the original article were the *Daily National
    Intelligencer*, *Richmond Enquirer*, and *Raleigh Register and North Carolina
    Gazette*.
28 Jarius Loomis to Daniel Patterson, August 13, 1816, *ASP: FR*, 4:559–60. Loomis
    was unclear on the day of the convoy's departure from New Orleans. For its
    departure on June 24 or 25, see Benigno García Calderón to Mauricío de
    Zuñiga, August 8, 1816, PC: LOC, Box 3090, leg. 1873, 111–14, and Edmund
    Gaines to Andrew Jackson, July 21, 1816, AJP, reel 20, respectively; for its
    departure on July 2, see Duncan L. Clinch to William Crawford, July 17, 1816,
    G-48, LRSW, reel 69. US gunboat policy is described in Gene A. Smith, *"For
    the Purposes of Defense": The Politics of the Jeffersonian Gunboat Program*
    (Newark: University of Delaware Press, 1995), 1–5, 73–93.
29 Multiple versions of Clinch's account of the army's role in the Battle of Negro
    Fort survive. Unless noted, the account here and below draws from Clinch's
    final draft, a "corrected copy" submitted to the War Department in 1819. See
    Duncan L. Clinch to Daniel Parker, October 29, 1819, and Duncan L. Clinch
    to Robert Butler, August 2, 1816, both in "Report of Colonel Clinch of the
    Capture of a Negro Fort on the Appalachicola River," National Archives and
    Records Administration, Washington, DC, RG45, Subject File, U.S. Navy,
    1775–1910, Box 181 (hereinafter cited as "Report of Colonel Clinch"). See also
    Duncan L. Clinch to William Crawford, July 17, 1816, G-48, LRSW, reel 69.
    For a description of the flatboats constructed by Clinch's men, see Edmund
    Gaines to William Crawford, March 20, 1816, and Edmund Gaines to Robert
    R. Ruffin, May 23, 1816, G-55, LRSW, reel 69.
30 Duncan L. Clinch to William Crawford, July 17, 1816, G-48, LRSW, reel 69.
31 "Articles of Agreement Entered into on the 18th of July 1816, by Lt. Col. D. L.
    Clinch, on the Part of the United States, and the Chiefs Capt Isaacs,
    Kotchahago, & Major McIntosh, on the Part of the Creek Nation," in
    National Archives and Records Administration, Washington, DC, RG45,
    Subject File, U.S. Navy, 1775–1910, Box 181.
32 Jarius Loomis to Daniel Patterson, August 13, 1816, *ASP: FR*, 4:560.
33 Ibid.
34 An abridged version of Buck's letter appeared in several newspapers shortly
    after the Battle of Negro Fort, including the *Nashville Whig*. "Extract of a

Letter from an Officer in the Southern Army, to His Father Near Winchester, Va, Dated Camp Crawford, Aug. 4, 1816," October 8, 1816, 2. For the full text, see "Gen. Clinch and the Indians," *Army and Navy Chronicle*, February 25, 1836, 115.

35 Duncan L. Clinch to Robert Butler, August 2, 1816, in "Report of Colonel Clinch."

36 "Gen. Clinch and the Indians," 116 (first quotation); Jarius Loomis to Daniel Patterson, August 13, 1816, *ASP: FR*, 4:560 (second quotation).

37 "Extract of a Letter to a Gentleman in Charleston, Dated Camp Crawford, August 4," *National Register*, September 7, 1816, 16.

38 "Report of Colonel Clinch."

39 Suspecting "treachery might be on foot" and being unfamiliar with Hambly, Loomis arrested the "white man" and one of the Indians, while ordering the other Indian to return to Clinch and inform him that all future messages must be delivered in writing by an American army officer. Jarius Loomis to Daniel Patterson, August 13, 1816, *ASP: FR*, 4:560.

40 "Chronicle. Shred of the Late War," *NWR*, August 31, 1816, 14–15.

41 *A Military Dictionary, Explaining and Describing the Technical Terms, Phrases, Works, and Machines, Used in the Science of War* (London: Robinson, Fielding, and Walker, 1778), H3. The word had not yet made it into any early American dictionaries. See, for example, Noah Webster's magnum opus: *An American Dictionary of the English Language* (New York: S. Converse, 1828).

42 "Gen. Clinch and the Indians," 116.

43 William Hambly to John Forbes, May 17, 1816, JFP, reel 2.

44 "Report of Colonel Clinch" (first, second, and third quotations). See also "Gen. Clinch and the Indians," 116. For the significance of the red flag, see Benerson Little, *The Sea Rover's Practice: Pirate Tactics and Techniques, 1630–1730* (Washington, DC: Potomac Books, 2005), 113 (fourth quotation).

45 "From New Orleans, August 19, 1816," *Washington Republican & Natchez Intelligencer*, August 28, 1816, 3.

46 Nathaniel Millett, *The Maroons of Prospect Bluff and Their Quest for Freedom in the Atlantic World* (Gainesville: University Press of Florida, 2013), 226.

47 Benjamin Hawkins to Edmund Gaines, May 3, 1816, *LJWBH*, 2:785.

48 Duncan L. Clinch to Edmund Gaines, June 14, 1816, AJP, reel 21.

49 Mauricio Zúñiga to Juan Ruiz de Apodaca, May 2, 1816, PC: LOC, Box 3073, Legajo 1796, 1823 ("del auxilio de los negros"). For the details of the conference, see Francisco Caso y Luengo to Mauricio de Zúñiga, April 28, 1816, PC: LOC, Box 3073, leg. 1796, 1827–29.

50 "Milledgeville, July 10," *NWR*, July 27, 1816, 368.

51 Alexander Durant to Mauricio Zúñiga, July 8, 1816, PC: LOC, Box 3090, Legajo 1873, 104–5 ("viveres, y un poco de aguardiente," "para entregar los

Negros sin ninguna resistencia"). See also Francisco Caso y Luengo to
Mauricio de Zúñiga, May 20, 1816, PC: UF, Legajo 79, 639–41, reel 479;
Francisco Caso y Luengo to Mauricio Zúñiga, July 12, 1816, PC: UF, Legajo 79,
664–66, reel 479. Summaries of the Spanish assault can be found in Claudio
Saunt, *A New Order of Things: Property, Power, and the Transformation of the
Creek Indians, 1773–1816* (Cambridge: Cambridge University Press, 1999),
286–87, and William S. Coker and Thomas D. Watson, *Indian Traders of the
Southeastern Spanish Borderlands: Panton, Leslie & Company, and John Forbes &
Company, 1783–1847* (Pensacola: University Presses of Florida, 1986), 306–9.

52 Saunt, *A New Order of Things*, 287.

53 The Governor of Pensacola to the Chiefs, July 23, 1816, Innerarity-Hulse
Papers, M1966–01, University Archives and West Florida History Center,
Pensacola; *Instrucciones aquel devera arreglarse el Capitan Don Benigno Garcia
Calderon, el desempeño dela Comisión que ha fiado a Su Cargo*, July 28, 1816, PC:
LOC, BOX 3090, Legajo 88, 107–11.

54 *Instrucciones aquel devera arreglarse el Capitan Don Benigno Garcia Calderon*,
107–11, 107 (first quotation, "el objeto principal)," 109 (second quotation and
third quotations, "para no causarles mas perjuicios de los que yah an sufrido
con la fuga de sus esclavos," "entregue los Esclavos si estuvieren en su poder").

55 For a discussion of how Spanish colonists "viewed the fort through a similar
lens and drew identical conclusions" as their American neighbors, see John
Paul Nuño, "'República de Bandidos': The Prospect Bluff Fort's Challenge
to the Spanish Slave System," *FHQ* 94, no. 2 (Fall 2015): 192–221 (quotation
on 215).

56 "Report of Colonel Clinch"; Jarius Loomis to Daniel Patterson, August 13,
1816, *ASP: FR*, 4:559–60; "Appalachicola," *NWR*, September 14, 1816, 37.

57 Ibid.

58 "Gen. Clinch and the Indians," 116.

59 "Report of Colonel Clinch."

60 Duncan L. Clinch to Robert Butler, August 2, 1816, and Marcus Buck to his
father, August 4, 1816, in "Gen. Clinch and the Indians," 115–16; "Chronicle,"
NWR, August 31, 1816, 14–15.

61 Jarius Loomis to Pedro de Alba, August 2, 1816, PC: LOC, Box 3090, Legajo
1873, 117 ("200 hombres, mujeres, y niños" and "como 25"); Jarius Loomis to
Daniel Patterson, August 13, 1816, *ASP: FR*, 4:559–60.

62 "From New Orleans, August 19, 1816," *Washington Republican & Natchez
Intelligencer*, August 28, 1816, 3.

63 "Report of Colonel Clinch." In contrast to Clinch's account, Spanish officials
noted the departure of significant numbers of maroons prior to the American
assault: As early as the fall of 1815, Francisco Caso y Luengo claimed that the
fort's commander, Prince, had already led a large contingent to the "Indians'

towns" ("en los Pueblos de Indios") nearby. The following summer, in his official report to Andrew Jackson, US Army captain Amelung recorded that according to the government administrators he met in Pensacola, "a great part" of the Negro Fort maroons had "abandoned the fort on account of scarcity of provisions." See Francisco Caso y Luengo to José de Soto, September 18, 1815, PC: UF, Legajo 147B, folio 568, reel 479; and Report of Captain Amelung to Andrew Jackson, June 4, 1816, *ASP: FR*, 4:557.

64 In a letter to the Spanish governor written just days before the Battle of Negro Fort, Creek trader Alexander Durant put the number of maroons inside the fort at seventy, "not counting the women and children" ("sin contar las Mugeres y niños"). Alexander Durant to Mauricio Zúñiga, July 8, 1816, PC: LOC, Box 3090, Legajo 1873, 105. Regarding the number of fatalities, Pensacola merchant John Innerarity claimed that only "about 40 negroes were blown up in the Fort besides about 20 that are left there wounded." John Innerarity to James Innerarity, August 13, 1816, in "Letters of John Innerarity and A. H. Gordon," *FHQ* 12, no. 1 (July 1933): 38. For historians citing the lower Spanish estimates, see Millett, *The Maroons of Prospect Bluff*, 144, and Saunt, *A New Order of Things*, 288 n.90.

65 Jarius Loomis to Daniel Patterson, August 13, 1816, *ASP: FR*, 4:560. See also Benigno García Calderón to Mauricio de Zúñiga, August 8, 1816, PC: LOC, Box 3090, Legajo 1873, 113.

66 "Destruction of a Fort in Florida," *Athens Southern Whig*, September 16, 1847, 2.

67 "Extract of a Letter to a Gentleman in Charleston."

68 Jarius Loomis to Daniel Patterson, August 13, 1816, *ASP: FR*, 4:560. See also the attached correspondence to "Report of Colonel Clinch." In reality, Loomis's naval convoy left with a great deal of the spoils of war, including four large cannons, hundreds of muskets, and more than one thousand bayonets. Jarius Loomis, "Inventory of Articles Shipped on Board the Schooner General Pike, from the Negro Fort to New Orleans," in *Letter from the Secretary of the Navy, Transmitting, in Obedience to a Resolution of the House of Representatives, of the Twenty-Sixth Ultimo, Sundry Documents relating to the Destruction of the Negro Fort in East Florida, in the Month of July, 1816* (Washington: E. De Krafft, 1819), 19.

69 Found uninjured among the ruins of Negro Fort by Clinch's men, the "negra" Maria belonged to Don Antonio Montero, a Pensacola politician who lost a total of eight slaves to the British Post during the War of 1812, including Garçon. Since only two of the escaped slaves belonging to Montero—the house servants Maria and Eugenia—were women of marriageable age, it is quite possible that Maria was Garçon's wife. For the Spanish account of this woman's survival and reenslavement, see Benigno García Calderón to Mauricío de Zúñiga, August 8, 1816, PC: LOC, Box 3090, leg. 1873, 113–14;

"Relacion de los Esclavos pertenecientes á los vecinos de Panzacola que se pudieron hallan con los Ingleses en Apalachicola," May 6, 1815, PC: LOC, Legajo 1796, Box 3069, 770–71. Further evidence of this woman's connection to Garçon comes from Edward Nicolls, who in a number of compelling yet contradictory statements made years later claimed that the wife of the "Black Serjeant-Major" who commanded the fort—whom Nicolls erroneously referred to as Wilson—counted among the fort's survivors. Unfortunately, many of Nicolls's later claims about Negro Fort and its survivors are unreliable. See John Wilson Croker to William Hamilton, April 7, 1818, LP; Edward Nicolls to Sir John Barrow, September 11, 1843, *Correspondence on the Slave Trade with Foreign Powers, Parties to Treaties, under Which Captured Vessels Are to Be Tried by Mixed Tribunals: From January 1 to December 31, 1844, Inclusive* (London: William Clowes and Sons, 1844), 13.

70 "Report of Colonel Clinch."

71 Mauricio de Zúñiga to José de Cienfuegos, August 22, 1816, PC: LOC, Box 3090, Legajo 1873, 102 ("inutiles y de poco valor porque sus edades abanzadas y otras tachas").

72 John Innerarity to James Innerarity, August 13, 1816, in "Letters of John Innerarity and A. H. Gordon," *FHQ* 12, no. 1 (July 1933): 38. See also "Relacion de nombre de los esclavos de la propiedad de las vecinos de Panzacola que se hallan en Apalachicola," May 8, 1815, PC: LOC, Box 3070, Legajo 1796, 768; "Relacion de los Esclavos," 665.

73 For Hawkins's death on June 6, 1816, see "The Journal," *GJ*, June 12, 1816, 3.

74 A List of Negroes, in "Report of Colonel Clinch."

75 "Report of Colonel Clinch."

76 Benigno García Calderón to Jarius Loomis, August 2, 1816, PC: LOC, Box 3090, Legajo 1873, 115 ("establecíada en territorio de S.M.C").

77 Jarius Loomis to Benigno García Calderón, August 2, 1816, PC: LOC, Box 3090, Legajo. 1873, 116, ("propiedad capturada," "esclavos profugos de los E.U.").

78 Benigno García Calderón to Mauricío de Zúñiga, August 8, 1816, PC: LOC, Box 3090, leg. 1873, 113 ("negros Españoles, Americanos y de Indios"). After receiving Loomis's response, Calderón ordered his men to return to Pensacola without visiting the grounds of the exploded fort. The decision would later draw criticism from Pensacola's slaveowners, who expected Calderón to return to the city with other captives who remained wounded at Prospect Bluff or were "scattered among the Seminoles." "Letters of John Innerarity and A. H. Gordon," 38. Benigno García Calderón to Mauricío de Zúñiga, August 8, 1816, PC: LOC, Box 3090, Legajo 1873, 113–14.

79 No record of the financial cost of the joint army-navy expedition exists because of its categorization as a regular military operation. David F. Ericson, *Slavery*

in the American Republic: Developing the Federal Government, 1791–1861
(Lawrence: University Press of Kansas, 2011), 111.

80 Andrew Jackson to Duncan Clinch, September 5, 1816, in "The Negro Fort in Florida," *DNI*, April 27, 1819, 2.

CHAPTER 5. THE BATTLE CONTINUES

1 "News," *GJ*, August 14, 1816, 2.
2 Ibid.
3 "Milledgeville, Ga. Aug. 14," *New-York Columbian*, August 28, 1816, 2.
4 "Milledgeville, Aug. 14. News," *Chillicothe Supporter*, September 10, 1816, 3.
5 "Appalachicola," *NWR*, September 14, 1816, 37.
6 "New Orleans, Aug. 16," *DNI*, September 18, 1816, 3. For northern reprints, see "From the New-Orleans *Gazette*," *New-York Columbian*, August 28, 1816, 2; "From the New-Orleans *Gazette*, Aug. 15," *New York Evening Post*, September 19, 1816, 2. Washington, DC's *National Intelligencer* carried a reprint as well on September 18, 1816, 3.
7 "Chronicle. Shred of the Late War," *NWR*, August 31, 1816, 14.
8 "Chronicle," *Augusta Chronicle*, October 18, 1816, 3. The same article also appeared in northern media. See "From the *Augusta Chronicle*, Oct. 18," *New York Evening Post*, October 21, 1816, 3.
9 "Extract of a Letter to a Gentleman in Charleston, Dated Camp Crawford, August 4," *Washington National Register*, September 7, 1816, 32.
10 "Extract of a Letter from a Gentleman in New Orleans to a Gentleman in This City," *New York Evening Post*, October 28, 1816, 2.
11 "Appalachicola," *NWR*, September 14, 1816, 37.
12 "Extract of a Letter from a Gentleman in New Orleans to a Gentleman in This City," 2 (first quotation); "The Appalachicola Fort," DNI, October 12, 1816, 3 (second quotation).
13 "New Orleans, Aug. 16," 3.
14 "From New Orleans, August 19, 1816," *Washington Republican & Natchez Intelligencer*, August 28, 1816, 3.
15 "New Orleans, Aug. 16," 3.
16 "Extract of a Letter from a Gentleman in New-Orleans," 2.
17 "Appalachicola," *NWR*, September 14, 1816, 37.
18 William Gibson to David B. Mitchell, September 7, 1816, SNAD.
19 [Zephaniah] L. Kingsley to David B. Mitchell, September 13, 1816, SNAD.
20 Duncan L. Clinch to Edmund Gaines, November 15, 1816, AJP, reel 22.
21 James M. Glassell to Duncan L. Clinch, December 26, 1816, in *Savannah Republican*, April 17, 1819, 2.
22 Edmund Gaines to Duncan L. Clinch, May 6, 1817, in *Savannah Republican*, April 17, 1819, 2.

23 Duncan L. Clinch to Andrew Jackson, October 28, 1816, AJP, reel 21.

24 Ibid.

25 "Washington: Saturday, November 30," *DNI*, November 30, 1816, 3.

26 Alexander Culloh [McCulloch] to Edmund Gaines, [no date], *ASP: FR*, 4:597.

27 Bowlegs to Don Jose Coppinger, November 18, 1816, *ASP: FR*, 4:589–90.
Prior to leaving the British Post on Prospect Bluff, Edward Nicolls
directed the Creeks "to have [as] little Communication with american
citizens as possible that being the best mode of preserving peace." He
moreover instructed them "to faithfully protect the black soldiers that
were with me and to permit all black men that fell into their hands to
join those at the bluff." Edward Nicolls to Alexander Gordon, September
24, 1816, LP.

28 Edmund Gaines to Andrew Jackson, April 2, 1817, *PAJ*, 4:106–7. See also
"Tuesday, March 4, 1817," *Augusta Herald*, March 4, 1817, 3, and "Indian Outrage,"
Augusta Herald, March 11, 1817, 3.

29 "The Southern Indians," *NWR*, May 31, 1817, 210–11.

30 Edmund Gaines to the Seminole Chiefs, [no date], *ASP: FR*, 4:585–86 (quotations on 586).

31 Kinache to Edmund Gaines, [no date], *ASP: FR*, 4:586.

32 "Look at This," *GJ*, May 6, 1817, 3 (first quotation); "On the 12th of This
Instant," *GJ*, June 3, 1817, 3 (second quotation).

33 "On or about the 12th or 13th of September Last," *GJ*, November 6, 1816, 4.

34 "Notice," *GJ*, April 21, 1818, 3.

35 "George Simmons," *GJ*, February 11, 1817, 1.

36 [Zephaniah] L. Kingsley to David B. Mitchell, September 13, 1816, SNAD.

37 John Innerarity to James Innerarity, October 5, 1816, JFP, reel 2.

38 Edmund Doyle to John Innerarity, December 10, 1816, JFP, reel 2.

39 Edmund Gaines to Andrew Jackson, November 21, 1817, *PAJ*, 4:150–51 (quotation
on 150). See also Edmund Gaines to Andrew Jackson, *PAJ*, 4:140–42.

40 George Perryman to Sands, February 24, 1817, *ASP: FR*, 4:596.

41 "Indian News," *Augusta Chronicle*, December 3, 1817, 2.

42 Edmund Gaines to Andrew Jackson, November 21, 1817, *ASP: IA*, 2:160. See also
Edmund Gaines to John C. Calhoun, November 26, 1817, *ASP: IA*, 2:160.

43 Edmund Gaines to William Rabun, *GJ*, December 16, 1817, 3; Edmund Gaines
to George Graham, December 2, 1817, *ASP: FR*, 4:598.

44 For the arrests of Hambly and Doyle and their journey to the Suwannee River,
see Matthew Arbuckle to Edmund Gaines, December 20, 1817, *ASP: MA*,
4:691; William Hambly Certificate, July 24, 1818, *ASP: FR*, 4:577; and William
Hambly and Edmund Doyle to Andrew Jackson, May 2, 1818, *ASP: FR*,
4:577–78.

45 Matthew Arbuckle to Edmund Gaines, December 20, 1817, *ASP: MA*, 4:691.

46 "Mobile, Feb. 3," *Augusta Chronicle, and Georgia Gazette*, April 4, 1818, 2.

47 Philemon Hawkins, "Extract from the Report of Cap't. Barnard," attached to Benjamin Hawkins to William Crawford, March 29, 1816, H-53, LRSW, reel 69.

48 Testimony of Peter B. Cook, *ASP: FR*, 4:582.

49 In a rare and unflattering account of Bowlegs's Town, a US Army captain wrote, "The Indians settled on Sawhanee were emigrants from different tribes— numbers seventy warriors under *Bowlegs*, a stupid and ill-disposed man—a body of worthless vagabonds. They had abundance of cattle and no arts except the manufacture of excellent moccasins. Cultivated a thin sandy soil on the west bank of Sahwanee river." Hugh Young, "A Topographical Memoir on East and West Florida with Itineraries of General Jackson's Army, 1818: Part I: The Memoir (Continued)," *FHQ* 13, no. 2 (October 1934): 89.

50 Philemon Hawkins, "Extract from the Report of Cap't. Barnard."

51 George Perryman to Sands, February 24, 1817, *ASP: FR*, 4:596.

52 Nathaniel Millett, *The Maroons of Prospect Bluff and Their Quest for Freedom in the Atlantic World* (Gainesville: University Press of Florida, 2013), 233.

53 Hugh Young, "A Topographical Memoir on East and West Florida," 100.

54 Overestimating the political advances of Negro Fort ("the Prospect Bluff community was governed by a sophisticated and modern political system"), Millett also asserts, without offering corroborating evidence, that the Nero's Town maroons recreated the "political system and military structure" they had enjoyed at Prospect Bluff. *The Maroons of Prospect Bluff*, 207 (first quotation), 233 (second quotation).

55 George Perryman to Sands, February 24, 1817, *ASP: FR*, 4:596.

56 Testimony of Peter B. Cook, *ASP: FR*, 4:582.

57 Susan R. Parker, "Success through Diversification: Francis Philip Fatio's New Switzerland Plantation," in Jane G. Landers, ed., *Colonial Plantations and Economy in Florida* (Gainesville: University Press of Florida, 2000), 69–82.

58 John Innerarity to John Forbes, November 15, 1815, GP. Two years after he absconded, Nero's name appears on two lists of slaves captured and returned to St. Augustine two years later—though a notation at the bottom of one of the undated documents suggests that he remained at large. See "Negros que se reclamen de los Estados Unidos," 1797, Untitled List of Slaves, 1797, and "Lista delos Esclavos fugitivos acogidos en los Estados Unidos de America," May 19, 1797, all of which are in To and from the United States, 1784–1821, East Florida Papers, New York Public Library, reel 42. See also Janes G. Landers, *Atlantic Creoles in the Age of Revolutions* (Cambridge, MA: Harvard University Press, 2010), 183–87, 190–94.

59 William Hambly Certificate, July 24, 1818, *ASP: FR*, 4:577. Hugh Young described Nero as "a *Mulatto* whose talents formed his only tie of

authority and who knew that the respect and authority of the negroes were the only security to the continuance of his magistracy." "A Topographical Memoir," 100.

60 Testimony of William Hambly, April 27, 1818, *ASP: FR*, 4:583.

61 William Hambly Certificate; Testimony of William Hambly.

62 John C. Calhoun to Andrew Jackson, December 26, 1817, *PAJ*, 4:163.

63 Andrew Jackson to John Coffee, January 14, 1818, *PAJ*, 4:169–70; Andrew Jackson to Edmund Gaines, January 20, 1818, *PAJ*, 4:171.

64 John Banks, *A Short Biographical Sketch of the Undersigned by Himself* (Austell, GA: E. Leonard, 1936), 12.

65 Andrew Jackson to John C. Calhoun, March 25, 1818, *ASP: FR*, 4:573.

66 Andrew Jackson to Isaac McKeever, March 25, 1818, *NWR*, March 20, 1819, 80.

67 "Baltimore, May 14, 1818," *New York National Advocate*, May 18, 1818, 2.

68 Robert Butler to Daniel Parker, May 3, 1818, in *NWR*, December 26, 1818, 317.

69 Andrew Jackson to Francisco Caso y Luengo, April 6, 1818, *ASP: FR*, 4:575.

70 Andrew Jackson to Francisco Caso y Luengo, April 7, 1818, *ASP: FR*, 4:576. See also Francisco Caso y Luengo to Andrew Jackson, April 7, 1818, *ASP: FR*, 4:575–76.

71 Andrew Jackson to John C. Calhoun, May 18, 1818, *PAJ*, 4:197–201. Francisco Caso y Luengo initially freed William Hambly and Edmund Doyle after both men promised they would "never return to that country, nor hold any communication, direct or indirect, with the United States Government, or any of her officers." However, both men met the US Navy fleet under the command of Captain Isaac McKeever, who returned them to Fort St. Marks. William Hambly Certificate. For Jackson's employment of Hambly and Doyle, see Francisco Caso y Luengo to Andrew Jackson, April 7, 1818, *PAJ*, 4:189; Andrew Jackson to John C. Calhoun, May 5, 1818, *PAJ*, 4:201; Andrew Jackson to James Monroe, June 2, 1818, *PAJ*, 4:214; James Monroe to Andrew Jackson, December 21, 1818, *PAJ*, 4:257. For a generation of men like Hambly and their part in securing American expansion, see Frank Lawrence Owsley Jr. and Gene A. Smith, *Filibusters and Expansionists: Jeffersonian Manifest Destiny, 1800–1821* (Tuscaloosa: University of Alabama Press, 1997).

72 Alexander Arbuthnot to John Arbuthnot, April 2, 1818, *ASP: FR*, 584.

73 "East Florida," *DNI*, November 7, 1817, 3. See also "East Florida," *NWR*, November 15, 1817, 190–91.

74 "Mobile, Feb. 3," *Augusta Chronicle, and Georgia Gazette*, April 4, 1818, 2.

75 Robert Butler to Daniel Parker, May 3, 1818, in *NWR*, December 26, 1818, 316–18 (quotation on 317). See also Andrew Jackson to John C. Calhoun, April 20, 1818, *PAJ*, 4:193–96.

76 "Late from the Army," *GJ*, May 5, 1818, 3.

77 Robert Butler to Daniel Parker, May 3, 1818, in *NWR*, December 26, 1818, 316-18 (quotations on 318). See also Andrew Jackson to John C. Calhoun, April 20, 1818, *PAJ*, 4:193–96.

78 *Testimony of Nero Bowlegs, a colored man, in Petition of the heirs of James Ormond, deceased*, 27th Cong., 2d Sess., H.R. 723, 5.

79 *Testimony of John Prince, a colored man, in Petition of the heirs of James Ormond, deceased*, 27th Cong., 2d Sess., H.R. 723, 4.

80 Ibid., 5.

81 Robert Butler to Daniel Parker, May 3, 1818, in *NWR*, December 26, 1818, 318.

82 *Extracts from the Minutes of the Proceedings of the Court-martial in the Trial of Ambrister, ASP: FR*, 4:604. Writing from Nassau, Bahamas, Ambrister's father described Cook as "a vendue master's clerk, who some time before quitted these islands, in consequence of having robbed his master, and who was afterwards imprisoned at Saint Marks for a similar offence against Mr. Arbuthnot, who had the misfortune to employ him in his mercantile concerns there." "Arbuthnot and Armbrister," *Richmond Enquirer*, September 29, 1818, 3. Cook's intrigues are also discussed in Andrew Jackson to John C. Calhoun, April 20, 1818, *PAJ*, 4:196, fn. 9.

83 While overseeing the post's construction several years earlier, Nicolls questioned the site's design, writing Alexander Cochrane, "Enclosed also is the plan Lieut. Christie of the Royal Artillery drew of the fort during my absence, but I found it so defective that I ordered Captain Henry to execute it differently as you will see by his plan." Edward Nicolls to Alexander Cochrane, December 3, 1814, ACP, MS2328, 118, reel 3. See also James W. Covington, "The Negro Fort," *Gulf Coast Historical Review* 5, no. 2 (Spring 1990): 89.

84 *Minutes of the Proceedings of a Special Court, Organized Agreeably to the Following Order*, April 26, 1818, *ASP: FR*, 4:581.

85 *Continuation of the Minutes of the Proceedings of a Special Court, Whereof Major General Gaines Is President, Convened by Order of the 26*th *April, 1818*, April 27, 1818, *ASP: FR*, 5:594. For the court's decision and the subsequent execution of the two defendants, see Andrew Jackson to John C. Calhoun, May 18, 1818, *PAJ*, 4:199, and various documents, *ASP: FR*, 4:581–96.

86 James Parton, *Life of Andrew Jackson* (New York: Mason Brothers, 1861), 2:483–84 (quotation on 483). For Fernando's story, see Richard Ivy Easter to Andrew Jackson, May 10, 1821, *PAJ*, 5:39–41; Catherine [Catalina] Satorios to Andrew Jackson, April 16, 1822, *PAJ*, 5:173–74; Bill of Sale, April 12, 1822, AJP, reel 31; Catalina Satorios to Andrew Jackson, June 7, 1822, and Catalina Satorios to Andrew Jackson, July 8, 1822, AJP, reel 31; Catalina Satorios to Fernando, June 14, 1822, AJP, reel 31.

87 Landers, *Atlantic Creoles in the Age of Revolutions*, 184, 191–92 (quotation on 192).

88 "Late from the Army," *GJ*, May 5, 1818, 3. For contemporary reports of the
Pensacola invasion, see "From the Southern Army," *DNI*, June 8, 1818, 2–3;
"From Pensacola," *DNI*, June 29, 1818, 2; "From Pensacola," *DNI*, July 3,
1818, 2.
89 Andrew Jackson to James Monroe, June 2, 1818, *PAJ*, 4:214 (first quotation), 215
(second and third quotations).
90 Ibid., 4:215.

CHAPTER 6. SLAVERY OR FREEDOM

1 Allan Nevins, ed., *The Diary of John Quincy Adams, 1794–1845: American
Diplomacy and Political, Social, and Intellectual Life, from Washington to Polk*
(New York: Scribner's, 1951), 203; "Our Relations with Spain," *DNI*, December
30, 1818, 2–3. For the paper's history, see William E. Ames, "The National
Intelligencer: Washington's Leading Political Newspaper," *Records of the
Columbia Historical Society* 66/68 (1966–1968): 71–83.
2 "Our Relations with Spain," *DNI*, December 30, 1818, 2.
3 Historian and biographer William Earl Weeks considers the letter "one of the
most famous state papers of his [Adams's] long life of public service." *John
Quincy Adams and American Global Empire* (Lexington: University Press of
Kentucky, 1992), 139–46 (quotation on 140).
4 For Adams's complex views on slavery, see David F. Ericson, "John Quincy
Adams: Apostle of Union," and Matthew Mason, "John Quincy Adams and
the Tangled Politics of Slavery," in David Waldstreicher, ed., *A Companion to
John Adams and John Quincy Adams* (Malden, MA: Wiley-Blackwell, 2013),
367–82, 402–21; William Lee Miller, *Arguing about Slavery: John Quincy Adams
and the Great Battle in the United States Congress* (New York: Vintage, 1998):
Leonard L. Richards, *The Life and Times of Congressman John Quincy Adams*
(New York: Oxford University Press, 1986).
5 Deborah A. Rosen, *Border Law: The First Seminole War and American
Nationhood* (Cambridge, MA: Harvard University Press, 2015), 166–67; Daniel
Walker Howe, *What Hath God Wrought: The Transformation of America,
1815–1848* (New York: Oxford University Press, 2007), 104–7; Robert V. Remini,
Andrew Jackson and His Indian Wars (New York: Viking Press, 2001), 166–68;
Robert V. Remini, *Andrew Jackson: The Course of Empire*. Vol. 1, *1767–1821*
(Baltimore, MD: Johns Hopkins University Press, 1998), 366–77; David S.
Heidler and Jeanne T. Heidler, *Old Hickory's War: Andrew Jackson and the
Quest for Empire* (Mechanicsburg, PA: Stackpole Books, 1996).
6 *Debate, in the House of Representatives of the United States, on the Seminole War,
in January and February, 1819* (Washington, DC: Office of the National
Intelligencer, 1819), 28 (first quotation), 201 (second quotation), 390 (third
quotation), 399 (fourth quotation).

7   *Debate, in the House of Representatives of the United States*, 313 (first and second quotations), 316 (third, fourth, and fifth quotations), 317 (sixth quotation).
8   Ibid., 58.
9   Ibid., 525.
10 Rosen, *Border Law*, 166 (first quotation), 167 (second quotation).
11 "Washington," *DNI*, January 19, 1819, 3.
12 Annals of Congress, 15th Cong., 2nd sess., 1132–38.
13 Report in the Senate of the United States, February 24, 1819, *ASP: MA*, 1:739–42. The bipartisan and cross-sectional committee consisted of Abner Lacock (Democratic-Republican, Pennsylvania), John Eaton (Democratic-Republican, Tennessee), John Wayles Eppes (Democratic-Republican, Virginia), Rufus King (Federalist, New York), and James Burrill Jr. (Federalist, Rhode Island). Never one to let any sort of criticism go unchallenged, Jackson, through his aides, published a rejoinder to the Senate report, calling it "unjustifiable in temper, argument, and statements. Its temper is harsh and vindictive, its arguments are childishly weak, and its statements are in many instances, grossly and unaccountably erroneous." "Strictures on Mr. Lacock's Report on the Seminole War," *DNI*, March 9, 1819, 2–3 (quotation on 2). A year later, Jackson offered a more extensive criticism of the Senate report entitled "General Jackson's Memorial," *DNI*, March 21 and 22, 1820, both on 2.
14 Robert V. Remini, *Andrew Jackson and His Indian Wars* (New York: Viking, 2001), 168.
15 Canter Brown Jr., "Tales of Angola: Free Blacks, Red Stick Creeks, and International Intrigue," in *African American History* (Tampa, FL: University of Tampa Press, 2005), 5–22; Canter Brown Jr., "The 'Sarrazota, or Runaway Negro Plantations': Tampa Bay's First Black Community, 1812–1821," *Tampa Bay History* 12, no. 2 (Fall/Winter 1990): 5–19.
16 Charles Vignoles, *Observations upon the Floridas* (New York: E. Bliss & E. White, 1823), 135. For the author's travels throughout Florida, see K. H. Vignoles, "Charles Blacker Vignoles in South Carolina and Florida, 1817–1823," *South Carolina Historical Society* 85, no. 2 (April 1984): 83–107.
17 Gabriel Perpall to Andrew Jackson, June 16, 1818, AJP, reel 25. For Hawkins first alerting the War Department to the migration of fugitive slaves to Tampa Bay in 1813, see Canter Brown Jr., "Tales of Angola," 6. One of the earliest mentions in national media can be found in "East Florida" and "Memoranda of the Geography, Population, &c. of East Florida," *NWR*, November 7, 1817, 189–91.
18 James Gadsden, "The Defences of the Floridas: A Report of Captain James Gadsden, Aide-de-Camp to General Jackson," *FHQ* 15, no. 4 (April 1937): 248.

19 Andrew Jackson to John C. Calhoun, November 28, 1818, *PAJ*, 4:252.

20 Horatio S. Dexter, "Observations of the Seminole Indians," in Mark F. Boyd, "Horatio S. Dexter and Events Leading to the Treaty of Moultrie Creek with the Seminole Indians," *Florida Anthropologist* 11, no. 3 (Summer 1958): 92.

21 "Nassau," *Nassau Royal Gazette and Bahama Advertiser*, October 2, 1819, 3. See also "Nassau," *Nassau Royal Gazette and Bahama Advertiser*, October 6 and 9, 1819, both on 3; Charles Vignoles, *Observations upon the Floridas*, 136. David E. Wood, *A Guide to Selected Sources for the History of the Seminole Settlements at Red Bays, Andros, 1817–1980* (Nassau, Bahamas: Department of Archives, 1980), 2–7. For some of these same Indians visiting Cuba, see William C. Sturtevant, "Chakaika and the 'Spanish Indians': Documentary Sources Compared with Seminole Tradition," *Tequesta* 13 (1953): 38–39.

22 For the treaty and related correspondence, see "Treaty with the Creeks," *ASP: IA*, 2:248–57. For a full list of American and Indian signatories, refer to *Treaties between the United States of America and the Several Indian Tribes, from 1778 to 1837* (Washington, DC: Langtree and O'Sullivan, 1837), 295.

23 Copy of the answer of the chiefs to the talk of the Georgia commissioners, delivered by General McIntosh, *ASP: IA*, 2:253. See also Copy of a talk delivered by the Georgia commissioners to the Creek chiefs, December 28, 1820, *ASP: IA*, 2:252.

24 Copy of a talk delivered by the Georgia commissioners to the Creek Indians, December 29, 1820, *ASP: IA*, 2:253.

25 From the outset, Jackson revealed his lack of enthusiasm for the assignment; nevertheless, he dutifully accepted the position after friends convinced him his presence was required to form a new government and attract "a respectable population" to the former Spanish colonies. Andrew Jackson to James Monroe, February 11, 1821, *PAJ*, 5:10.

26 Andrew Jackson to John Quincy Adams, April 2, 1821, in Clarence Edwin Carter, *Territorial Papers of the United States* (Washington, DC: U.S. Government Printing Office, 1956), 22:29.

27 Among those pointing to Jackson for the raid are Nathaniel Millett, *The Maroons of Prospect Bluff and Their Quest for Freedom in the Atlantic World* (Gainesville: University Press of Florida, 2013), 250; and Canter Brown Jr., "Tales of Angola," 11. While Secretary of War Calhoun denied having any prior knowledge of the "excursion," Indian agent John Bell promised Calhoun he would send a force from St. Augustine to stop further Indian aggression and "at the same time secure what runaway negroes we can and keep them in Safety to be given up to their real owners when properly identified." John C. Calhoun to John R. Bell, August 4, 1821, and John R. Bell to John C. Calhoun, July 17, 1821, both in Carter, *Territorial Papers*, 22:164 (first quotation), and 126 (second quotation).

28 Several weeks before the Tampa Bay expedition began, Jackson formally
requested that President Monroe and Secretary of State Adams offer instructions on the proper course of action regarding Indians and slaves in Florida now
that the United States had formally taken possession of the territory, but the
Indian expedition had already begun before he received an answer.

29 "For the City Gazette, Advice to the Southern Planters," *Charleston City
Gazette and Commercial Daily*, November 24, 1821, 2. The anonymous writer
was probably Peter Chazotte, a South Carolinian who traveled through south
Florida at the time of the Creek expedition. See "Proposals," *Washington
Gazette*, April 27, 1822, 3.

30 Mrs. Dunbar Rowland, *Mississippi Territory in the War of 1812* (Baltimore, MD:
Genealogical Publishing Company, 1968), 47. See also Remini, *Andrew Jackson:
The Course of Empire*, 1:219, and Angie Debo, *The Road to Disappearance: A
History of the Creek Indians* (Norman: University of Oklahoma Press, 1967), 82;
George Carry Eggleston, *Red Eagle and the Wars with the Creek Indians of
Alabama* (New York: Dodd, 1878), 342.

31 John Bell reported that William McIntosh led the Tampa Bay raid, and a
Charleston, South Carolina, newspaper credited Chief "Charles Miller" with
leading the expedition. However, War Department records make it clear that
the force's commander was the mestizo Creek William Miller. John R. Bell to
John C. Calhoun, July 17, 1821, Carter, *Territorial Papers*, 22:164; "For the City
Gazette," 2; "Description of the Negroes Brought to This Place, by a
Detachment of Indians under the Command of Capt. Wm. Miller, an Indian
of the Creek Nation, from Florida," enclosed in John Crowell to John C.
Calhoun, August 20, 1821, LRSWIA, reel 3.

32 "For the City Gazette," 2.

33 "Description of the Negroes in the Possession of the Indians Commanded by
Capt. Wm. Miller (an Indian)," July 28, 1821, B-95, LRSW, reel 92. See also
"Description of the Negroes Brought to This Place" and "Descriptive List of
the Negroes Brought into the Creek Nation by a Detachment of Indian
Warriors under the Command of Col. William Miller, a Half-breed Indian.
viz & the Disposition Made of Them," enclosed in John Crowell to John C.
Calhoun, July 24, 1823, LRSWIA, reel 4.

34 "Description of the Negroes Brought to This Place," 3. For the domestic slave
trade, see Damian Alan Pargas, *Slavery and Forced Migration in the Antebellum
South* (Cambridge: Cambridge University Press, 2014), and Steven Deyle,
Carry Me Back: The Domestic Slave Trade in American Life (New York: Oxford
University Press, 2006).

35 For examples of the advertisement, see "Notice," *Pensacola Floridian*,
September 22, 1821, 4, and *St. Augustine Florida Gazette*, September 22, 1821, 1.
See also John Crowell to John C. Calhoun, August 20, 1821, LRSWIA, reel 3.

36 "Descriptive Roll of Negroes," January 22, 1822 (second quotation), enclosed in
    John Crowell to John C. Calhoun, January 22, 1822, LRSWIA, reel 4 (first
    quotation).

37 Horatio S. Dexter to John R. Bell, August 24, 1821, B-95, LRSW, reel 92.

38 John Crowell to John C. Calhoun, January 22, 1822, LRSWIA, reel 4.

39 "A Card," *St. Augustine Florida Gazette*, December 22, 1821, 1. See also
    "Descriptive Roll of Negroes."

40 "For the City Gazette," 2. As many as forty wreckers plied the Florida Keys
    annually between 1819 and 1822. John Viele, *The Florida Keys: The Wreckers*, vol.
    3 (Sarasota, FL: Pineapple Press, 2001), 25.

41 Rosanne Marion Adderley, *"New Negroes from Africa": Slave Trade Abolition
    and Free African Settlement in the Nineteenth-Century Caribbean* (Bloomington:
    Indiana University Press, 2006).

42 "Nassau," *Nassau Royal Gazette and Bahamas Advertiser*, March 20, 1822, 3.

43 Vignoles, *Observations upon the Floridas*, 136.

44 Wood, *A Guide to Selected Sources*, 8, 19 (quotation on 8).

45 Though historians long suspected the origins of the town's name, Kevin
    Mulroy was among the first to insist upon the connection to Edward Nicolls,
    writing of the town's residents, "They established a settlement in the north of
    the island and called it Nicholls town after the British officer who built the
    Negro Fort at Prospect Bluff." More recently, Nathaniel Millett remarked of
    the significance of the town's name, "It is difficult to imagine stronger
    evidence of Nicolls's impact on the former slaves' lives than the completely
    independent decision to name their community in his honor." Kevin Mulroy,
    *Freedom on the Border: The Seminole Maroons in Florida, the Indian Territory,
    Coahuila, and Texas* (Lubbock: Texas Tech University Press, 1993), 26; Millett,
    The Maroons of Prospect Bluff, 252. For further discussion of the founding and
    naming of Nicholls Town and surrounding communities, see Rosalyn Howard,
    "The 'Wild Indians' of Andros Island: Black Seminole Legacy in the
    Bahamas," *Journal of Black Studies* 37, no. 2 (November 2006): 282; Rosalyn
    Howard, *Black Seminoles in the Bahamas* (Gainesville: University Press of
    Florida, 2002); Wood, *A Guide to Selected Sources*; John M. Goggin, "The
    Seminole Negroes of Andros Island, Bahamas," *FHQ* 24, no. 3 (January 1946):
    201–6; Kenneth W. Porter, "Notes on Seminole Negroes in the Bahamas,"
    FHQ 24, no. 1 (July 1945): 56–60.

46 Wood, *A Guide to Selected Sources*, 9.

47 Ibid., 8. For Grant's generally sympathetic stance towards black islanders, who
    named one of their communities after him, see Whittington B. Johnson, *Race
    Relations in the Bahamas, 1784–1834: The Nonviolent Transformation from a
    Slave to a Free Society* (Fayetteville: University of Arkansas Press, 2000), 115, 147,
    148, 171.

48 Wood, *A Guide to Selected Sources*, 8–13 (quotations on 12).

49 Ibid., 12.

50 James G. Forbes to John Quincy Adams, July 14, 1821, in Carter, *Territorial Papers*, 22:118.

51 Wood, *A Guide to Selected Sources*, 15.

52 Harry A. Kersey Jr., "The Seminole Negroes of Andros Island Revisited: Some New Pieces to an Old Puzzle," *Florida Anthropologist* 34, no. 4 (December 1981): 169–76 (quotation on 174). See also Wood, *A Guide to Selected Sources*, 15. For the case in which Roberts testified, involving a free black man enslaved in Cuba, see "Late and Interesting from Cuba," *New York Herald*, October 19, 1853, 2; "Cuban Affairs," *New York Daily Times*, October 19, 1853, 2.

53 Horatio Dexter, "Observations on the Seminole Indians," 82.

54 Abraham Eustis to William Pope Duval, October 16, 1822, in Carter, *Territorial Papers*, 22:549.

55 For an example of these requests and the government's response, refer to the following: William Pope Duval to John C. Calhoun, September 23, 1823, in Carter, *Territorial Papers*, 22:744; "Petition to the President by Inhabitants of the Territory," October 4, 1823, in Carter, *Territorial Papers*, 22:762–64; John C. Calhoun to Samuel Cook and Others, December 30, 1823, 820–21, in Carter, *Territorial Papers*, 22:820-21; "Petition to Congress by Inhabitants of East Florida," March 8, 1824, in Carter, *Territorial Papers*, 22:857–59; *Journal of the House of Representatives of the United States*, 18th Cong., 1st sess., 298, 301, 319.

56 More than a decade of angry protests by southern slaveowners and their allies in the American government resulted in Great Britain's agreement in 1826 to pay more than one million dollars in compensation for delivering more than thirty-five hundred slaves from the United States to various parts of the British Empire during the war. The Spanish government proved far less successful in securing reimbursement for the escaped slaves from East and West Florida. "Great Britain paid the American slaveowners," wrote the authors of the definitive history of John Forbes & Company, "but still refused to pay Forbes and the other inhabitants of the Floridas so much as a farthing for their losses." William S. Coker and Thomas D. Watson, *Indian Traders of the Southeastern Borderland: Panton, Leslie & Company and John Forbes & Company, 1783–1847* (Pensacola: University Presses of Florida, 1986), 298; Alan Taylor, *The Internal Enemy: Slavery and War in Virginia, 1772–1832* (New York: Norton, 2013), 429–35; Don E. Fehrenbacher, *The Slaveholding Republic: An Account of the United States Government's Relations to Slavery*, ed. Ward M. McAfee (New York: Oxford University Press, 2001), 94–98; Arnett G. Lindsay, "Diplomatic Relations between the United States and Great Britain Bearing on the Return of Negro Slaves, 1783–1828," *Journal of Negro History* 5, no. 4 (October 1920): 391–419; J. S. Pott, *A Plain Statement of Facts,*

in Which Appears a Question of International Law of Great Importance to Colonial Proprietors, Arising out of the Claims of the Inhabitants of East and West Florida on the British Government, for Aggressions Committed by the British Forces during the War with the United States of America in 1814 (London: Cunningham and Salmon, 1833).

57 In the spring of 1835, Jackson informed the Seminoles that he preferred that they leave Florida voluntarily but that if they refused, he would send American troops "to remove you by force. "To the Chiefs and Warriors of the Seminole Indians in Florida," [1835], in Woodburne Potter, *The War in Florida: Being an Exposition of Its Causes, and an Accurate History of the Campaigns of Generals Clinch, Gaines, and Scott* (Baltimore, MD: Lewis and Coleman, 1836), 79–81.

58 "Indian Massacre!!" *Tallahassee Floridian*, January 23, 1836, 3.

59 "The Last of Major Dade's Command: From the Charleston Courier," *NWR*, August 20, 1836, 419. See also W. S. Steele, "Last Command: The Dade Massacre," *Tequesta* 46 (1986): 5–19.

60 "Hostilities of the Seminoles," *Washington Globe*, January 19, 1836, 3.

61 "Affairs in Florida," *DNI*, January 29, 1836, 3.

62 "From the Mobile *Commercial Register*, Jan. 18," *New Orleans Commercial Bulletin*, January 21, 1836, 2.

63 For Abraham's biography see Kenneth Wiggins Porter, "The Negro Abraham," *FHQ* 25, no. 1 (July 1946): 1–43 (quotation on 10); "Abraham," *Phylon* 2, no. 2 (second quarter 1941): 102–16; George A. McCall, *Letters from the Frontiers: Written during a Period of Thirty Years' Service in the Army of the United States* (Philadelphia: Lippincott, 1868), 302; "Relacion de nombre de los esclavos de la propiedad de las vecinos de Panzacola que se hallan en Apalachicola," May 8, 1815, PC: LOC, Box 3070, Legajo 1796, 768.

64 Myer M. Cohen, *Notices of Florida and the Campaigns* (Charleston: Burges & Honour, 1836), 239 (first quotation), 81 (second quotation).

65 "Relacion de los Esclavos pertenecientes á los vecinos de Panzacola que se pudieron hallan con los Ingleses en Apalachicola," May 6, 1815, PC: LOC, Legajo 1796, Box 3069, 665. At least three slaves named Harry left Pensacola with the British in the fall of 1814; however, one returned to the city while the other had no provable connection to Abraham. The black Seminole Harry, however, shared an owner and occupation with Abraham in Pensacola and as late as 1836 was still considered Abraham's "intimate." "War with the Seminoles," *NWR*, January 30, 1836, 367; "Relacion de nombre de los esclavos," 768, 770, 774.

66 "War with the Seminoles," 367. For a description of the town of Tolokchopko see Dexter, "Observations on the Seminole Indians," 82, 91. While Harry's fate is unknown, Abraham removed to the west following the war. "Registry of

Negro Prisoners Captured by the Troops Commanded by Major General Thomas S. Jesup, in 1836 and 1837, and Owned by Indians, or Who Claim to Be Free," *ASP: MA*, 7:852.

67 Jackson undoubtedly would have utilized the services of William McIntosh as well, but the Lower Creek chief was assassinated by fellow tribesmen in 1825. Benjamin W. Griffith Jr., *McIntosh and Weatherford, Creek Indian Leaders*, 248–54.

68 James W. Silver, *Edmund Pendleton Gaines: Frontier General* (Baton Rouge: Louisiana State University Press, 1949), 171–90; Rembert W. Patrick, *Aristocrat in Uniform: General Duncan L. Clinch* (Gainesville: University of Florida Press, 1963), 116–36.

69 Reliable accounts of the Second Seminole War include John Missall and Mary Lou Missall, *The Seminole Wars: America's Longest Indian Conflict* (Gainesville: University Press of Florida, 2004); John K. Mahon, *History of the Second Seminole War, 1835–1842* (Gainesville: University Press of Florida, 1967); John T. Sprague, *The Origin, Progress, and Conclusion of the Florida War* (New York: Appleton, 1848). For the war's expense, see David F. Ericson, *Slavery in the American Republic: Developing the Federal Government, 1791–1861* (Lawrence: University Press of Kansas, 2011), 112–16. The fate of the Native Americans and African Americans in Florida following the war is examined in Jill Watts's "Seminole Black Perceptions and the Second Seminole War," *UCLA Historical Journal* 7 (1986): 23.

70 "An Act for the Relief of Jarius Loomis and Heirs of James Basset," Private Law 178, 25th Cong., 3d sess. (March 3, 1839), 778. The bill was first presented to the House of Representatives by New York congressman Henry Storrs in January 1818 and periodically considered over the next twenty-one years. For example, see *Journal of the House of Representatives of the United States: Being the First Session of the Twenty-First Congress, Begun and Held at the City of Washington, December 7, 1829* (Washington, DC: Duff Green, 1829), 50.

EPILOGUE

1 Philo A. Goodwin, *Biography of Andrew Jackson, President of the United States, Formerly Major General in the Army of the United States* (Hartford, CT: Clapp and Benton, 1832), 207. The biography's success resulted in several reprints before the Civil War.

2 At least one contemporary considered the biography "on the whole, the best life yet written of any of our public men." "Reviews and Literary Notices," *Atlantic Monthly* 7, no. 41 (March 1861): 382.

3 James Parton, *Life of Andrew Jackson* (New York: Mason Brothers, 1861), 2:400 (first and second quotations), 403 (third quotation), 407 (fourth and fifth quotations).

4 The movement claimed as estimated 250,000 active supporters at its height.
   The best full treatment of American abolitionism is Manisha Sinha's *Slave's
   Cause: A History of Abolition* (New Haven, CT: Yale University Press, 2016), 253.

5 "The Seminole War," *Liberator*, November 24, 1837, 4.

6 "The Admission of New States into the Union, No. VI," *New York
   Emancipator*, January 31, 1839, 1. For the first five parts of Parburt's essay, see
   December 6, 1838, 1–2; December 13, 1838, 2; December 20, 1838, 1–2; January 10,
   1839, 1–2; January 17, 1839, 2.

7 "Slavocracy," *New York Emancipator*, April 25, 1839, 2. The word first appeared
   in the *Massachusetts Abolitionist*.

8 At the Manhattan headquarters of the American Anti-Slavery Society, the
   book sold for sixty-two and a half cents per copy, or fifty dollars per one
   hundred copies. "Just Received," *New York Emancipator*, March 28, 1839, 3.

9 "Jay's View," *Boston Emancipator and Free American*, February 8, 1844, 3. A
   more recent observer calls the work "one of the unappreciated classics of
   abolitionist literature." James Oakes, *Freedom National: The Destruction of
   Slavery in the United States, 1861–1865* (New York: Norton, 2013), 347.

10 William Jay, *A View of the Action of the Federal Government, in Behalf of Slavery*,
   2nd ed. (New York: American Anti-Slavery Society, 1839), 65. This volume was
   a revised and slightly expanded edition of the book first published several
   months earlier by J. S. Taylor. In the introduction to the second edition, Jay
   wrote of the book's remarkable reception, "The rapid sale of the first edition
   of this work, and the almost immediate call for another, afford gratifying
   evidence of the awakening attention of the public, to the action of the Federal
   government in behalf of slavery."

11 Jay raged about the bonus, "Hence, after the lapse of twenty-three years, the
   government has deemed it good policy to evince their estimation of such
   services, by rewarding the heroes of Appalachicola." Jay, *A View of the Action of
   the Federal Government*, 65.

12 Paul Finkelman, *Slavery and the Founders: Race and Liberty in the Age of Jefferson*,
   3d ed. (New York: Routledge, 2015), 177.

13 *The Congressional Globe: New Series: Containing Sketches of the Debates and
   Proceedings of the First Session of the Thirtieth Congress* (Washington, DC: Blair
   & Rives, 1848), 199.

14 *Speech of Hon. George W. Julian, of Indiana, on the Slavery Question, Delivered in
   the House of Representatives, May 14, 1850* (Washington, DC: Congressional
   Globe Office, 1850), 10.

15 Biographies include James Brewer Stewart, *Joshua R. Giddings and the Tactics
   of Radical Politics* (Cleveland, OH: Press of Case Western Reserve University,
   1970) and George W. Julian, *The Life of Joshua R. Giddings* (Chicago: A. C.
   McClurg, 1892), 91–101.

16 Joshua Giddings, *The Rights of the Free States Subverted; or, An Enumeration of Some of the Most Prominent Instances in Which the Federal Constitution Has Been Violated by Our National Government, for the Benefit of Slavery* (n.p.: [1844?]), 7.

17 Julia Griffiths, ed., *Autographs for Freedom* (Auburn, NY: Alden, Beardsley, 1854), 16–26 (first quotation on 16 and passim, second quotation on 19, third quotation on 21).

18 Ibid., 24 (first quotation), 26 (second quotation).

19 "From the 'Autographs for Freedom.' Massacre at Blount's Fort, by Hon. Joshua R. Giddings," *Liberator*, January 13, 1854, 1.

20 William Cooper Nell, *The Colored Patriots of the American Revolution, with Sketches of Several Distinguished Colored Persons: To Which Is Added a Brief Survey of the Condition and Prospects of Colored Americans* (Boston: R. F. Wallcut, 1855), 256–63.

21 Joshua R. Giddings, *The Exiles of Florida; or, The Crimes Committed by Our Government against the Maroons, Who Fled from South Carolina and Other Slave States, Seeking Protection under Spanish Law* (Columbus, OH: Follett, Foster, 1858), 44.

22 John Brown, "A Declaration of Liberty by the Representatives of the Slave Population of the United States of America," in Richard J. Hinton, ed., *John Brown and His Men: With Some Account of the Roads They Traveled to Reach Harper's Ferry* (New York: Funk & Wagnalls, 1894), 642.

INDEX

Daniels, Edward, 115–116, 124, 160
Darley, James, 170
Dauphin Island, 55–56, 65
Declaration of Independence, 4, 188
Delisle, 43
Dexter, Horatio, 165, 169, 173
Dinsmoor, Silas, 34
Dooly, Colonel, 90
Doyle, Edmund, 68, 141, 143, 145–146, 150, 230n44, 232n71
Dulendo, 125
Dunmore's Proclamation, 20
Durant, Alexander, 78, 120, 143, 208n2, 227n64

Early, Peter, 26, 91, 221n85
Erving, George, 157

Fatio, Francis, 145
Forbes, John, 43, 96
Fort Gadsden, 147–148, 155
Fort Gaines, 108, 116, 130, 140
Fort Hawkins, 27, 91, 109, 140–141
Fort Mitchell, 103, 169–170
Fort St. Marks (Fort San Marcos de Apalache), 85, 94, 110, 120, 146–151, 153, 155, 232n71
Fort San Carlos de Barrancas, 45
Fort San Miguel, 25
Fort Scott, 110, 142, 146. See also Camp Crawford
Fort Stoddert, 43, 69
Fowltown, 59, 109, 223n18; Battle of, 141–142
Francis, Josiah, 24, 30, 48, 50, 72, 147, 150
free men of color: Fort St. Marks, 168; New Orleans, 15, 52–54; Pensacola, 44, 67, 208n81. See also Creoles; Ned; Prince, John
fugitive slave bounties, 27–28, 109–110, 114–115, 121, 167

fugitive slave reimbursements, 27, 60, 174, 211n33, 239n56
fugitive slaves (maroons): Abraham (Georgia), 125; Ambrosio, 64; Barrott, 90; Battrice, 125; Ben, 173; Betsey; 81; Billy, 81; Bob, 140; Carlos, 64; Carlos Congo, 81; Carlos Muyamba, 81; Castalio, 125; Charles, 125; Congo Tom, 81; Dick, 90 (Georgia); Dick (South Carolina), 140; Dominique, 81; Eduardo, 81; Elijah, 125; Eugenia, 227n69; Fernando, 154; Francisco, 81; Francois, 63; Frank, 81; Green, 90; Grigg, 90; Jacob, 125; Jaque, 81; Jean-Baptiste, 55–56; Jim, 91 (Milledgeville, Georgia); Jim, 140–141 (Savannah, Georgia); Jo, 125; Joe, 152; John, 141; Lamb, 125; Lucas, 63; Moises, 63, 81; Nelson, Ruben, 63–64; Paris, 81; Pedro, 81; Polly, 140; Sally, 63; Sam, 81; Samson, 63; Santiago, 81; Simon, 63 (West Florida); Simon, 90 (Georgia); Tom, 81 (West Florida); Tom, 90 (Georgia); Tom, 140 (Georgia); William, 125. See also Abraham; Cyrus; Garçon; Harry; Jim; Maria; Phil, Prince; Roberts, Mitchell

Gadsden, James, 147, 163–164
Gaines, Edmund, 2, 69, 87, 95, 100–101, 103–104, 106–111, 119, 134–135, 138–142, 178, 184, 203n21, 222n10, 223n13; racial attitudes of, 104
Garçon (Negro Fort captain), 86–87, 94, 115, 119, 124–125, 227–228n69
Garrett, Obediah, 138
Garrison, William Lloyd, 182, 187
German Coast slave rebellion, 51, 54
Gibson, William, 133

ABOUT THE AUTHOR

MATTHEW J. CLAVIN, Professor of History at the University of Houston, is the author of *Aiming for Pensacola* and *Toussaint Louverture and the American Civil War*.